G

9

KUWASI BALAGOON★
A SOLDIER'S STORY

Revolutionary Writings by a New Afrikan Anarchist

*Edited by Matt Meyer
and Karl Kersplebedeb*

D1596187

2019

A Soldier's Story:
Revolutionary Writings by a New Afrikan Anarchist
By Kuwasi Balagoon

Edited by Matt Meyer and Karl Kersplebedeb

This edition copyright PM Press, 2019

ISBN 9781629633770
LCCN 2017942917

Kersplebedeb Publishing and Distribution
CP 63560
CCCP Van Horne
Montreal, Quebec
Canada H3W 3H8
www.kersplebedeb.com
www.leftwingbooks.net

PM Press
P.O. Box 23912
Oakland, CA 94623
www.pmpress.org

Cover Design by John Yates

Printed in the USA by the Employee Owners of
Thomson-Shore in Dexter, Michigan
www.thomsonshore.com

Table of Contents

Introduction to 2019 Edition

Close to twenty years after the publication of the first edition of this collection of writings by Kuwasi Balagoon, his light and legacy shine brighter than ever. The project to publish a new edition of *A Soldier's Story* was born out of expedience: the many printings of the previous editions were running out, and over the course of time we accumulated some new writings and much new commentary about this freedom fighter so defiant of the state and all forms of oppression—and so defying of easy definition and labeling. Even the word "anarchist" which graces the subtitle of this book can in some circles be controversial: Kuwasi was an active revolutionary nationalist whose love for his people (and all people) was a central element of his being, as was his hatred of authoritarian structures and styles. This new collection, then, following the course of the previous collections, seeks to deepen our understanding of the nuances that made up the life and thought of Kuwasi Balagoon—and, in so doing, to help us prepare for the nuances so needed in forging new fightback movements of resistance and revolution.

In the course of preparing this edition of *A Soldier's Story*, the editors received invaluable assistance from former comrades of Kuwasi's, some of whom still had in their possession writings by Kuwasi that had never been published or widely circulated. The status of these writings is unclear; we do not know if Kuwasi considered them complete or if they were drafts he would have wanted to return to. In at least one case, given that the document ends abruptly, it is clear that his intention was to write more. We present them all here, with little editing, to present as broad and wide a scope of Kuwasi's contributions to radicals who hold him in deep esteem, and to the many who are just learning about this too often overlooked and complex revolutionary. Some of what is included here are new reflections from those closest to him or those influenced by him who in some way help carry on his work. Surely Kuwasi would have rejoiced at some of the interpersonal openness not quite acceptable in his day; surely he would have spent most of his time working to free all political prisoners—including his still imprisoned New York Panther 21 codefendant Sundiata Acoli—and to rid the world of all injustice. If we are to remain true to his spirit, we would do well to redouble our efforts along these very lines.

In a sense, this book is the result of almost twenty years work, as it was the very end of the twentieth century when comrades first started assembling some of these texts for what was then imagined would be a pamphlet of maybe sixty or seventy pages, building on work that had been done previously by the New Jersey chapter of the Anarchist Black Cross Federation. Besides those listed in the contributors section of this volume, we would like to thank those who were involved in Solidarity, a short-lived Montreal-based publishing collective, Prison News Service, and the Arm the Spirit collective based in Toronto (not to be confused with the prisoner newspaper of the same name) for the contributions to and work done on that first edition. Also, much thanks goes to J. Sakai, without whose guidance and encouragement that first edition would have never happened. For this most recent edition, we also thank the comrades from Freedom Archives, and Mary Patten and the Madame Binh Graphics Collective Archives, for their assistance in providing images and documents for inclusion in this volume.

Introduction to the First Edition

Solidarity, Montreal 2001

This is a collection of writings by Kuwasi Balagoon, a man who many anarchists, nationalists, and anti-imperialists may have heard of in passing, but about whom very little has been made broadly available. As you read on, this state of affairs may perplex or even anger you, for certainly what we have here are important and eloquent words by a man who devoted his life to the cause of freedom — freedom from colonialism and national oppression for New Afrika and freedom from the mental shackles we all wear around our minds.

A staunch advocate of New Afrikan liberation and the eradication of capitalism, Balagoon was also an anarchist and a participant in armed struggle. Serving a stint in the U.S. army in Germany, he and other Black GIs formed a clandestine direct action group called De Legislators, which set out to punish racist soldiers with beatings or worse. Upon his return to North America he got involved with the Black Panther Party for Self-Defense. Balagoon was one of the Panther 21, whom the government attempted (unsuccessfully) to frame in 1969. Many of his earliest writings can be found in the collective autobiography of the Panther 21, *Look for Me in the Whirlwind*. As the Black Panther Party disintegrated due to both outside pressure from the police and FBI and internal contradictions between different personalities and political lines, Balagoon joined that faction that became the Black Liberation Army, an important formation that engaged in armed confrontation with the state, breaking comrades out of prison, attacking the police, and carrying out expropriations (aka robberies) of capitalists.

Throughout his political journey, Balagoon remained a critical observer, often committing his thoughts and ideas to paper.

Luckily, we have been able to assemble at least a portion of his writings in this booklet. Our goal in publishing this is not so much to tell people about an unknown superhero or prophet of revolution—there are too many of those already. We have no doubt that Balagoon had his faults and made errors just like the rest of us, and indeed we are in no way claiming to agree with each and every one of his ideas. Yet it is important that these words be published together, at long last, not only as a tribute to someone who provides a good example of what a freethinking and uncompromising revolutionary can be but also for our own sake. As revolutionaries there is a lot we can learn from Balagoon's words, as well as from his deeds. While hopefully keeping our own critical sense—how else would he have wanted it?—there is much to be found in his observations, strategies, and ideas that should be taken seriously and discussed by those who fight for a better day now, almost fifteen years after his death.

B.L.A.

Albert Nuh Washington, March 14, 1986

Black
      is a political condition,
      a state of oppression and consciousness
      a nation seeking to become,
                   A people who hope.
Liberation
      is freedom from oppression
      freedom to define, to determine one's destiny
      free from despair
                   A slave to hope.
Army
      is a politically armed unit
      to defend and preserve
      after it achieves
                   Liberation for those who hope.

Albert Nuh Washington was a member of the Black Liberation Army and prisoner of war (one of the New York Three). He died of cancer on April 28, 2000, at the Coxsackie Correctional Facility prison in New York State.

KUWASI IN THE
TWENTY-FIRST CENTURY

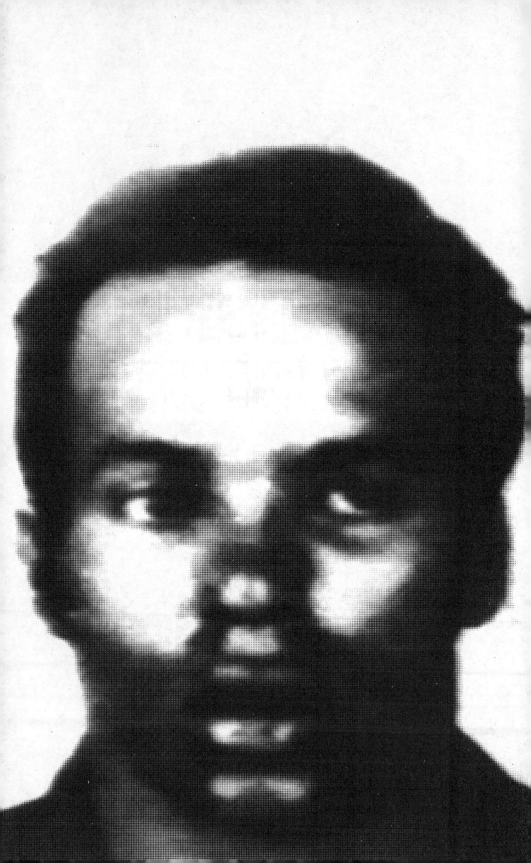

Maroon: Kuwasi Balagoon and the Evolution of Revolutionary New Afrikan Anarchism

Akinyele Umoja[*]

On October 20, 1981, Black revolutionaries and their white radical allies engaged in an attempted "expropriation" of a Brink's armored truck in Rockland County, New York. That day Rockland police apprehended three white activists and one Black man. A manhunt ensued, and on January 20, 1982, Black revolutionary Kuwasi Balagoon was apprehended in New York City. The alliance of Black and white radicals captured were part of a radical formation called the Revolutionary Armed Task Force (RATF) under the leadership of the Black Liberation Army (BLA). Balagoon was the lone anarchist among the RATF defendants; others identified themselves as Muslims, revolutionary nationalists, and Marxist-Leninists. While Balagoon was closely aligned with and respected by his comrades in the BLA and RATF, his anarchist position set him apart ideologically.[1]

Informants told the U.S. government investigators that his BLA and RATF comrades called Balagoon "Maroon." The term "Maroon" originates from enslaved Africans in the Western Hemisphere who escaped and formed rebel communities in remote areas away from slaveholding society. Balagoon earned this nickname due to his multiple escapes from incarceration. This article will explore how Balagoon was also an ideological and social "Maroon" in the context of the Black Liberation Movement and will examine his legacy in the contemporary struggle for self-determination and social justice.

This essay first appeared in *Science & Society* 79, no. 2 (April 2015): 196–220.

From Donald Weems to Kuwasi Balagoon:
The Development of a Revolutionary

Kuwasi Balagoon chronicles his early life and political development in the collective autobiography of New York Black Panther
Party defendants titled *Look for Me in the Whirlwind*. He was born
Donald Weems in the majority Black community of Lakeland in
Prince George's County, Maryland, on December 22, 1946. Early
experiences prepared young Donald Weems to become an activist who would militantly resist white supremacy and unjust
authority.[2]

He was also inspired by the militant movement led by Gloria
Richardson in Cambridge in the Eastern Shore region of Maryland. Protests in Cambridge evolved into violence in 1963. Blacks
organized sniper teams to defend nonviolent protesters from
white supremacist violence. In June 1963, the National Guard was
sent to Cambridge to quell the accelerating disturbance and was
deployed there for a year. U.S. Attorney General Robert Kennedy
and the Justice Department were forced to intervene and negoti-
ate a "treaty" between Richardson and the white power structure.
Nation of Islam national spokesman Malcolm X Shabazz would
mention the Cambridge movement as an example of developing
"Black revolution" in his legendary speech "Message to the Grassroots." The militancy of the Cambridge Movement inspired and
impressed the teenaged Weems.[3]

Weems joined the U.S. Army after graduating from high
school and was stationed in Germany after basic training. Like
most Blacks in the army, he experienced racism and physical
attacks from white officers and enlisted men. Weems believed
Black soldiers were unjustly and disproportionately punished
after altercations with whites. Black soldiers formed a clandestine
association called "Da Legislators," in his words, "based on fucking up racists ... because we were going to make and enforce new
laws that were fair." Donald prided himself in his ability to exact
revenge on racist war soldiers. In London, he also connected with
Africans and African descendants. He described the experience of
socializing with African descendants from around the globe and

other people of color in London as a "natural tonic," which motivated him to ground himself in Black consciousness and culture. He stopped "processing" his hair, wore a more natural hairstyle, and also "became more committed to Black Liberation." He was honorably discharged in 1967, after three years serving primarily in Germany.[4]

After his discharge and return home to Lakeland, Weems ultimately moved to New York City, where his sister Diane lived. In New York, he involved himself in rent strikes and was eventually hired as a tenant organizer for the Community Council on Housing (CCH). The principal leader and spokesman of the CCH was Harlem rent strike organizer Jesse Gray. Gray used the rhetoric of militant Black nationalism to recruit lieutenants for his activist campaigns. He once told a Harlem audience that he

"My father worked for the U.S. Printing Office, and my mom and Mary Day worked at Fort Meade, Maryland. Their love for my other sister Diane and for me, the only boy and the baby of the family — and the concept that you've got to work somewhere, and all-suffering determination — enabled them to rush to the job, and getting there, work and teach white folks how to do the type of work encountered, and then watch them climb the governmental ladder quickly, while they themselves rose slowly and painfully step by slow step. They did that for twenty-five years, so we could have food and clothes and goodies." (From: *Look for Me in the Whirlwind* [PM Press, 2017])

(WX12) WASHINGTON, Aug. 7--ARRESTED, THEN RELEASED--Jesse Gray, r[...]
[H]arlem rent strike leader, and Donald Weems, left, stand outside
[p]olice headquarters in Washington late today. They were arrested

needed "one hundred Black revolutionaries ready to die." Gray exhorted:

> There is only one thing that can correct the situation and that's guerrilla warfare…. [A]ll you Black people that have been in the armed services and know anything about guerrilla warfare should come to the aid of our people. If we must die, let us die scientifically![5]

Like many of his generation, Weems was ready to join an uncompromising movement for Black freedom and human rights. He joined Gray in protesting the conditions in New York housing, particularly the infestation of rats in public housing. In 1967, Gray, Weems, his sister Diane, and two other tenant activists were arrested for disorderly conduct in Washington, DC, where, unannounced and uninvited, they attended a session of Congress and brought a cage of rats to the assembly to highlight urban housing conditions. Due to the protests, the CCH lost its funding and Gray his ability to pay his organizers.

After Weems left CCH, he participated in the Central Harlem Committee for Self-Defense in solidarity with student protests at Columbia University. The Committee brought food and water to students who occupied buildings on the Columbia campus.

Weems would also associate himself with the Yoruba Temple in Harlem, organized by Nana Oserjiman Adefumi. The Detroit-born Adefumi was initiated in Cuba in the Lukumi rites of Yoruba origin. He saw the West African religious and cultural heritage as a means to cultural self-determination and peoplehood for African descendants in the United States. Explaining the nationalistic aims of the Yoruba Temple, Adefumi offered, "We must Africanize everything! Our names, our hats, our clothes, our clubs, our churches…etc., etc., etc." Many of the youth of Weems's generation rejected their "slave" names and adopted African or Arabic names. Through his association with the Yoruba temple, Weems was renamed. He would be Donald Weems no more, adopting an Ewe day name, "Kuwasi," for a male born on Sunday, and the Yoruba name "Balagoon," meaning "warlord." He would later say that the name Kuwasi Balagoon "reflects what I am about and my origins."[6]

Revolutionary Nationalism:
Balagoon and the New York Black Panther Party

While Balagoon found his cultural bearing in the Yoruba Temple, he was attracted to the Black Power politics of revolutionary Black nationalism. The revolutionary Black nationalism of the Black Power movement was a political expression that argued that Black liberation would not be possible without the overthrow of the U.S. constitutional order and capitalist economic system. Revolutionary Black nationalism represented a confluence of ideological influences on the Black freedom movement. Significant numbers of Black militants of the 1960s Black Power movement did not see classical Marxism-Leninism as a framework they could identify with. Many were inspired by the influence of Marxism in the Chinese and Cuban Revolutions and other national liberation movements in Africa, Asia, and the Americas, but were critical of the racism of the Old Left and sought a theoretical vehicle and self-definition that gave them ideological self-determination. A significant number of Black youth identified with the direct action of the Civil Rights Movement but were not committed to nonviolence as a way of life. Some Black radicals also identified with Black nationalism and rejected the integration and pro-assimilationist tendencies within the Civil Rights Movement. Young Black Power militants also sought a more insurgent political program than they observed from the Nation of Islam and fundamental Black nationalists. As a new ideological development in the Black freedom movement, the Revolutionary Black nationalism of the Black Power movement incorporated the Marxian critique of capitalism, the historic tradition of Black nationalism and self-determination, and the direct action approach that characterized the Civil Rights Movement.[7]

In his own words, Balagoon "became a revolutionary and accepted the doctrine of nationalism as a response to the genocide practiced by the United States government." He began to read literature like the *Autobiography of Malcolm X*, Robert F. Williams's book *Negroes with Guns,* and the newsletter *The Crusader.* SNCC leader and Black Power movement spokesman H. Rap Brown also inspired Balagoon. Brown was elevated to spokesman of SNCC in 1967. He became one of the most recognized voices of the Black Power movement and the rebellion of urban communities of the late 1960s. Balagoon also came to embrace the position that Black liberation would only come through "protracted guerrilla warfare."[8]

Balagoon would actualize his revolutionary nationalist politics as a member of the Black Panther Party. Originally the Black Panther Party for Self-Defense (BPP) had distinguished itself in Oakland, California, by its armed patrols to monitor police abuse and its armed demonstration at the California State Legislature in Sacramento on May 2, 1967. Balagoon first heard of the BPP after the October 28, 1967, shootout between BPP founder Huey Newton and one of his comrades and members of the Oakland Police Department. The shooting left Officer John Frey fatally wounded and Newton and Officer Herbert Heanes injured; Newton's companion fled the scene. Newton became a national hero to urban Black youth after the shootout. While Newton was wounded in the exchange, the thought that a militant Black Power activist actually survived a gun battle with white police automatically propelled him to legendary heights. After he was charged with Frey's murder, the defense of Newton and the call to "Free Huey" became a popular cause in Black Power and left circles.[9]

The BPP came to New York in the summer of 1968. An alliance between the Student Nonviolent Coordinating Committee (SNCC) and the Revolutionary Action Movement (RAM) had attempted to create a Black Panther Party in New York in June 1966, but this grouping became dysfunctional due to internal conflict.[10] The Oakland-based Black Panther Party for Self-Defense became a national organization after the assassination of Martin Luther King Jr. in April 1968. The organization grew from a regional organization with chapters in the California Bay Area, Los Angeles, and Seattle to a national movement with thousands of members and supporters throughout the United States. Building a chapter in New York was one of the most important events of this development. The same month as Dr. King's assassination, national BPP Central Committee members Bobby Seale and Kathleen Cleaver came to New York and appointed eighteen-year-old SNCC member Joudon Ford as acting captain of defense of the BPP on the East Coast. Ford was soon joined by forty-year-old David Brothers to found the New York chapter of the BPP in Brooklyn in the summer of 1968. The national leadership sent Ron Pennywell, a trusted member of its cadre, to give direction to the New York chapter. Pennywell had reached the rank of captain in the BPP ranks. Pennywell was described as "a very grass-root brother, who would always ask the cadre for suggestions."[11]

Lumumba Shakur would found the Harlem branch of the New York chapter. Shakur was the son of a Malcolm X Shabazz associate Saladin Shakur. The elder Shakur also served as a mentor and surrogate father for many members of the New York BPP chapter. Lumumba Shakur and his friend Sekou Odinga traveled to Oakland in 1968 to learn about the BPP. Shakur and Odinga met in prison in the early 1960s and embraced Islam and revolutionary nationalism through the teachings of Malcolm X and under the tutelage of Saladin Shakur, a member of Shabazz's Muslim Mosque Incorporated and the Organization of Afro-American Unity. After the assassination of Malcolm X, both young men attempted to find a revolutionary organization to replace the fledgling Organization of Afro-American Unity. They returned to meet Pennywell and Brothers in April 1968. Shakur was the section leader of Harlem, and Odinga was assigned to organize the Bronx with Bilal Sunni-Ali, who had introduced them to Pennywell. The New York chapter of the BPP would grow to be among the largest, if not the largest, in the organization, with approximately five hundred members.[12]

When Balagoon found out the BPP was organizing in New York, he located the organization and ultimately joined. He had affinity with the BPP's ten-point program, which he believed was "community based." He also identified with the organization's appropriation of Mao Zedong's axiom that political power "comes from the barrel of a gun."[13] The assertion of the necessity of armed struggle was not the only principle the BPP borrowed from Mao. Mao and the Chinese Revolution profoundly influenced the BPP, as it did other radical movements of the 1960s.

The Chinese Communist Party and its Leninist model of democratic centralism was the model of organization for the BPP. The BPP's National Central Committee (NCC) was the highest decision-making body of the organization. The first NCC was concentrated in Oakland, with the overwhelming majority of the body composed of associates of BPP founder Huey Newton.[14] The BPP also functioned as a paramilitary organization, with Newton, as Minister of Defense, being the principal leader and with military positions (*e.g.*, Captain, Field Marshal, etc.) integrated into the organization's chain of command. The BPP system and style of governance would become a factor in Balagoon's attraction to antiauthoritarian politics.

Balagoon was able to engage in militant, grassroots organizing, combined with revolutionary ideology, as a member of the BPP in Harlem. In the Party he found comrades ready to participate in working with poor and oppressed Black communities around basic issues and willing to challenge the system with insurgent action. The New York City BPP engaged in grassroots organizing. In September 1968, BPP members participated in a community takeover of Lincoln Hospital. Lincoln was a "dilapidated and disinvested public hospital in the [predominately Black and Latino] South Bronx." The BPP would ultimately align itself with the Puerto Rican Young Lords and the

Lincoln Detox~

The People's Program

Lincoln Detox, staffed mainly by people who were themselves detoxified at the program, is known as "The People's Program." It is located in the South Bronx and has detoxified 35,000 victims of methadone and heroin in the five years of its existence.

Other Detox acti
Program court colle
sists lawyers to help
of poor people who

Provisional Government of the Republic of New Africa to take over and reform the Detox Program at Lincoln Hospital.[15] New York Panther branches were also involved in tenant organizing and in fights for community control of the school system and of the police. BPP leaders, along with the Emergency Civil Liberties Committee, Center for Constitutional Rights, and the National Lawyers Guild, filed a lawsuit calling for decentralization of the police in October 1968.[16] While Balagoon's previous experience as a tenant organizer helped him become a key member of the organization, he was attracted to the military wing of the BPP.

Repression and BPP Internal Contradictions: Catalyst Towards Antiauthoritarianism

Balagoon and New York BPP member Richard Harris were arrested in February 1969 on bank robbery charges in Newark, New Jersey. On April 2, 1969, less than one year after the founding of the New York chapter of the BPP, twenty-one Panther leaders and organizers (including Balagoon and Harris) were indicted, twelve arrested on conspiracy charges in a thirty-count indictment. This case became known as the case of the New York Panther 21. The charges included conspiracy to bomb the New York Botanical Gardens and police stations and to assassinate police officers. After their arrest, most of the defendants were released on a hundred thousand dollars bail. Balagoon was held without bail.[17]

A central charge in the indictment was the accusation that on January 17, 1969, Balagoon and Odinga planned to ambush New York police but were interrupted by other officers coming on the scene. This charge was based on testimony from a nineteen-year-old BPP member Joan Bird, who, defense attorneys argued, had been beaten by police to elicit a statement to favor the prosecution. Bird's mother reported arriving at the police station and hearing her daughter screaming. She was startled when she was taken to her daughter, who had visibly been beaten, with a black eye, swollen lip, and bruises on her face.[18]

Odinga escaped police and went underground on the day he was charged, after hearing of Bird's arrest and alleged torture. He escaped arrest on April 2, when his comrades were apprehended, fled the United States, and eventually received political asylum in Algeria. Balagoon was severed from the case of thirteen of those who had been arrested originally, to face charges in New Jersey. After over two years behind bars, the thirteen defendants were acquitted of all charges. It only took the jury one hour of deliberation to acquit. While this was a significant legal victory, the incarceration of key organizers and leaders of the New York BPP significantly crippled the organization's momentum and activities. After the acquittal of most of his comrades, Balagoon pleaded guilty to the charge that he and an unidentified person did attempt to shoot police officers, making him the only one of the twenty-one original defendants to be convicted. If these charges were true, Balagoon had committed himself to participate in offensive guerrilla warfare as early as 1969.[19]

The BPP national leadership's handling of the New York Panther 21 case played a significant role in the transition of Balagoon from revolutionary nationalism and democratic centralism to antiauthoritarian politics. The members of the New York BPP, including the defendants in the Panther 21 conspiracy trial, became disenchanted with the national leadership in Oakland. Division between the Oakland-based national leadership and the New York chapter increased after the purge of Geronimo Pratt by the national leadership. Pratt, a U.S. Army veteran who served as an Army Ranger in Vietnam, distinguished himself by training BPP members and other Black liberation forces in paramilitary tactics. He went underground to develop a clandestine apparatus but was captured in Dallas, Texas, on December 8, 1970. On January 23, 1971, Huey Newton, the BPP Minister of Defense, expelled Pratt from the organization for "counterrevolutionary behavior." Newton's expulsion of Pratt created confusion within the ranks of the organization. Many BPP rank-and-file members considered Pratt a hero, and he was well-respected in the New York chapter.[20]

The expulsion of Pratt is connected to a series of expulsions by the national leadership of BPP members engaged in armed struggle. The initial orientation of the BPP encouraged the development of an armed underground capacity to wage guerrilla warfare. Combined with the image of armed Panthers patrolling against the police, many Blacks who believed in armed confrontation with the state were attracted to the BPP. The New York BPP had developed an armed clandestine capacity from its inception. One police officer reported at a congressional hearing: "Members of the Panthers are not secret, with the exception of those who have been designated 'underground.' This group are secret revolutionaries and their identities are kept secret." New York police and the FBI suspected the BPP in an August 2, 1968, shooting of two police officers in Brooklyn and an attempted bombing of a New York City police station on November 2, 1968.[21]

Tensions also developed when the BPP national leadership sent Oakland cadres Robert Bey and Thomas Jolly to New York to assume leadership of the chapter. Years later, Balagoon publicly criticized the decision to import a new leadership group to New York, as opposed to promoting indigenous leadership from the local community. He saw this as critical to destabilizing the revolutionary vitality of the organization. Other New York BPP members shared Balagoon's criticism of the NCC appointment of supervisory leadership over Panther activity in New York and on the East Coast. Unlike Pennywell, the newly imported leadership possessed a more autocratic and hierarchical style of decision-making. In her autobiography, Assata Shakur questioned the quality of some of the West Coast leaders sent to New York. Shakur noted:

> We [New York BPP members] had a bit of a leadership problem with Robert Bey and Jolly who were both from the West Coast. Bey's problem was that he was none too bright and that he had an aggressive, even belligerent, way of talking and dealing with people. Jolly's problem was that he was Robert Bey's shadow.[22]

Members of the Harlem BPP branch, along with historian Kit Holder, argued the "lack of indigenous leadership on the local level was one of the major contributing factors to the initial differences of opinions and misunderstandings" between the national leadership and the New York chapter.[23] Holder argued these factors "inhibited the growth of the Party." One of the factors Holder identified was "cultural nationalism."

Due to conflict with elements of the Black Arts Movement in the Bay Area and the US Organization in Los Angeles, the California-based BPP developed an aversion to African Americans who identified with African culture. The New York group, on the other hand, embraced African and Arabic names (*e.g.*, Kuwasi, Afeni, Assata, Lumumba, Dhoruba, Zayd, etc.) and African clothing. Some were Muslims or influenced by African traditional religion. Holder reports that the national leadership barred New York BPP members from participating in nationalist-oriented community events or displaying the red, black, and green flag that originated in the Pan-African nationalist Universal Negro Improvement Association (aka the Garvey movement). The decision by nationally appointed leadership to take emphasis away from the local activism of the New York BPP around tenant issues and reassign cadre to "serve the people" programs that were popular on the West Coast was also resented by New York cadre.[24]

The incarcerated members of the New York BPP conspiracy case also believed the national leadership did not provide sufficient financial support for their legal defense. Balagoon would comment on how the national leadership selectively determined who would be released on bail. He stated: "Those who were bailed out were chosen by the leadership, regardless of the wishes of the rank-and-file or fellow prisoners of war or regardless of the relatively low bail of at least one proven comrade." It must also be noted that the U.S. government, particularly the FBI through its Cointelpro program, worked to increase the division within the national leadership of the BPP, the New York chapter, and the New York Panther 21 defendants.[25]

After a series of attempts to send criticisms of the national leadership to the *Black Panther* newspaper, New York Panther 21 defendants publicly took what was interpreted as a critical position on the BPP national leadership in an open letter to the Weather Underground published on January 19, 1971. The Weather Underground was a clandestine organization of white radical anti-imperialists who initiated a campaign of armed propaganda by bombing U.S. government facilities in solidarity with national liberation movements, particularly in Vietnam. The open letter applauded the insurgent actions of the Weather Underground and acknowledged them as part of the vanguard of the revolutionary movement in the United States. Without naming the BPP national leadership, the statement of the incarcerated New York Panthers also critiqued "self-proclaimed 'vanguard' parties" that abandoned the actions of the radical underground struggle and the political prisoners.[26] Balagoon agreed with this criticism of the national leadership of the BPP.

> Under their leadership, "political consequences" (attacks) against occupation forces [police] ceased altogether. Only a fraction of the money collected for the purpose of bail went towards bail. The leaders began to live high off the hog … leaving behind so many robots [in the rank and file] who wouldn't challenge policy until those in jail publicly denounced the leadership.[27]

The differences between the national leadership and the New York BPP accelerated after the publication of the New York Panther 21 open letter. Newton immediately expelled the Panther 21 on February 9, 1971. The cover of the February 13 *Black Panther* newspaper would declare New York BPP leaders and New York Panther 21 defendants Richard Dhoruba Moore, Cetawayo Tabor, and Newton's personal secretary Connie Matthews "Enemies of the People." Moore and Tabor, out on bail, went underground rather than return to court proceedings. They would ultimately surface in Algeria at the BPP international section. Later that month, members of the New York BPP would hold a press conference and call for the purge of Huey Newton and BPP Chief of Staff David Hilliard and the formation of a new National Central Committee. The New York chapter officially split from the national organization.[28]

Balagoon's involvement in the New York BPP was an important part of his political development. On the one hand, he was inspired to be a part of a dynamic revolutionary movement with comrades that he respected, loved, and trusted. On the other, Balagoon's experience with the BPP national leadership left him questioning its decision-making and the nature of democracy in the organization. While acknowledging that state repression disrupted this revolutionary nationalist organization, Balagoon wanted to correct the internal and ideological weaknesses that compromised the fighting capacity and solidarity of the liberation movement.

Besides his disenchantment with the BPP national leadership, Balagoon's receptivity to antiauthoritarian politics was also supported by his role in organizing fellow inmates as a Panther political prisoner. His comrade Kazembe Balagun argues that Kuwasi's experience in prison awaiting trial influenced his transition to anarchism. The New York Panther 21 were incarcerated at a variety of jails in different boroughs of New York City. Kit Holder called a series of inmate protests at each of these institutions in 1970 a "coordinated rebellion." Balagoon, Lumumba Shakur, and New York Panther 21 defendant Kwando Kinshasa were all incarcerated in the Queens House of Detention, where inmates organized an uprising that took seven hostages, including a captain, five correctional officers, and a Black cook, holding them from October 1 to 5, 1970. The slogan for the multiethnic (Black, Latino, and white) inmate takeover was "all power to the people, free all oppressed people." The primary demand of the inmates was for speedier trials. Instead of attempting to play a "vanguard" role in the decision-making, Kazembe Balagun argued, even before formally declaring his commitment to anti-authoritarian politics, Kuwasi Balagoon's "primary concern was a consensus process for all inmates in decision-making, including access to food being brought from the outside." He and the other incarcerated Panthers in Queens were concerned that the weight of the Panther leadership was too influential on the general consensus of other prisoners, so Kuwasi and his comrades skipped general meetings to allow prisoners to "determine what was true and what was bullshit." The Panthers also promised to go with the majority.

The prisoners formed committees to coordinate their uprising. The inmates agreed to release the Black cook and one prison guard as a "sign of good faith." The prisoners ultimately released all of the hostages and suffered physical abuse and charges from the uprising. Kazembe Balagun argues that while Kuwasi was disappointed at the outcome, he believed the power the inmate resisters felt by "holding the state at bay" was a valuable experience. As an organizer, he saw the uprising as "'growing pains' to those of us who believe oppressed people *will* rise up and seek justice."[29]

From Black Panther Party to Black Liberation Army

Balagoon's experience in the BPP and the repression of the New York chapter also convinced him of the necessity of being involved in a clandestine fight against the state. He concluded that repression turned the BPP away from grassroots organizing the Black masses around issues that most affected their daily survival (housing, education, and police abuse) to defending the political prisoners. Balagoon stated:

> The state rounded up all the organizers pointed out to it by its agents who infiltrated the party as soon as it had been organizing in New York. It charged these people with conspiracy and demanded bails so high that the party turned away from its purpose of liberation of the Black colony to fundraising [for legal defense].

This experience convinced him that "to survive and contribute I would have to go underground and literally fight."[30] Balagoon was committed to building a Black Liberation Army and saw his role in the Black Liberation Movement as a clandestine freedom fighter.

On September 27, 1973, Balagoon would escape from New Jersey's Rahway State Prison shortly after his conviction for armed robbery in New Jersey. Approximately eight months after his escape, on May 5, 1974, Balagoon was captured attempting to assist New York BPP member and New York Panther 21 defendant Richard Harris escape from custody while being transported to a funeral in Newark. Balagoon and Harris were apprehended after being wounded in a gun battle with correctional and police officers. Risking being recaptured to free Harris demonstrated Balagoon's commitment to his comrades and willingness to sacrifice for the liberation struggle.[31]

New Afrikan Anarchism

Balagoon's imprisonment and expulsion from and disillusionment with the BPP did not discourage his involvement or commitment to revolution. He began to explore anarchist politics during his incarceration. Balagoon received and studied literature from solidarity groups such as Anarchist Black Cross, an antiauthoritarian organization that provided material and legal support to political prisoners. Anarchism provided an analytical lens to sum up his critique of his experience in the BPP. According to Balagun, he worked to "apply the theories of Wilhelm Reich, Emma Goldman and others to the Black liberation struggle." He began to ask critical questions about the practice of his comrades and himself in allowing the national hierarchy to weaken the resolve and fighting capacity of the BPP. He concluded:

> The cadre accepted their command regardless of what their intellect had or had not made clear to them. The true democratic process which they were willing to die for, for the sake of their children, they would not claim for themselves.[32]

He desired a democratic process that would unleash the revolutionary potential of the masses and not make them prey to new oppressors.

> It is to say the only way to make a dictatorship of the proletariat is to elevate everyone to being proletariat and deflate all the advantages of power that translate into the wills of a few dictating to the majority …. Only an anarchist revolution has on its agenda to deal with these goals.[33]

Balagoon clearly believed that true Black liberation could only be achieved through anarchism.

While incarcerated he read and identified with certain radical anarchists, particularly those men and women of action advocating insurrection against the oppressive order and the necessity and right of the oppressed to expropriate resources from their oppressors. One of his inspirations was Italian anarchist Errico Malatesta, who exhorted that revolutionary struggle "consists more of deeds than words." Another influence was Spanish revolutionary José Buenaventura Durruti Dumange, who organized the anarchist guerrilla movement *Los Justicieros* (The Avenging Ones). Like their name, *Los Justicieros* were thought to be involved in political assassinations in retaliation for political repression and guerrilla raids on the military forces of the Spanish dictatorship. Balagoon was also motivated by the example of Italian exile

Severino Di Giovanni, known for his campaign of bombing as armed propaganda in solidarity with executed anarchists Sacco and Vanzetti. Durutti and Giovanni both engaged in expropriation of capitalist institutions as a mean of supporting the revolutionary movement.[34]

Another ideological influence on Balagoon was Russian immigrant and pioneer of American anarchism Emma Goldman. Another advocate of revolutionary armed struggle, Goldman supported the attempt by her comrade Alexander Berkman to assassinate a wealthy industrialist, Henry Clay Frick. The methods used by Frick to suppress the Homestead Steel strike in Pennsylvania "justified the means." Goldman's encouragement of "free love" also resonated with Balagoon, as he was open to sexual relationships with both men and women.[35]

Balagoon continued to believe the original BPP position that Black people were an internal colony of the United States and interpreted the Black liberation struggle as a national liberation movement. Like other BLA members, he also began to identify with the New Afrikan Independence Movement. The Provisional Government of the Republic of New Africa (PGRNA) viewed Black people as a "subjugated nation" within the USA. The PGRNA was founded in March 1968 at a conference of five hundred Black nationalists who declared their independence from the United States and demanded five states in the Deep South (South Carolina, Georgia, Alabama, Mississippi, Louisiana) as reparations for the enslavement and racial oppression of Blacks. "New Afrika" was declared the name of the new nation and the five states as its national territory. Some New York BPP members developed a political relationship with the PGRNA from its inception. Kamau Sadiki (aka Freddie Hilton) of the Queens BPP branch remembers PGRNA member Mutulu Shakur facilitating political education sessions for him and other BPP members. Corona (in the borough of Queens) BPP branch leader Cyril Innis remembers taking the oath of allegiance to the New Afrikan nation in 1969, when the PGRNA and BPP collaborated around struggles for community control of education in New York's public schools.[36]

Like many of the New York BPP and BLA comrades, Balagoon began to ideologically unite with the political objective of the PGRNA for independence and adopted "New Afrikan" as his national identity. Balagoon believed that:

> We say the U.S. has no right to confine New Afrikan people to redlined reservations and that We have a right to live on our own terms on a common land area and to govern ourselves, free of occupation forces such as the police, national guard, or GIs that have invaded our colonies from time to time. We have a right to control our own economy, print our own money, trade with other nations.... We have a right to control our educational institutions and systems where our children will not be indoctrinated by aliens to suffer the destructive designs of the U.S. government.

His position for Black self-determination was also combined with an anti-capitalist perspective. Balagoon proposed that New Afrikans would

> enter a workforce where We are not excluded by design and where our wages and the wages of all workers cannot be manipulated by a ruling class that controls the wealth.

The New Afrikan Independence Movement was consistent with Balagoon's belief in the necessity of national liberation of the colonized Black nation. He identified himself as a New Afrikan anarchist to express his national identity, aspiration for self-determination, and desire for whatever type of society he wished to inhabit.

Balagoon's identity as a New Afrikan anarchist set him ideologically apart from Black Marxist-Leninists and revolutionary nationalists who had the objective of seizing state power from the white power structure of U.S. capitalism and imperialism. But he still desired a land for Black people to achieve self-determination and space to build a society based on antiauthoritarianism and freedom. His continued support for New Afrikan politics also distinguished him from the majority of the anarchist movement in the United States, many of whom opposed any form of nationalism.

Balagoon would share his New Afrikan anarchist viewpoint and ideologically struggle with Marxist-Leninist and revolutionary nationalist political prisoners incarcerated with him. He recruited soldiers for the BLA, as well as converts to antiauthoritarian and New Afrikan politics. In Trenton State Prison, in New Jersey, his fellow New York Panther 21 defendant Sundiata Acoli and BLA members James York and Andaliwa Clark formed a political study group inside the penitentiary.[37]

Political education behind bars became a vehicle for recruitment into the BLA. Clark and Kojo Bomani were both inmates who had been politicized by Balagoon and other political prisoners after being incarcerated and recruited into the BLA.[38] Bomani was released in 1975 and arrested in December of the same year in a failed BLA expropriation of a financial institution. A BLA member captured with Bomani was Ojore Lutalo. Lutalo provides testimony concerning Balagoon's influence on his transition from Marxism-Leninism to antiauthoritarian thinking:

> In 1975 I became disillusioned with Marxism and became an anarchist (thanks to Kuwasi Balagoon) due to the inactiveness and ineffectiveness of Marxism in our communities along with repressive bureaucracy that comes with Marxism. People aren't going to commit themselves to a life-and-death struggle just because of grand ideas someone might have floating around in their heads. I feel people will commit themselves to a struggle if they can see progress being made similar to the progress of anarchist collectives in Spain during the era of the fascist Bahamonde.[39]

Like his teacher and comrade, Lutalo identified himself as a "New Afrikan/Anarchist Prisoner of War."

A New Afrikan Freedom Fighter:
Balagoon and the Revolutionary Armed Task Force

Balagoon would again escape from Rahway State Prison in New Jersey on May 27, 1978. He would rejoin a clandestine network of BLA soldiers in alliance with white radicals in solidarity with the Black Liberation Movement and other national liberation struggles. This ideologically diverse network of insurgent militants was known as the Revolutionary Armed Task Force (RATF). The RATF was described as "a strategic alliance…under the leadership of the Black Liberation Army." The BLA members in the alliance identified themselves as Muslims or revolutionary nationalists and the white radicals as anti-imperialists or communists. Balagoon appeared to be the sole anarchist in this formation. Balagoon's BPP comrade Sekou Odinga had returned from political exile in Algeria and the People's Republic of the Congo to be a major leader in this formation. While Balagoon was critical of Marxism and nationalism, he decided to join comrades he loved and trusted in a common front against white supremacy, capitalism, and imperialism. He and his comrades in the RATF also had political unity on the question of New Afrikan independence. This wing of the BLA identified themselves as "New Afrikan Freedom Fighters." Balagoon, who was considered a "free spirit," viewed most nationalist formations as "too rigid." His RATF comrades, despite ideological differences and his sexual orientation, respected Balagoon due to his commitment to revolutionary struggle and his history of sacrifices on behalf of his comrades and for the liberation movement. In terms of his sexuality, comrades stated, "That's Kuwasi's business." Differences over ideology and sexual orientation were tolerated and subordinated to the pragmatic unity necessary to carry out the clandestine work of armed propaganda, expropriations of resources from capitalist financial institutions, or assisting comrades in escaping from incarceration.[40]

The RATF came together in response to an increase in violent acts against Black people in the late 1970s and early 1980s, including the murders of Black children and youth in Atlanta and Black women in Boston and shootings of Black women in

Alabama. The increase in white supremacist paramilitary activity, including the Ku Klux Klan, was a related motivator for this alliance. The whites in the RATF participated in intelligence gathering on white supremacist and right-wing activity to ascertain its capability and connection with elements of the U.S. military. The RATF also engaged in "expropriations" to obtain resources to build the capacity of the Black Liberation Movement to resist the white supremacist upsurge.[41]

The two most well-known actions of this New Afrikan Freedom Fighters wing of the BLA and the RATF were the escape of Assata Shakur and the attempted "Brink's expropriation" in Nyack, New York. Assata Shakur was a member of the New York BPP who was forced underground in response to the repression of the organization. She was captured on May 2, 1973, after a shootout with New Jersey state troopers and BLA members. State trooper Werner Foerster and New York BPP member Zayd Shakur were both killed in the shootout. Assata Shakur was wounded and paralyzed from the shooting. Former New York Panther 21 defendant and BLA member Sundiata Acoli was captured two days after the shootout, having escaped the scene. The FBI identified Assata Shakur as the "soul of the BLA" and hailed her capture as a significant event in "breaking the back" of the Black underground. While forensic evidence proved she did not fire a gun, and although she was paralyzed at the outset of the shooting, Assata Shakur was convicted of the murder of Foerster and Zayd Shakur and sentenced to life plus sixty-five years. She was considered a political prisoner by human rights organizations in the United States and internationally.

According to the FBI, an armed team of four BLA members, including Odinga and Balagoon and two white allies, facilitated the escape of Shakur from Clinton Correctional Institution for Women in New Jersey on November 2, 1979. Prison officials stated the raid was "well planned and arranged." Shakur's escape was hailed and celebrated as a "liberation" by the Black Liberation Movement and demonstrated the continued existence of the BLA.[42]

An attempt by the BLA and RATF to expropriate 1.6 million dollars from a Brink's armored truck in the New York city of

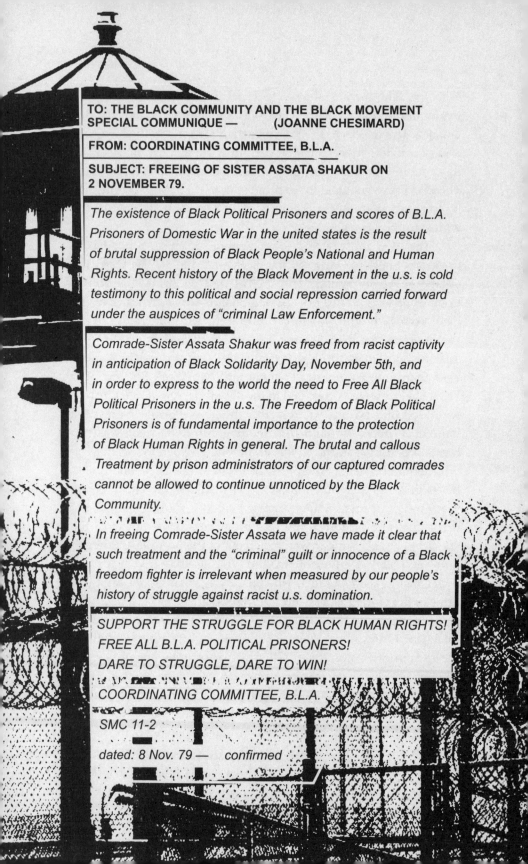

TO: THE BLACK COMMUNITY AND THE BLACK MOVEMENT
SPECIAL COMMUNIQUE — <u>(JOANNE CHESIMARD)</u>

FROM: COORDINATING COMMITTEE, B.L.A.

SUBJECT: FREEING OF SISTER ASSATA SHAKUR ON
2 NOVEMBER 79.

*The existence of Black Political Prisoners and scores of B.L.A.
Prisoners of Domestic War in the united states is the result
of brutal suppression of Black People's National and Human
Rights. Recent history of the Black Movement in the u.s. is cold
testimony to this political and social repression carried forward
under the auspices of "criminal Law Enforcement."*

*Comrade-Sister Assata Shakur was freed from racist captivity
in anticipation of Black Solidarity Day, November 5th, and
in order to express to the world the need to Free All Black
Political Prisoners in the u.s. The Freedom of Black Political
Prisoners is of fundamental importance to the protection
of Black Human Rights in general. The brutal and callous
Treatment by prison administrators of our captured comrades
cannot be allowed to continue unnoticed by the Black
Community.*

*In freeing Comrade-Sister Assata we have made it clear that
such treatment and the "criminal" guilt or innocence of a Black
freedom fighter is irrelevant when measured by our people's
history of struggle against racist u.s. domination.*

SUPPORT THE STRUGGLE FOR BLACK HUMAN RIGHTS!
FREE ALL B.L.A. POLITICAL PRISONERS!
DARE TO STRUGGLE, DARE TO WIN!

COORDINATING COMMITTEE, B.L.A.

SMC 11-2

dated: 8 Nov. 79 —   confirmed

Nyack on October 20, 1981, led to an exchange of fire, resulting in the deaths of one Brink's security guard and two police officers. Three white radicals — Judy Clark, David Gilbert, and Kathy Boudin — and one Black man — Solomon Brown — were captured. A manhunt ensued for others who were believed to have escaped the scene or assisted in the attempt. Physical evidence, electronic surveillance, and informants led to arrests of other revolutionaries and the death of BLA member Mtayari Sundiata. The Joint Terrorist Task Force (JTTF) apprehended Balagoon in New York City at a Manhattan apartment three months later. The JTTF was organized after the escape of Assata Shakur to provide a coordinated investigation by FBI and local police. The FBI believed Balagoon was a part of the BLA team that initiated the expropriation attempt in Nyack. It was also believed that this wing of the BLA had successfully expropriated funds from financial institutions in a series of raids dating back to 1976. The funds had been utilized to support the development of an underground infrastructure, families of political prisoners, Black Liberation Movement political activities and institutions, and freedom struggles on the African continent.[43]

New Afrikan Anarchist Prisoner of War

After his capture, Kuwasi Balagoon publicly spoke to the movement for the first time since the publication of *Look for Me in the Whirlwind* eleven years earlier, in 1971. Defining himself as a New Afrikan anarchist, Balagoon represented New Afrikan and antiauthoritarian politics in public statements. In captivity, he defined himself as a prisoner of war not a criminal. Balagoon acted *pro se* (served as his own attorney) at the Rockland County trial where he was charged with armed robbery for the Nyack expropriation and the murders of the Brink's guard and two police officers. This gave him the opportunity to speak to the public about his politics and to make his intentions clear for history. In his opening statement, Balagoon declared:

i am a prisoner of war. i reject the crap about me being a defendant, and i do not recognize the legitimacy of this court. The term defendant applies to someone involved in a criminal matter.... It is clear that i've been a part of the Black Liberation Movement all of my adult life and have been involved in a war against the American Imperialist, in order to free New Afrikan people from its yoke.[44]

Balagoon wanted it acknowledged that his armed actions were politically motivated to win national liberation for New Afrikan people and to eliminate capitalism, imperialism, and ultimately authoritarian forms of government.

Once convicted and sentenced to life imprisonment, Balagoon continued to speak to New Afrikan/Black Liberation forces and anarchist gatherings through public statements. As well as his continued support for armed struggle, he advocated the building of an insurgent movement and building of autonomous communities. On July 18, 1983, at a Harlem rally for imprisoned New Afrikan Freedom Fighters, Balagoon's statement was read: "We must build a revolutionary political platform and a universal network of survival programs."[45] In another statement directed to anarchists, Balagoon stated:

Where we live and work...We must organize on the ground level. The landlords must be contested through rent strikes and rather than develop strategies to pay rent, we should develop strategies to take the buildings.... Set up communes in abandoned buildings.... Turn vacant lots into gardens. When our children grow out of clothes, we should have places we can take them, clearly marked anarchist clothing exchanges.... We must learn construction and ways to take back our lives.[46]

He also challenged anarchists to move from theory to practice. In the tradition of the insurgent anarchists of previous generations who inspired him, Balagoon argued:

We permit people of other ideologies to define anarchy rather than bring our views to the masses and provide models to show the contrary.... In short, by not engaging in mass organizing and delivering war to the oppressors, we become anarchists in name only.[47]

Balagoon also continued to organize and provide political education to other prisoners. He died in prison on December 13, 1986, from pneumocystis pneumonia, an AIDS-related illness.

Legacy

While Balagoon is not in mainstream discourse, his name is evoked in some Black/New Afrikan, anarchist, and queer spaces. In 2005, the Malcolm X Grassroots Movement (MXGM), a New Afrikan activist organization, dedicated its annual Black August celebration to Kuwasi Balagoon. That year MXGM highlighted the need for awareness of the AIDS virus in Africa and among the African diaspora. A few radical hip-hop artists, such as Dead Prez and Zayd Malik, also mention Balagoon's name. But Balagoon's name is not commonly used, even in socially conscious hip-hop, as much as other Black revolutionaries such as Marcus Garvey, Huey Newton, Assata Shakur, Geronimo (Pratt) ji Jaga, and Mutulu Shakur.

Anarchist collectives have republished Balagoon's statements. After his incarceration and self-identification as an anarchist, a Canadian antiauthoritarian collective that published the newsletter *Bulldozer*, which later became known as *Prison News Service*, published Balagoon's writings. The Patterson Anarchist Collective in New Jersey reprinted his trial statement and tributes to his life in 1994. The Quebec collective Solidarity issued a Collected Works of Balagoon's trial statements, essays, poetry, and acknowledgements from comrades titled *A Soldier's Story: Writings by a Revolutionary New Afrikan Anarchist*; subsequently reissued by Kersplebedeb. [The first edition of this book was published in 2001; the most recent edition is the book you are holding in your hands today, now copublished with PM Press.]

Radical queer liberation forces also embraced Balagoon's legacy. He acknowledged his bisexual identity within a primarily heteronormative Black Liberation Movement. ACT UP, a direct action organization emerging from queer liberation forces, joined forces with anarchists and revolutionary Black/New Afrikan nationalists to commemorate Balagoon in December 2006. His sexual identity has become a vehicle to challenge homophobia within the broader Black Liberation Movement. Elements of the queer liberation movement and their allies have criticized Black liberation forces for being silent on Balagoon's sexuality. Balagun, in a posthumous statement honoring Kuwasi Balagoon, offered this:

> One of the silences that engulfed Kuwasi's life was his bisexuality. The official eulogies offered by the New Afrikan People's Organization and others omitted his sexuality or that he died of AIDS-related complications. These erasures are a reflection of the ongoing internal struggle against homophobia and patriarchy within the larger society in general and the movement in particular.[48]

This issue will remain so long as heteronormativity remains the dominant sexual orientation of the Black Liberation Movement.

Kuwasi Balagoon is remembered and saluted by revolutionary nationalists, radical anarchists, and queer liberation forces. He remains a "Maroon" isolated from mainstream Black and left political dialogue and memory. His legacy will only be secure with the survival and empowerment of the political tendencies he represented. Balagoon's name will only be saved from obscurity when insurgent Black nationalists and anarchist collectives take up his charge to organize oppressed people to build a revolutionary program that challenges capitalism and institutional racism in the United States.

ENDNOTES

1.Arnold H. Lubasch, "Key Suspect is Arrested in Brink's Car Robbery," *New York Times,* January 22, 1982, accessed October 24, 2018, https://www.nytimes.com/1982/01/22/nyregion/key-suspect-is-arrested-in-brink-s-car-robbery.html.

2. Kuwasi Balagoon, in *Look for Me in the Whirlwind: From the Panther 21 to 21st Century Revolutions,* ed. dequi kioni-sadiki and Matt Meyer (Oakland: PM Press, 2017), 201–6; Tim Blunk and Ray Levasseur, eds., *Hauling Up the Morning: Writings and Art by Political Prisoners and Prisoners of War* (Trenton, NJ: Red Sea Press, 1990), 373; Kazembe Balagun, "Kuwasi at 60," *Monthly Review* (December 2006), accessed October 24, 2018, mrzine.monthlyreview.org/2006/balagun311206.html.

3. Balagoon, *Look for Me in the Whirlwind,* 255–6; Sharon Harley, "'Chronicle of a Death Foretold': Gloria Richardson, the Cambridge Movement, and the Radical Black Activist Tradition," in *Sisters in the Struggle: African-American Women in the Civil Rights-Black Power Movement,* ed. Betty Collier-Thomas and V.P. Franklin (New York: New York University Press, 2001), 174–96; Paula Giddings, *When and Where I Enter: The Impact of Black Women on Race and Sex in America* (New York: Bantam, 1994), 290–92.

4. Balagoon, *Look for Me in the Whirlwind,* 372, 392.

5. Jesse Gray, quoted in Peter Noel, "By Any Means Unnecessary," *The Village Voice,* September 2, 1999.

6. Balagoon, *Look for Me in the Whirlwind,* 368–72; David Gilbert, "In Memory of Kuwasi Balagoon, New Afrikan Freedom Fighter," see page 201 in current volume. Kuwasi Balagoon, "Anarchy Can't Fight Alone," see page 150 in current volume.

7. Harold Cruse, "Revolutionary Nationalism and the Afro-American," *Studies on the Left* 2, no. 3 (1962), accessed October 24, 2018, http://brotherwisedispatch.blogspot.com/2009/12/revolutionary-nationalism-and-afro.html. The first self-described revolutionary nationalist organization, the Revolutionary Action Movement, stated in 1963 that it was "somewhere between the Nation of Islam (Black Muslims) and SNCC (the Student Nonviolent Coordinating Committee)"; Max Stanford, in *Black*

Nationalism in America, ed. John Bracey, Elliot Rudwick, and August Meier (Indianapolis: Bobbs-Merrill, 1970), 508; Akinyele Omowale Umoja, "From One Generation to the Next: Armed Self-Defense, Revolutionary Nationalism, and the Southern Black Freedom Movement," *Souls: A Critical Journal of Black Politics, Culture and Society* 15, no. 3 (Fall 2013): 224–25.

8. Balagoon, *Look for Me in the Whirlwind,* 438; Balagoon, see page 150 in current volume.

9. Akinyele Omowale Umoja, "Set Our Warriors Free: The Legacy of the Black Panther Party and Political Prisoners," in *Black Panthers Reconsidered,* ed. Charles E. Jones (Baltimore, MD: Black Classics Press, 1998), 418–19.

10. Muhammad Ahmad, *We Will Return in the Whirlwind: Black Radical Organizations 1960–1975* (Chicago: Charles H. Kerr, 2007), 167–70.

11. Murray Kempton, *The Briar Patch: The Trial of the Panther 21* (New York: Da Capo Press, 1997), 43; Sundiata Acoli, "A Brief History of the Black Panther Party: Its Place in the Black Liberation Movement," February 4, 1985, accessed October 24, 2018, http://www.hartford-hwp.com/archives/45a/004.html; Balagoon, *Look for Me in the Whirlwind,* 463.

12. Lumumba Shakur, in *Look for Me in the Whirlwind,* 463; Acoli, "A Brief History of the Black Panther Party"; Kalonji Changa, "Tupac and the Revolutionary Shakur family: Interview with Bilal Sunni-Ali," *New Afrikan* 77, accessed October 24, 2018, tpmovement.tumblr.com/post/50587379244/shakur-family-tree; Ahmad, *We Will Return in the Whirlwind,* 191.

13. Balagoon, *Look for Me in the Whirlwind,* 438.

14. Kit Holder, "The History of the Black Panther Party 1966–1971" (PhD diss., University of Massachusetts, 1990), 255.

15. James Tracy, "Rising Up: Poor, White, and Angry in the New Left," in *The Hidden 1970s: Histories of Radicalism,* ed. Dan Berger (New Brunswick, NJ: Rutgers University Press, 2010), 223.

16. Holder, "The History of the Black Panther Party 1966–1971," 227.

17. Morris Kaplan, "Bomb Plot is Laid to 21 Panthers: Black Extremists Accused of Planning Explosions at Macy's and Elsewhere," *New York*

Times, April 3, 1969, accessed October 24, 2018, https://www.nytimes.com/1969/04/03/archives/bomb-plot-is-laid-to-21-panthers-black-extremists-accused-of.html; "Panther 21 Trial: Another Chicago," February 20, 1970, accessed October 24, 2018, http://jfk.hood.edu/Collection/Weisberg%20Subject%20Index%20Files/B%20Disk/Blacks%20Miscellaneous/049.pdf.

18. T.J. English, *The Savage City: Race, Murder, and a Generation on the Edge* (New York: Harper Collins, 2011), 267–68.

19. Sekou Odinga, in *Can't Jail the Spirit: Political Prisoners in the U.S.* (Chicago: Committee to End the Marion Lockdown, 1990), 143; Lubasch, "Key Suspect Is Arrested in Brink's Car Robbery"; Juan M. Vasquez, "One of Panther 21 Admits Helping Anti-Police Sniper," *New York Times,* October 8, 1971, accessed October 24, 2018, https://www.nytimes.com/1971/10/08/archives/one-of-panther-21-admits-helping-antipolice-sniper.html.

20. Akinyele Omowale Umoja, "Repression Breeds Resistance: The Black Liberation Army and the Radical Legacy of the Black Panther Party," *New Political Science* 21, no. 2 (June 1999): 138–39.

21. Thomas Courtney, Testimony of Sgt. Thomas Courtney in Hearings Before the Permanent Sub-Committee of the Committee Investigations of Government Operations United States Senate, Ninety-First Congress, First Session, Riots, Civil and Criminal Disorders, June 26 and 30, 1969, Part 20, Washington, DC, U.S. Government Printing Office, 4235.

22. Assata Shakur, *Assata: The Autobiography of a Revolutionary* (Chicago: Lawrence Hill, 2001).

23. Holder, "The History of the Black Panther Party 1966–1971," 258.

24. Ibid., 258–61.

25. Umoja, "Repression Breeds Resistance," 141; Balagoon, see page 151 in current volume.

26. Umoja, "Set Our Warriors Free," 421–22; Umoja, "Repression Breeds Resistance," 138–39.

27. Balagoon, see page 151 in current volume.

28. Umoja, "Repression Breeds Resistance," 141-43.

29. Balagun, "Kuwasi at 60"; Balagoon, *Look for Me in the Whirlwind*, 494–515; "6 Are Arraigned in 1970 Jail Riots: 2 Panthers Acquitted Last Week Among Defendants," *New York Times*, May 19, 1971, accessed October 26, 2018, https://www.nytimes.com/1971/05/19/archives/6-are-arraigned-in-1970-jail-riots-2-panthers-acquitted-last-week.html; "Prison Struggle 1970–1," n.d., accessed October 26, 2018, https://abolitionistpaper.files.wordpress.com/2012/03/fa-war-behind-walls-1970-1.pdf; "Queens House Of Detention Prison Riot" (photo), October 1970, accessed October 26, 2018, http://www.flickr.com/photos/nycdreamin/6735842575/.

30. Balagoon, see pages 150-1 in current volume.

31. Gilbert (2003), p. 9; Commission on Criminal Justice Services, New York State Report of the Policy Group on Terrorism, November 1985, 99–100; "Panther 21 Trial: Another Chicago"; Mutulu Shakur, "To Our Brother Kuwasi Balagoon," *Campaign to Free Dr. Mutulu Shakur*, 1986.

32. Balagoon, see page 151 in current volume.

33. Ibid.

34. Ashanti Alston, correspondence with author, September 7, 2013. Alston is a former Black Liberation Army member, political prisoner, and anarchist activist. See Ashanti Alston, "Propaganda of the Deed," *Workers' Solidarity* (October 1998); Abel Paz, *Durruti in the Spanish Revolution* (Oakland: AK Press, 2007), 9–22, 87, 88, 116.

35. Ojore Lutalo, phone interview with author, October 12, 2013.

36. Kamau Sadiki, discussion with author, Atlanta, Georgia, November 27, 2003; Cyril Innis, discussion with Charles E. Jones and author, Bronx, New York, June 5, 2013.

37. "Bashir Hamed: Black Liberation Army Political Prisoner," *It's About Time* 5, no. 4 (Fall–Winter 2001).

38. Clark would be killed in an attempted escape on January 19, 1976; Commission on Criminal Justice Services, *New York State Report of the Policy Group on Terrorism* (November 1985), 102.

39. Ojore Nuru Lutalo, in *Can't Jail the Spirit: Political Prisoners in the U.S.* (Chicago: Committee to End the Marion Lockdown, 2002), 132.

40. Umoja, "Repression Breeds Resistance," 154; "Sekou Odinga—New Afrikan Prisoner of War," *Arm the Spirit* 14 (Fall 1982): 1, 9.

41. Black Liberation Army, "On Strategic Alliance of Armed Military Forces of the Revolutionary Nationalist and Anti-Imperialist Movement," in *America the Nation-State: The Politics of the United States from a State Building Perspective,* ed. Imari Obadele (Baton Rouge, LA: The Malcolm Generation, 1998), 423-24.

42. Umoja, "Set Our Warriors Free," 425; Umoja, "Repression Breeds Resistance," 148-49.

43. Lubasch, "Key Suspect Is Arrested in Brink's Car Robbery"; Eileen Putman, "Jury Indicts Eighth Suspect in Brinks Robbery," *Schenectady Gazette,* January 16, 1982, accessed October 27, 2018, http://news.google.com/newspapers?nid=1917&dat=19820116&id=amxGAAAAIBAJ&sjid=f-kMAAAAIBAJ&pg=2539,12813.

44. Balagoon, see pages 95-6 in the current volume. In the grammar of the New Afrikan Independence Movement the first personal singular is not capitalized ("i") and the first letter in first person plural is capitalized ("We"). This is the application of a principle of the New Afrikan Creed, "The community is more important than the individual."

45. See pages 148-9 in this volume.

46. See page 152 in this volume.

47. See page 153 in this volume.

48. Balagun, "Kuwasi at 60."

3 Haiku That Barely Suggest
the Sparkle of Kuwasi Balagoon

David Gilbert, September 6, 2017

Coffee/dab-of-cream
color. Maroon spirit. Laugh;
irrepressible

Syncopated jazz
whistle; surreal art; poetry—
both sharp and touching

Lion heart courage
but puppy dog loving heart,
our freedom fighter

Kuwasi: A Virtual Roundtable of Love and Reflection

Compiled and coordinated by Matt Meyer, with Joan P. Gibbs and Meg Starr, featuring Sekou Odinga, Bilal Sunni-Ali, Kim Kit Holder, Meg Starr, Danielle Jasmine, Amilcar Shabazz, Ajamu Sankofa, David Gilbert, dequi kioni-sadiki, Kai Lumumba Barrow, Dhoruba Bin Wahad, and Ashanti Alston

Unique. The single word most often used to describe Kuwasi Balagoon when discussing his life and legacy with those closest to and most affected by him is "unique"—that Kuwasi's way of living and looking at life set him apart in special and wonderous ways. Even in the midst of amazing friends and colleagues, and even while living and working in extraordinary times, Kuwasi stood out. Distinctions surrounding other labels and descriptors—New Afrikan revolutionary nationalist and anarchist; gay, bisexual, and/or queer; poet, militant, housing activist, Panther—can be discussed and debated and reflected upon, but Kuwasi's greatest quality was surely his lasting love for the people and his ability to transform that love into tangible acts of resistance.

"I probably met Kuwasi in the spring or early summer of 1968," remembered Sekou Odinga, "and he was always a real energetic brother. You were always going to hear him telling a story or joke or enjoying one." A fellow Panther and codefendant in the infamous New York Panther 21 case, Odinga noted that Kuwasi was always "full of life, always ready to volunteer for any work that needed to be done: the more dangerous the work, the more ready he was. He was real, sincere, and dependable. That was what struck me early on. He was always ready to step up, even if you didn't need him. He would volunteer; it wasn't something where you ever had to go find him. He and his wife at the time were working on housing issues—trying to get the landlords to do the right thing."

Sekou and Kuwasi also shared an interest in building the clandestine movement, and both were part of the formation of the Black Liberation Army. Though Sekou recalled that the two of them "connected militarily," he added that "as much of a military inclination as Kuwasi had, he had—as Che said—even more of a love for the people. He loved children and the elderly and was always ready to help and talk with them. Kuwasi lived with my family and I for a few months, and he'd get right down there on the floor with the kids and became one of them—creating games and playing. He was full of love, always wanting to participate in all aspects of life."

"My first impression of Kuwasi came from a poetry reading," recalled New York Panther and famed jazz musician Bilal Sunni-Ali. "The Black Panther Party for Self Defense was at its early, infant stages—not to be confused with the earlier New York Black Panthers organized by the Revolutionary Action Movement (RAM). Sekou and I and Lumumba Shakur were there, and this brother got up and read this poem called 'Disrupt!' I don't remember a word of the poem, but it described so well what power we have—that we have the power to disrupt what was going on, to stop the injustices. The delivery of the poem struck me so hard that I made it a point of saying to Sekou and Lumumba, 'Please reach out to that brother who did that poem and get him in the Party.' That was the spring of 1968."

"Kuwasi was drawn to poetry, to Amiri Baraka and the Last Poets. He was a very articulate brother," added Sekou. "He always had a comeback, the right thing to say. He had a comedic side as well, and always had a name to call you. For example, I was known to control the finances pretty tightly, while he was kinda loose with his money. Sometimes he'd have to come to me to borrow some money, so he might call me the Banker!"

One of Kuwasi's most striking and unique strengths was his ability to articulate seemingly contrasting ideas in ways that made sense. "He was definitely a Pan-Africanist," noted Sekou, "and he was also a nationalist, an anarchist, and very antiauthoritarian. He was a revolutionary nationalist—an internationalist—and he didn't just talk it, he lived it. I don't know anyone else who fit into those categories like that. He was a contradiction himself: a real warrior but a babysitter too. You'd want to leave the kids with him! He was one of the few brothers whose nationalism had no basis in racism, and in a racial USA that is a hard thing to say. Kuwasi had white friends growing up, in the military, in school, and he always had an openness about all people, even though he was very clear about America being very racist. He was, way before the rest of us, really open to working with white folks."

"He enjoyed getting high," Sekou continued, "and would experiment with any kind of drug except heroin. He used to tell me about drugs I'd never even heard of! He was a living dude — all about getting the most out of life. He loved music: jazz, rhythm and blues, rock and roll, heavy metal, really eclectic stuff. That was the uniqueness of Kuwasi. He fit into almost every category. You couldn't put him into a category: Kuwasi was Kuwasi."

Professor Kim Kit Holder, whose dissertation *The Black Panther Party 1966–1971: A Curriculum Tool for Afrikan-American Studies* helped usher in a new wave of academic interest in the Party, first remembers becoming aware of Kuwasi at the time of the New York Panther 21 trial. "I joined the Party a month later," Holder reflected, "and looked at Kuwasi in three categories: as a guerrilla, as a queer, and as an anarchist — intersectionally. As a guerrilla, I put him up there with Harriet Tubman and George Jackson. The first thing that made an impression on me was the New York City 1970 jail uprisings, later learning about his key role in it. I remember saying 'Wow … we are going to *win* this, because Panthers never give up the fight!' It gave us rank-and-file Party members strength; it didn't matter where we were, we were going to struggle. That was profound."

Holder was struck by Kuwasi's shift towards anarchism after the trial of the 21. "At first, he insulted us, calling us 'robots', but at the same time he gave us voice, articulating our problems with the leadership structure and the people in it. I was just a kid in New York City when I joined the Party, but remember one of the things that pissed me off was that we earned five cents for every Panther newspaper that we sold, while the West Coast folks got ten cents from the sale. There were a bunch of other things, and while Kuwasi's thoughts on anarchism weren't always taken up as a new philosophy, we could use them as tools in our work. Kuwasi aligned himself with what made sense. The needs of the people were more important than any particular ideology."

Theory and practice collided intensely in the events of 1981, when the attempted robbery of a Brink's truck to fund clandestine work of the Black Liberation Movement and their allies ended in disaster. Two police officers and a security guard were killed, and those involved in the movement—including Kuwasi and codefendant David Gilbert, as well as Sekou Odinga and many others—were captured, tortured, tried, and imprisoned. Many younger activists first learned of Kuwasi at this time, including Free Puerto Rico Committee leader and author Meg Starr.

"Kuwasi was arrested the night before my twenty-second birthday," Meg sharply recalls. "I had met his codefendant Judy Clark and other white anti-imperialists some scant six months earlier, through the Women's Committee Against Genocide. My roommates brought me some ice cream, and we watched the news about the Brink's Case on television. I spent most of the night throwing up." Shortly after that, Meg became a regular visitor of Kuwasi, David, and Judy.

"It was a very difficult time," reflects Meg. "In those years of rallies outside of courthouses, wheat pasting posters on billboards across town, and having our apartments broken into and covered in fingerprint dust, you became used to a level of repression. In contrast, visiting these political prisoners was inspiring. Kuwasi's energy and passion lit up the dank visiting room. He got out of me the fact that I loved punk rock, even though I knew already that most of the older activists around me thought that punk was 'degenerate white music.' But Kuwasi loved punk. He connected to the part of me that was a natural nonconformist to anything at all, including radical political correctness. He explained things to me that I didn't really understand till later. And he sent me long amazing letters."

One of those letters, from December 1983, revealed some of Kuwasi's own reflections on the intersection of political and social aspects of life, and the tasks ahead.

Kuwasi wrote:

i had been led to believe i was an oddity. Even on the
street, i had to separate political from social dealings.
The people i met at the Mud Club and other clubs
and the people i knew from the Liberation movement
were distinctly different! But there's no separation in
my mind about cultural and political things, so i write
you and want to see you and convince you to aid me
in being a more complete person. i not only intend to
survive but to grow, not only because to survive i'm
gonna have to grow, but also because i've resolved to
deal with this condition not merely as a fall, but as a
step in the evolution of myself, just as i am trying to
influence the movements to transform this defeat into
a victory by using the information from the experience:
to become what we must to really transform the world.

The question of ideology and practice were also part of Meg's
in-person communications with Kuwasi, as he tried to explain
to this young, lesbian, radical punk his own political journey. "I
was too new to political work to understand or imagine the com-
promises that led Kuwasi to where he ended up," Meg notes
with some regret. "But a few minutes of one visit stick out in
my mind like a short and powerful video. Long before I read or
even heard of Audre Lorde, surrounded by the grey walls, focusing on Kuwasi's shining eyes, I listened intently to his musings
about how he landed exactly where he was, the trajectory to that
exact spot. Kuwasi said: 'I am down with the Black nationalists
because I looked around, and they were the ones that were actually doing something, that were really down to fight the state.'
My respect for Kuwasi and the others was immense: they were
actually engaged in attempting revolutionary action, instead of
just talking about it."

One concrete action which the Women's Committee Against
Genocide took was to help single mothers escaping from abusive
relationships. The matriarch of one such family became deeply
involved in a relationship with Kuwasi, remembered here by her

grand-daughter, poet Danielle Jasmine.

"My Grandma loved a man," Danielle wrote, "who was a great many things to a great many people, but to her: a man…a passionate, supportive, inspiring man. I lost my Grandma many years ago and after she passed, I came across her letters from Kuwasi from 1983–1985. Through them, I've gotten a glimpse into what they shared and the love and support they provided for each other. Throughout his letters, he offered support for her sobriety, health, and family. We all have walls built up around us, and my Grandma worked on dismantling the ones she could. I like to think I've continued this process (for her and for me) in some of my writing.

"Beyonce's song 'Halo' has been an anthem for me throughout this process and I often listened to it while reading Kuwasi's letters, feeling their presence in the lyrics 'remember those walls I built. Well, baby, they're tumbling down.' All of Kuwasi's letters end similarly, yet on one particular day, in one particular letter, he asks my Grandma to give her daughter, my Aunt, 'a Halo hug for him.' To balance the struggle for freedom and justice with peace and light is a remarkable feat in any case. That Kuwasi could understand and accomplish this, despite the physical walls around him, is a remarkable thing, something he offered to all of us in his life. As he ended each letter: 'Love, Power, & Peace by Piece.'"

Another young activist at the time of the Brink's trial was Texas-based Amilcar Shabazz, now chair of the W.E.B. Du Bois Department of Afro-American Studies at the University of Massachusetts Amherst and vice president of the National Council for Black Studies. By 1981, Shabazz had already worked with leaders of the Republic of New Afrika (including Minister of Education Fulani Sunni-Ali and New Afrikan People's Organization leader Ahmed Obefemi) and been given permission to start a local chapter of the National Committee to Honor New Afrikan Freedom Fighters. After Brink's, that group changed its name from an emphasis on "honor" to the National Committee to *Defend*, and Shabazz moved to New York, became a volunteer paralegal, and worked with Attorney Chokwe Lumumba on the cases of Kuwasi, Sekou Odinga, and the rest. His thoughts of that time are much more than fond memories: "Kuwasi was warm and generous in a way you would not believe."

"I was able to get through the daunting security system at the jail where Kuwasi, David Gilbert, and Judith Clark were being held," Shabazz recalled, "because I'd go in with an attorney working with Gilbert and Clark. Kuwasi represented himself at trial, but he'd come to these face-to-face legal meetings so that he and I could sidebar in the meeting room. Under these conditions, we got to know each other and had frank talks about how to reach New Afrikans about what this case was really about, and who the real criminals were. In the first of these meetings, Kuwasi expressed to me his dislike for the very name of the National Committee. He did not like the term 'freedom fighter.' A fire fighter is someone who fights fires. A crime fighter is someone who, what? Fights crime. So, isn't a freedom fighter someone who fights against freedom? That was my first lesson in understanding Kuwasi's ironic wit and political nonconformism."

Kuwasi and Shabazz became quite close, with Shabazz serving as liaison between Kuwasi and the outside defense committees. Instrumental in producing the original booklet of Kuwasi's "Statement of a New Afrikan Prisoner of War," Shabazz notes Kuwasi's intention "for his statement to be a clear and truthful articulation of exactly who he was and why he did the things he did." It was here that Kuwasi first articulated the now popularly cited adage that "repression breeds resistance," and that he called out the U.S. for many of the crimes against Afrikan peoples that Kuwasi himself witnessed, as a soldier in Vietnam and as a housing rights activist in the tenements of Harlem.

"Kuwasi was a warlord," Shabazz concludes, "in the best sense of the word. He did not elevate the revolutionary methods by which he fought or the level of resistance he was best at above what others in the struggle contributed. He gave us some of his ideas on 'PT,' or physical training, in his handwriting with sketches of different exercises, especially what could be performed in the tight confines of the small cells he spent many hours, days, and years of his life locked up inside prisons and devoid of human contact. His body was as solid as iron from his PT practice, which was a key to his life and power to escape. 'We are human,' he said, 'and nobody wants to live under or bring offspring into a confined atmosphere with an artificial sky.' I have never met a comrade that could make me think, laugh, and strive for liberation like Kuwasi."

Already a lawyer at the time of the Brink's trial, Joan Gibbs was employed by the National Lawyers' Guild's Grand Jury Project in 1981 and was a member of Dykes Against Racism Everywhere (DARE). A supporter of the Black Panther Party, Gibbs explains that she "never joined the Party for a couple of reasons, among them their seeming militarism and the hyper-masculinity of some of their members." In addition, she adds, "at the time, I was more attracted to Marxism, Leninism, and Trotskyism. The August 1970 publication of Huey P. Newton's 'To the Revolutionary Brothers and Sisters about the Women's Liberation Movement and Gay Liberation Movements' tempered but did not entirely erase my feelings that because of my sexuality I would be not welcomed with open arms in the BPP." Years later, Kim Kit Holder would report that he used Kuwasi's life as an example, especially for LGBTQ people, to "show the possibility of the universality" of Panther politics and to "use Kuwasi as a badge to deconstruct the concept that armed struggle is a hyper-masculine phenomenon."

But even in the more backwards 1980s, Brink's, for a young, radical, lesbian, New York–based Black lawyer, was impossible to ignore. "In the aftermath of the Brink's incident," Gibbs recalls, "a federal grand jury was impaneled in the United States District Court for the Southern District of New York. Activists were sub-poenaed to appear before it from both in and outside of New York City. Consequently, at the Grand Jury Project, I worked to educate organizations and individuals about federal prosecutors' abuse of grand jury subpoenas to harass and sometimes incarcer-ate dissidents from the United States foreign and domestic pol-icies, and the risks of talking to the FBI. In DARE, we worked to build support for both those arrested and those subpoenaed, an arduous task as many of the people purportedly on 'the left' considered those arrested to be, at best, 'adventurists.' DARE principally focused on building support among LGBT folks. To this end, DARE, among other things, organized forums on non-collaboration with the FBI and grand juries and published leaflets on these issues. I believed, then and now, that for revolutionaries the principle contradiction is between us and the state. The contradictions among those of us working to fundamentally transform the U.S. are secondary. For these reasons, I also support the freedom of all U.S. political prisoners and prisoners of war." Joan Gibbs, it should be noted, has served as defense counsel to some of the most significant BPP-related political prisoners of the past half-century, including Jericho Movement cofounder Herman Ferguson and former NASA mathematician Sundiata Acoli (still in jail as of this writing, well over eighty years old).

"As for Kuwasi's sexuality," Gibbs recalled, "his arrest with his transvestite lover garnered tabloid headlines. The circumstances of his arrest were negatively greeted by some alleged supporters of the Black Liberation Movement, including some alleged supporters of the Black Liberation Army. And, if my memory serves me correctly, when he died in December 1986, only a few openly spoke about the fact he had died from an AIDS-related illness. None of this should be surprising given the times. In 1982, when Kuwasi was arrested, and in 1986 when he died, support for LGBTQ people was far less than it is today, in society generally and also within the left and the Black Liberation Movement. Heterosexism, homophobia, and transphobia were the norm."

Reflecting on Kuwasi's legacy, Joan has noted that "while I am not an anarchist, his writings on anarchism have challenged and caused me to rethink my beliefs with respect to the need for 'a vanguard party,' with democratic centralism, and with the meaning of leadership itself. In other words, his writings have deepened my understanding, as well as my appreciation, of the theory and practice of anarchism—understanding its popularity today, particularly among younger activists. Like Harriet Tubman, Kuwasi should long be remembered for his steadfast, decades-long commitment to the fundamental transformation of the U.S. Kuwasi demonstrated his repeated willingness to risk liberty and life in furtherance of the liberation of people of African descent in the United States, by non-queer and queer people committed to that same goal. With a white supremist, misogynist, homophobe in the White House, with the far right, Nazis, and Klan rallying and marching unmasked, we especially need people with Kuwasi's revolutionary, free, loving spirit."

Regarding Kuwasi's sexual orientation, the ways in which he freely expressed his love—spiritually and otherwise—has perhaps been the most complicated aspect of his legacy; the prejudices, then and now, which Joan Gibbs poignantly notes, are not the only reason for this. Questions of self-determination—of how Kuwasi defined or would have defined himself—need also be considered. Sekou Odinga, one of his oldest and closest comrades, asserts: "I often hear people say that Kuwasi was part of the queer community, but he never called himself that. Clearly, he would not have called himself gay. From what I'm told—I didn't know it at the time—Kuwasi was bisexual; he had a homosexual relationship which continued while he was in prison. I did meet [his lover] Chicky, but didn't know her much. I was out at their house but didn't know that Chicky was transsexual. Was Kuwasi a gender rebel? Yes. He wasn't caught up in people's bourgeois ways of looking at things. He had his own way of looking at things."

Bilal Sunni-Ali remembered one time late in Kuwasi's life when he had to pick Kuwasi up at a hospital. "He told me that he had a sexually transmitted disease, and he said he had a male partner. That was the first and the only time that I heard him talk about his private life." This memory reinforces an assessment made by revolutionary educator and lawyer Ajamu Sankofa, who concluded that "Kuwasi viewed sexual expression as fundamentally a private matter, not to be regulated by systems of domination." Though he never met Kuwasi, Sankofa—a member and leader of the African Liberation Support Committee, the National Independent Black Political Party, the Socialist Workers Party, the National Conference of Black Lawyers (NCBL), and the American Civil Liberties Union (ACLU)—is one of many who have spoken and written about the great impact Kuwasi's life had on their own thoughts and practice. Sankofa concluded that Kuwasi's own fluid and liberated ways of approaching relationships could serve as "a perspective that if fully practiced could help lead humanity out of the horrible dungeons of sexual oppression."

Ajamu Sankofa remarked of his own experience, "Up until I encountered Kuwasi's writings, my only Black male radical role model was James Baldwin and, of course, as a proud Gay Black man, I had to process the fact that the mainstream Black-led civil rights movement hid Baldwin from view whenever it could. I fervently hung on to the words of Huey P. Newton, who said, "[q]uite the contrary, maybe a homosexual could be the most revolutionary." In the late 1980s Sankofa "became aware of Kuwasi as an *out* Black bisexual prisoner of war of African descent who was public with his transvestite lover."

In Sankofa's assessment, Kuwasi was "one who lived a life that put into concrete practice an ever-evolving set of ideological principles that rested within a dynamic pyramid of intention, where one point was anti-imperialist anarchism, another was Marxism-Leninism, and the other was revolutionary Black nationalism. Each point existed in dynamic tension with the other recreating itself while influencing each other point. I found that to be pretty unique indeed." In 1989, several years after Kuwasi's death, Sankofa joined the staff of the ACLU Prisoners' Rights Project, which filed lawsuits against state prison systems because they were deliberating denying necessary health care to prisoners with HIV/AIDs in violation of the Eighth Amendment to the United States Constitution. At the same time, as Sanfoka experienced and remembered, "The radical left held hateful and reactionary views towards gay people. The Black community, especially the clergy, was notably hostile towards gay people and prisoners."

"During the decade of 1980s," Sankofa continued, "the Black community was under siege by the triple threat of drugs, violence, and AIDS. Black people despised drug dealers in their communities, as opportunistic politicians manipulated them to support mass incarceration. Accordingly, during this period the prison population was disproportionately filled with prisoners with HIV/AIDS due to the correlation of drugs, sex, and HIV. Prisoners with

HIV/AIDS terrified and repelled many prison medical staff." It is noteworthy that one leading exception to leftist denial of and distancing from the AIDS epidemic and people with AIDS came from within the prison system itself—and from one of Kuwasi's closest comrades and codefendants. White anti-imperialist David Gilbert, who still languishes in prison at the time of this writing (and who did time behind bars with Kuwasi during the last years of his life), pioneered a peer-centered support and education program for prisoners with HIV/AIDs in New York State. This program, used as a model for inmate education across the U.S., was formally begun just one year after Kuwasi's passing; Gilbert's instructive and challenging booklet *AIDS Conspiracy? Tracking the Real Genocide*, was dedicated to Kuwasi: "a Black Liberation warrior with a giant heart, who died of AIDS on December 13, 1986."

Sankofa's perceptions about Kuwasi's legacy is that his story might lead revolutionaries to "take a far deeper and humble dive into the physics of small stuff, such that we are ever fortifying ourselves against dogmas, against navel gazing, and for greater openness to new revolutionary ideas." He concluded that "Kuwasi's definitions and practice of revolutionary nationalism and anarchism seem to me to have been 'in formation.' ... They do provoke new thinking regarding the existing meanings of ideological categories. This is very healthy for vibrant revolutionary movements." Finally, Sankofa asserted, "the signature lesson that I glean from Kuwasi's definitions is the necessity to be authentic in your revolutionary practice."

Authenticity, humility, and an openness to working across personal and political categorization were also the key Kuwasi legacy points raised by Sister dequi kioni-sadiki, coordinator of the Malcolm X Commemoration Committee. "We can all learn from Kuwasi's ability to work with all kinds of people across the board," observed dequi, "accepting people from where they are and helping them develop without writing anyone off. We don't talk about the human side of our revolutionaries often enough, but Kuwasi's humanity shone through." A cofounder of the Northeast Political Prisoner Coalition along with her husband Sekou Odinga, dequi reminisced that Kuwasi, like Sekou, was committed to "finding more ways to work with people than reasons not to work with them." That, she noted, is a great legacy indeed.

In the words of Black liberation artist and Gallery of the Streets founder Kai Lumumba Barrow, Kuwasi was no less than a contemporary Maroon. As a performance and visual artist, Kai has incorporated Kuwasi's "character" into her theatrical and political work, including a current piece titled *[b]Reach: adventures in heterotopia*. A multimedia traveling act, *[b]Reach* works to "consider the notion of Black fugitivity as a point of departure, a place to discuss the questions ... a third space — between confinement and freedom," which situates Black fugitivity as a "location of disobedience, consistent among resistance movements for structural change." As a founder of the prison industrial complex abolitionist organization Critical Resistance, a leader of the Malcolm X Grassroots Movement and Southerners on New Ground, and a key activist with the Black Panther Newspaper Committee, INCITE! Women of Color Against Violence, FIERCE!, UBUNTU, and the Student Liberation Action Movement, Kai has been at the center of many of the major strategic organizing efforts since the time of Kuwasi's transition. "As a queer Black feminist artist," she wrote, "I was, and am, inspired by Kuwasi's life and example.... His escapes were operatic; his sexuality the stuff of gossip and pride, and his practice, a model for aspiring revolutionaries. Kuwasi's trial statements were the work of a surrealist shaman — Abracadabra and Whoop there it is — he transformed the kourtroom into a space of political education, revealing the farce that is the amerikkkan justice system."

Bilal Sunni-Ali agreed with this larger-than-life imagery. During the time when Bilal was released from California's Soledad Prison in the 1970s and returned to New York, Kuwasi had masterminded one of his prison breaks. "The newspapers," Bilal recalls, "were describing someone who was nine feet tall, leaping over two cars at a time while still shooting at the police who were chasing him!"

Dhoruba Bin Wahad, Black Panther Party New York Field Secretary and a New York Panther 21 codefendant of Kuwasi, vividly recalls how his powerful words back then continue to echo in the struggles of today. "Once on a run down south," Dhoruba remembered, "Kuwasi was called upon to bust a verse or two. He began his poem about 'Black self-hatred' and ended it with an existential metaphor for white supremacy that, to me, also presaged Black Lives Matter. He matter-of-factly juxtaposed 'social justice' with racial equality as a question of 'mind over matter'; Kuwasi poetically proclaimed to all who were listening that from a white supremacist mindset: 'White folks don't mind, and Black folks don't matter.'"

Former Black Liberation Army militant and political prisoner Ashanti Alston, who adopted the moniker "Anarchist Panther" in the 1980s, speaks of how he "was drawn to Kuwasi, because he seemed to have a daringness not just to say bold things but to do things and to be certain ways outside of the norm.... He opened up many doors at a time when it was important for more and more people to see that they have a part to play—whether they be queer, whether they be nationalist but still critiquing top-down structures. [Former New York Panther 21 defendant] Ali Bey Hassan and Panther political prisoner Bashir Hameed—the Jersey crew—would tell stories of this great loyalty they had to one another. One of them was in prison on a road work crew, and another was out...so they were going to get their brother free. They organized some plan to come by in a fast car and pick the one off the road! That's how they rolled, that kind of daringness—and if you're going to have a revolutionary movement, you cannot be passive about this, you cannot be on the fence about what you're going to do. Sometimes you've got to step outside the box. And Kuwasi became that person willing to step outside the box on many different levels."

Ashanti, who served as national cochair of the Jericho Movement to Free All U.S. Political Prisoners, noted that "how Kuwasi saw himself in relation to other human beings, and his own sexuality, was in deep contrast to the European concepts of sexuality and what is a man, what is a woman. The Black nationalist movement just didn't deal with that and were in some ways aligned with the Western model which Kuwasi challenged by the way he lived his life. The public statement Kuwasi made was how he chose to live. How people look at these choices after his death is like a piece of art: it is up to the viewer to get something from that. It is like how people look at Malcolm X after his death: some people may only focus on what Malcolm said about voting, others focus on what he said about the land, and others just focus on what Malcolm said about armed struggle.

"What do you get when you see the life of Kuwasi Balagoon?" Ashanti asks us all. "That is what becomes important. In the times that we live in, when so many people have been oppressed and repressed in so many ways in terms of their very being, it is important to have someone like Kuwasi saying, 'You don't have to fit that norm. You are trying to be free in the spirit that you're in, doing it in the course of struggle.' That is the importance of Kuwasi Balagoon; it is all *in the course of the struggle to change this world*. His anarchism, his sexuality, all of the parts of his life fit into the whole of his revolutionary-ness. That is what I think people miss: it was still *all* him—as a revolutionary, but a revolutionary who is also willing to be free in some areas that we might not all have the courage to be free in." No matter who Kuwasi loved from one moment to the next, Kuwasi's love—for the people as a whole and for individual peoples of all kinds—was the revolutionary context for his life of militant action.

Perhaps Sekou Odinga's concluding words serve as the best summary of all: "Kuwasi loved life! He clearly loved life and loved living life. He was always ready to live.... He was a living dude, and most of us all really loved him."

Viva Kuwasi Libre!
Kuwasi Balagoon Presente!
Ashe, ashe, Baba Kuwasi.

Black Cats Named Kuwasi

A reflection by Kai Lumumba Barrow

Back in the day, we had a couple of black cats: Kuwasi and Merle, named to honor Merle Africa, of MOVE, and Kuwasi Balagoon, BLA anarchist, anti-imperialist, AIDS activist, and bisexual poet. Both Kuwasi and Merle died in the underbelly of the belly of the beast and we wanted to recognize their contributions to Black liberation. To quote Ashanti, "There are Cats, and there are Cats.... There is Kuwasi Balagoon"

As a queer Black feminist artist and cat lover, I was, and am, inspired by Kuwasi's life and example. I never knew Kuwasi, but his reputation was the stuff of legend. In my cadre, Kuwasi was described as bold, brazen, wild, and sharp. His escapes were operatic; his sexuality the stuff of gossip and pride, and his practice, a model for aspiring revolutionaries. Kuwasi's trial statements were the work of a surrealist shaman—Abracadabra and Whoop there it is—he transformed the kourtroom into a space of political education, revealing the farce that is the amerikkkan justice system.

Kuwasi was a Trickster in our midst, a contemporary Maroon determined to live free or die trying.

As if taking on the spirit of his namesake, Kuwasi the cat refused to stay confined to the house. A frequent flier and escape artist, no amount of threats, punishments, product, or cajoling would make that cat behave. No solo act, he even learned how to open our Brooklyn brownstone sliding door (the locks are on the bottom), unlocking the latch and sliding the barrier aside so that both he and Merle could escape. "It's better inside," I told him one day, after catching him on his way out and trapping him back in the house. "It's dangerous out there with cat snatchers and roaming Toms and ruffneck felines on every corner. We'll give you toys and catnip and scratching posts and take care of your basic needs," I pleaded. "Just stay inside, and definitely stay away from the upstairs apartment. The old lady who lives above is not a fan. These are the rules," I said walking away, hoping that the cat would pick up what I was putting down, and pretty sure that he would not.

Minutes later, I peeked back into the room curious to see the effect of my rules. Kuwasi was gone. And so was Merle. The door cracked open stood as a reminder of Balagoon's words, "This is the place to begin erasing borders." Kuwasi indeed, was one of them Cats.

your honor

your honor
since i've been convicted of murder
and have taken time to digest
just what that means
after noting what it means to my family
and how it affects people who read the newspapers
and all
i see now that i've made a terrible mistake!
and didn't approach this trial
in a respectful, deliberate or thoughtful manner
didn't take advantage of the best legal advice
and based my actions on irrelevant matters
which i can see now in a much more sober mind
had nothing to do with this case
i must have been legally insane thinking about:
the twenty-five murders of children in atlanta since
Wayne Williams' capture
the recent murder of a man in boston by the police
the recent murders of two in chicago by police
the shooting of a five-year-old little boy in suburban calif
the lynchings in alabama
the mob murder of a transit worker in brooklyn
the murders of fourteen women in boston
feeling that this is evidence of something
and that there must
be a lesson in all this—i thought
murder was legal

with no questions

the leaves are changing
to sheaves of fire
rust 'n indigo
in waves
And all at once
And one by one
different in their deaths
like all times
and loved ones
and memories of places
faded from lack of presence
and fallen from the attention of today
to lie like a quilt on the earth
and winter
and change to the rich pungent ground
that feeds realities to come
with no questions.

secretary watts*

Secretary Watts
saz that Native Americans have suffered the effects of socialism
and with his rubber stamps and memo machines
leaves mining companies the rights to dig up and poison
whatever space they have left
and it's no big deal

But when that cracker saz something saz something about
the "Beach Boys"
the turd president and his wife and the white house staff
makes him apologise   right away
after all what's the meaning of the 4th of July

---

* James Watts was the notorious "libertarian" right-wing secretary of the
interior during the Reagan administration, who favored turning over public
lands to oil and mining interests and agribusiness.

spring comes

spring comes
and mail
trickles in
and trickles out
as if written in blood
winter's talk
hangs unresolved and useless as smoke
and well-reasoned routines are questioned
with a runaway mind
that doesn't stop to sleep
and has come to expect
the bare minimum
for the sake of an argument
that will only make sense
when it is a fight
spring comes
shiny grey
and coiled
in a box

big ben*

Benjamin Ward
Likes to entertain
and be entertained
on the rocks, in his office
likes to mix a little business with pleasure
likes to loosen up
before he hurrahs the boys
at police ceremonies
with a few drinks
and mop his brow
and shift his weight from foot to foot
at press conferences
and stutter
and entertain everyone who watches the news
This is no uncle tom
or some neocolonial fixture
of a city that suddenly found itself third world
and unable to stomach a Minter or Alvarez
as school chancellor
and as i picture him at the podium
i can't help but hear Michael Jackson
singing Ben
or maybe i only hear the recording
is it live or is it memorex?
the mayor, his honor no less, who couldn't stand
Back Minter or Brown Alvarez
loves Black Ben
and saz, everybody makes mistakes
Ben saz, he'll never drink again
will cut the playboy routine
mops his brow, shifts his weight to the right

---

* In the 1980s, Benjamin Ward became the first Black police chief of
New York City. He was notorious as a hard-drinking front man for the
blue mafia.

he's asked, if he will resign
mops his brow, shifts his weight to the left
"Not today," he musters a mumble
and his owner, looks at him, "Oh, come on Ben"
and i can almost hear him say, he'll never come again
his honor explains, these are just a couple of instructions
in an otherwise flawless career as commissioner of
department of corrections, NYC
commissioner of department of corrections, New York State
and now as the city's Top Cop
police commissioner
This is no handpicked uncle tom
The first black police commissioner of New York City
where more kids showed up to the airport to meet
Menudo in 84
than showed up to meet the beatles in 64
was appointed!
This is the one responsible for the Michael
Stewart investigation
This is the one responsible for bringing the
murderers of Willie Turks to justice
This is the one responsible for investigating
police brutality charges in Harlem
This is a symbol for how far a black man
can go in the United States.
A man mentioned in the Centurion!
making this videotape with his honor
like Michael Jackson did with Paul McCartney
"say, say, say, what you want" how am i doin?
Why are people complaining to koch about the police?
This in 1984—not 1964
Why are people complaining about racism?
ain't whites in Staten Island complaining
about police brutality?
and Big Ben is checking into it
and being the top cop he knows about those things
how many times have you heard of cops

blowin somebody away because the cop thought
that the play gun the child had was real
or that the comb or bottle or whatever
made a bulge in a black teenager's
pocket was a gun or knife?
but black cops, like Big Ben
have better vision than white cops
i don't know if they do better on the firing range
but when have you heard of a black
cop blowing a white child away because
he thought the toy gun was real?
And how many times have you heard of a black
cop mistaking a comb or
bottle or bulge in a white teenager's
pocket for a gun?
Is the ratio of these types of mistakes
the same as the ratio of black to white
cops?
how many times have you heard of
white cops shooting black cops?
OK, how about the other way around?
don't whites carry combs and bottles
or otherwise have bulges in their
pockets?
don't black cops accidentally discharge their weapons
So now you know who the guardian society guards
cause niggers know the law
and the law is
If you are black you can't be white
and you can't be yourself
Other speakers have takened a nip before addressing a
        convention
and entertained friends on business hours
but what else does that nigger apologize for?

i remember

i remember her asking me if i thought her shoes were pretty
while limping beside me down the avenue
in a din of pain
the cops turning the block for the second time
slowing up traffic to glare at us to see how we would react, like
      dobermans
the beer cans and wrappers on the sidewalk
the shadows of the young trees
the slight friendly breeze of the night of holding hands
the expensive shops filled with non-sense
and wondering who could afford such folly
you know, it's the little things ...

life is rough

Life is rough when your attitude is bad
the routine you're going through seems a curse
     everything is boring
there is no reason to do the things that are possible
and the things that there is good reason for ... appear impossible
A voice in the back of your head tells you, "so and so"
     is full of shit
and "so and so" wears different contentiousness and murkiness
and swarms into a swirling mass down the drain
     of a thousand years
like rust and gravel dust in the painted desert
that looks like a place but ain't really nowhere
and every offered niche a place for a mole
or labrador retriever or longhorn steer
or some position not applied for in the dung heap you'll stick in.

<u>the klan marched</u>

the Klan marched through a town
      with an economically deprived New Afrikan
      and Chicano community
accompanied by police
who followed the Klan demonstrators around
      and beat a Chicano woman for being a
      Chicano woman, and clearly
opposed to racism
      and beat a Chicano man after following him
      around
cause he was there
but it wasn't really the Klan
it was just Austin
the Klan has been active
a beating here a murder there
"the good ole boys"
and you say that you will deal with the Klan
but first we got to live together
      that is not so. We don't have to live together.
      We won't be living together.
when we try, you do the living and we do the
dying, for 400 years
so we will die together
like Sundiata, Zayd and Twyman
or like those working-class armed agents of the
      state in Nyack
      until our survivors understand and make
      suitable rearrangements
cause it's not the Klan
it's Austin
it's Amerikkka

mother of pearl sky

Mother of pearl sky
crystalline phantom trees
sheering wind
harvesting the residue of feelings past
and depositing them into the icy void
of space, that is permitted
because there is *no one* inclined to wonder
where questions fret and pace
by seashores empty since labor day
watching the reruns of reflections
etched through the eyes
to souls that shudder
only when undistincted
a kind word, for being left alone
which can be distinctive
like footprints that spoil the snow

rain

Rain, rain, rain all day
Wash this stinking town away
down the river and out to sea
every home and every building and everybody

Rain rain rain all night
so we can see things in a different light
grab the inner tubes and logs
save the people and drown the hogs

some solo piano or guitar

Some solo piano or guitar
and sun filtering through the curtains
she hasn't picked out yet
in some little ticky tack
or old abode stacked in the crowded heights
like a chamber
where all the ghosts
can stretch their arms and yarn
and settle in the folds of blankets and unpacked clothes
giving us their blessings
assured in our resolve
when she awakes, after sleeping like a baby
happy to be alive and awake
and to see me
and i'll be *myself*

filtered through the roof

The rain filtered through the roof
collected in some unseen crevice
    and fell
    in cadence
    in some unseen spot
like some lost drummer
summoning phantoms
having taken refuge in the night
and fusing themselves with those of us
    who were wet
    and dark
    and listening

we've got to

We got to stop meeting this way
looking for an apartment
and negotiating with supers,
         who want two months security rent
and an extra month's security to nod in our favor
going from building to building
and giving up and dropping by to see
         what your mom may have the
         inside scoop on
Cleaning the hoods of cars with our jeans
as she climbs out on the fire escape
and explains that all those bastards are full of shit
and we wander the streets
stopping for coffee and plans
till finally you can't wait
         and i have to go

We got to stop meeting
         in clubs
that the police close down
because they see people leaving at six in the morning,
         on weekdays,
         giving them the finger
and the owners have smoked up the graft
and had to pitch in with Mr Big, Franz Fringey
         and Tootsie Roll for
         cab fare
to turn angles in the bronx
where he forgets the name and systematically rings all the bells
until someone who doesn't even know him
         hits the buzzer and then
         goes back to sleep
leaving those harlequins to roaming the hall
until i get up that evening to pick up Sunday morning's paper

having a late start on living like other people
       or sort of
other people don't part every two weeks
or go for years making do with dreams and reflections
or hunger until the mind waters and pours through the eyes
       to only be blocked by masks

they jog and come home
      and watch T.V.

when the world is stale

When the world is stale
and springs brings warnings instead of promises
and old acquaintances drop out of sight
        for reasons of their own
and new ones who need help for problems of their own
saturate your every waking moment
with noise
you find yourself raking coals
        of friendships past
turning over in your head
designs of better days
        or at least adventures
rather than the endless sitcom

lock step

They march in formation
lock step
in cadence
so that their bodies don't betray
their fear
by jerky-hesitant motions.
Head straight
on order
by order
so that the folder
cannot confirm under-certain eyes.
They make noises
"hut, two"
to think "hut, two"
and whatever they are told
instead of possible death.
And they think of dying anyway
even though they are used to thinking whatever they are told.
And they think they should be honored for this.
And they shall be
increasingly
with grenades.

refused

i remember
being refused
by a lover
and being put up
and being put up with
by a friend
and making myself scarce
to make it easier

walkin the streets
in the cold
thinking
that it's really gonna take some doin
wondering
which nut would crack first?
when could we do another raid?
'n start from scratch and git back to basics
and how could i find who i needed
and looking at my watch
while checking a frozen muck
and walking into the happy cheery juke joint
'n ordering a double 'n another
and looking up and seeing an acquaintance
and leaving
'n going back — to where i was put up with

walkin into the darkness
feeling the warmth spread like an invisible glow of
a kerosene lamp
and thinking, how amazing
with so many problems
and no answers to what to do next
but here,
a simple chemical, could make me feel so much better!
i laugh at hypothetical warnings
and sap rap about the virtues of feeling miserable

carefully folding my clothes
and dropping them on the floor
twirlin my feet 'n body, in a quilt 'n charcoal sofa
i heard my host announce
that a friend who was supposed to be there already
should be coming at any time
they called 3 hours ago
and "i didn't know what could have takened so long?"
and "could stay up to open the door?"

These are the times that try men's souls
and as the cloud ascended to my head
from the fire in my belly
and made the darkness sweet 'n heavy
and reflections from the street lamp and objects
aimed at though caprice inhabit images in
a whirlpool, lighter than the gross planet at
many points where, making yourself go is a prerequisite for getting nowhere
i remember
      thinking as much in paraphrase and what a time to be
      called upon to muster an
      extra effort, just a little reframe, reprieve,
      a break from consciousness for a soul who had
      had it with reality
      All in my head and unsorted
      And i remember explaining that i was …

i remember
thinking as much in paraphrase and what a time to be called upon to muster an
extra effort, just alittle reframe, reprieve, a break from consciousness for a soul who had
had it with reality
All in my head and unsorted
and i remember explaining that … was finding first

rockland

Up in Rockland
they like to believe
that they can get up in the morning in their mortgaged banes
eat breakfast at McDonalds
drive down to Hill Street
sit on each other's desks drinking coffee
pack their state-issued revolvers, bulletproof vest, heads and
      tales in state-issued cars
and ride around Harlem, the South Bronx, the Lower East Side,
      Bedford Sty, Brownsville, Jamaica
looking for trouble, shaking down suspects, chasing "Niggers
      and Puerto Ricans" around maybe git some overtime
and drive back up to Rockland, across the tappan zee bridge to
      manicured lawns, fresh air, space, HBO
Eat pizza, soak up suds and shoot the shit about the "Animals"
and go back to the jungle
as if nothing had happened
and nothing will happen
Up in Rockland county
they like to believe
that they can go on some shift at a crowded concentration kamp
count the blacks, latins, Indians, an whites who for some reason
      couldn't get a job and add up the total
complain about the fuel they feed the "inmates"
watch them
take them to Kangaroo court
maybe get some overtime and
      thumb through a couple of cunt books
and Gang up on some "Animal"
and drive back up to Rockland, across the river,
      Aw! feeling better already,
unwind, loosen up, curse "fucking scumbags"
& "go back to work" maybe taking a coupla weeks off in the
      Caribbean
As if today was yesterday

Up in Rockland
they like to believe
that they can come to the city
collect rents, make their commissions, sell their tax credits,
        do the wall street hustle
take in a couple of shows, a couple of drinks,
        some entertainment on the company card and drive back
        up to Rockland, across the tappan zee bridge,
        surrounded by loyal cops
and firemen, a boat on the river,
year-round swimming and tennis at the spa
the good life maybe invite the boss over to dinner, cocktails and
        maybe when the economy is better, God
Up in Rockland
they like to believe
that they can count money indefinitely with no interruptions
because the Criminal Law and Natural Law are the same,
        because the guys on the legal tender
look like
them, and either made a killing in slaves or Government
And plus the cops, punch drunk viet veterans would rather die
        than look for a job
they are really strange up there
Not that there ain't merchants, paperboys, waitresses,
        gas station attendants, nurses,
teachers, housewives, bartenders
Nuclear plant workers, domestics, students, unemployed,
        butchers, bakers, candlestick makers, laborers — if i was a
        laborer, and you were in labor, and you had a daughter of
        mine, would you let them enslave her
But whoever hears of these folks, or us, we could be the same for
        all we know
but they could never be the same in Rockland
they like to believe they could.

KUWASI SPEAKS

Top BANANAS

In the Other Army

Excerpted from Look for Me in the Whirlwind (PM Press, 2017)

I hit it off all right later in the third platoon, being a field soldier in the field, and being in good understandings with the brothers. But there was a lot of shit that had been bugging me for a long time. Besides the ridiculous changes that all enlisted men went through, there was an added factor: rampant racism on all levels. A captain who was black was demoted to sergeant E-6 before our very eyes and shipped out. Brothers would spend 34 or 35 months of a 36-month enlistment and then get dishonorable discharges—white soldiers had to make successive superduper fuck-ups before the same would happen to them (like throw a German citizen off a bridge into the river in the month of January). If a brother whipped a white boy, under just about any circumstances, then disciplinary action was on the way—but not vice versa. And motherfuckers were still rapping that A-Company/C-Company shit. I rapped anti-American.

We blacks who felt we were marked men, on whom designs had been made to take care of 208-style, looked at the injustices on the post, had a secret meeting, and formed an organization based on fucking up racists. We called ourselves De Legislators, because we were going to make and enforce new laws that were fair. We were De Judge, De Prosecutor, De Executioner, Hannibal, and De Prophet. We said we would go to jail for a reason and not the season. We would get 208, but would make the brass go gray and bawl and stay up a whole lot of nights giving it to us.

From then on, every time a racial situation appeared, we did. Every time white GIs ganged a black GI, we moved to more than even the score. One at a time we would catch up with them and beat and stomp them so bad that helicopters would have to be used to take them to better hospitals than the ones in the area. We were not playing. We would plan things so that we could kick something off inside a club that would instantly turn into a riotous condition—once everything was in chaos it was impossible to pick us out. We then broke faces and bodies of whoever we planned to get, and made our escape. Afterward we would have critiques, just like in the end of war games; get our alibis together; and keep the whole thing under our hats.

The CIDo began investigating us, and the Provost Marshal. We began to want 208s but were beating motherfuckers up so bad they wouldn't name us. One of my partners, Huff, had a very high moral character, and broke me out of the habit of talking about people's mothers. He was an earnest social student and passed on worthy literature. He and Rhodes were the best of company. Rhodes was serious-minded about the struggle; and he ofttimes related that he grew up with the four sisters who were murdered by the racists in Birmingham in the explosion of the church. [...]

There were some hip dudes in De Legislators. Hannibal had earned his name by kicking ass. I had earned the name De Prophet by prophesying that so-and-so was going to get fucked up in a predetermined amount of time, and then going on and fucking the chump up. Brothers had asked how come I had never got busted. First, we were careful; and second, we were decisive, never saying, "One more ass to kick and then I'm going to stop"—always five more asses to kick. I wish that I'd kept in touch with the Legislators, and a few other brothers from that time, because sincere comrades are hard to come by.

Statement at Preliminary Hearing
September 2, 1982

As an anti-imperialist and a warrior of African descent, dedicated to the overthrow of the United States government, as an urban guerrilla in the ranks of the Black Liberation Army, i will not only resist the designs of a sham hypocritical system of law, but outright refuse to take any part in court proceedings. At large, i do not pay taxes, aid the fascist law enforcement authorities, or pass up reasonable opportunities to strike the oppressors, and find no reason to change now or any time in the future. As long as the United States government keeps the masses of Black and other Third World people as cannon fodder, and uses force to maintain its domination over us, and i am alive, i will resist, knowing that my fate as a resister irregardless of the state's consequences is better than the fates of those who accept oppression and pass it on to coming generations.

The gang of bullies under the banner of the American flag who practice genocide against Black, Latin, and Native American peoples within its confines, while harboring nazis and secret police from other fascist regimes, and arming and training Ku Klux Klanners and domestic Nazis, deserves no respite, and it's a sad day whenever they do. The United States, Israel, and South Africa stand as expanding imperialist settler states, rotten to their cores, from inception. Their fall will mark the end of a tragic era in history, worth all truly revolutionary efforts.

courtesy of Mary Patten and Madame Binh Graphics Collective Archives

Brink's Trial Opening Statement
July 11, 1983

My name is Kuwasi Balagoon. The name is of Yoruba origin. Yoruba is a name of a tribe in Western Africa in what was called the Slave Coast, and now called Nigeria. Many if not the bulk of slaves brought to the Western Hemisphere were Yoruba, and throughout slavery and U.S. colonialism the religion, customs, and even part of the language were maintained in the United States and throughout the Caribbean, Central, and South America. When the people of Nigeria threw the British out, they sent representatives to Oriente Province in Cuba to relearn the culture and the Yoruba religion, which was kept intact throughout slavery, Spanish, and American colonialism. i was renamed by my peers in the Yoruba temple and was married in a Yoruba ceremony like thousands of people before and since.

The english translation of Kuwasi is "born on Sunday," and the translation of Balagoon is "Warlord," and it suits me to have a name which reflects what i am about and my origins, i accept that name. Donald Weems, the name that the prosecutor likes to use, is an alien european name. Donald is a Christian name—and i am not a Christian; and Weems is a Scottish name, and i am not Scottish. It's a name that some slaver decided to brand what he considered his property with, and it is the name the state likes to use to propagate a colonial relationship. The english translation of Weems is "cave dweller." i reject all that it means.

i am a prisoner of war, and i reject the crap about me being a defendant, and i do not recognize the legitimacy of this court. The

---

This is the statement Kuwasi wrote in his defense, to explain the events that had brought them all there. He began reading this but was prevented from finishing by Judge Ritter. Unless otherwise noted, all footnotes in this and other texts in the "Kuwasi Speaks" section were added by the publishers of the first edition of *A Soldier's Story*, in 1999.

term defendant applies to someone involved in a criminal matter, in an internal search for guilt or innocence. It is clear that i've been a part of the Black Liberation Movement all of my adult life and have been involved in a war against the American Imperialist, in order to free New Afrikan people from its yoke. i am not treated like a criminal, am never in the company of prisoners with non-political charges. Never have i had a bail or parole once captured, and out of ten years in County Jails and prisons, seven years were spent in isolation, administrative segregation, management control, incorrigible units, or some separate, punitive arrangement or prison within a prison.

Before becoming a clandestine revolutionary i was a tenant organizer and was arrested for menacing a 270-pound colonial building superintendent with a machete, who physically stopped the delivery of oil to a building i didn't live in but had helped to organize. Being an organizer for the Community Council on Housing i took part in not only organizing rent strikes but pressed slumlords to make repairs and maintain heat and hot water, killed rats, represented tenants in court, stopped illegal evictions, faced

Kuwasi with his sister Diane, late 1960s

off with City Marshals, helped turn rents into repair resources and collective ownership by tenants, and demonstrated whenever the needs of tenants were at stake. In 1967, the U.S. Congress killed the rat bill which would have provided funding for killing rats. At that time, it was estimated that there were at least one rat for every person in New York City. So we decided to demonstrate at the U.S. House of Representatives. Once we got there we decided that instead of walking around with signs in the sun waiting for reporters, we would just go in and tell those creeps how we felt. Once we began to practice our First Amendment rights and refused to leave, Speaker of the House Tip O'Neill instructed the Capitol Police to "Get those niggers out of here," at which time the Boy and Girl Scouts and other spectators were ushered out and we and the Capitol Police had a free-for-all in the halls of Congress, down the front steps, and all over the lawn. Five of us, including myself and my sister, were arrested for "disorderly conduct," which the FBI files advise me was lodged because of resulting publicity that court proceedings might have entailed. The U.S. Congress response to us was to have plexiglass installed between them and the gallery where people affected by their actions and inactions would have to sit.

Although i was naive, i didn't think so, having been honorably discharged from the U.S. Army and seeing countless New Afrikan and Mexican GIs dishonorably discharged after serving thirty-four months of a thirty-six-month enlistment. Being stigmatized for life and denied employment and the right to vote for what white GIs were reprimanded for. Being told by a company commander that he was told that he would have to pay graft before our combat scores would be correctly calculated. i thought i knew the U.S. government.

We found it unacceptable that the same government who drafted New Afrikans and demanded that we fight the Vietnamese who had forced the French to surrender at Dien Bien Phu and leave Indochina, and who had mauled the 1st Cavalry Division in hand-to-hand combat in the jungles, as well as retaking Hamburger Hill at least four times, could not allocate a little money for killing rats, who were attacking countless infants and children, causing nervous disorders as well as poisoning, and traumatizing, mauling mothers nursing their infants. Members of Congress laughed straight out when the bill was brought before it and promptly voted it down.

There were people in the Community Council on Housing who worked at other jobs during the day and organized and conducted meetings at night until all matters were decided and business conducted; there were people who got up early in the morning to go with tenants to "tenants and landlords" court to argue out specific injustices, with pictures, inspection data, and building and apartment histories, and then walked all over West Harlem to organize meetings, because we couldn't afford our fare back and forth across town. We would stop illegal evictions at the door with court orders, arranged repairs, got heat and hot water for tenants, and outright threatened and stood off City Marshals who received hundreds of dollars for each eviction. i had gone to apartments and waited with my carbine a few times.

Then i began to realize that with all this effort, we couldn't put a dent in the problem. There's thousands of buildings with wiring eaten away by rats, holes in the floors, ceilings that had crashed on people, bathtubs that had fallen through the floors. There were always electrical fires; in the winter, 90 percent of the people i ran into heated their apartments with their ovens. i could confront building superintendents every day and a job and a free apartment would draw a replacement just as rotten. These conditions didn't come about through accident or people in high places not being aware. It was not even a question of the government not caring. The City of New York is the greatest slumlord, and the other slumlords get tax breaks and make superprofits on buildings that have been paid for hundreds of times over. i began to know that these inhuman conditions were not only perpetrated in Harlem, Brownsville, El Barrio, and the South Bronx where had originated and aided other organizers. These conditions were and are perpetrated in New Afrikan reservations in Washington, DC, in Miami's Overtown, the Hill District of Pittsburgh, the Central Ward of Newark, North Philadelphia, the Southside of Chicago, and all over the confines of the U.S.

We say that the U.S. has no right to confine New Afrikan people to redlined reservations, and that we have a right to live on our own terms in a common land area and to govern ourselves, free of occupation forces, such as the police, national guard, or GIs who have invaded our colonies from time to time. We have a right to control our own economy, print our own money, trade with other nations, and enter a workforce where we are not excluded by design and where our wages and the wages of all workers can be manipulated by a ruling class that controls the wealth. We have a right to build our own educational institutions and systems where our children will not be indoctrinated by aliens to suffer the destructive designs of the U.S. government.

When i say we New Afrikan people are colonized, i mean that our lives socially, economically, and politically, with the exception of our war of liberation, are controlled by other people, by imperialist euro-americans. Imperialist euro-americans tell us where to live and under what conditions, euro-american invaders, colonizers, decide what laws we should obey and what jobs we will get. It's no mystery why such a proportion of GIs, hospital workers, domestic workers, farmworkers, or athletes are New Afrikans or why we are 10 percent of the population within the confines of the U.S. and 50 percent of the prison population. We suffer 50 percent unemployment. Likewise, there is no mystery why the Black Liberation Army (BLA) was formed well over a decade ago and, despite captures and many instances of tortures and executions on the part of the U.S. government, has managed to continue the struggle and fill a lot of cops full of holes and continue to enjoy our people's support, in spite of raids and threats by the U.S. government and outright political and military blunders on our part. Despite claims that our backs have been broken or that we were out of existence, we of the BLA have continued to fight. Repression breeds resistance. There is no mystery how the Fuerzas Armados de Liberacion Nacional* (Armed Forces of National Liberation—FALN) continues, or how

---

* A clandestine Puerto Rican nationalist organization that engaged in armed struggle.

the Irish Republican Army (IRA) continues in Ireland, or the African National Congress continues to oppose America's 51st state: South Africa. Or why, despite helicopters and bloodthirsty advisers, the guerrillas in El Salvador continue to struggle and advance or why the Palestine Liberation Organization, despite the massive invasion of Lebanon, Israeli- and American-backed massacres, and internal conflicts, struggle on.* We have legitimate support from peoples who have been victimized and have a right to self-determination. We are human and nobody wants to live under or bring offspring into a confined atmosphere with an artificial sky.

That is what it is all about. The state knows that of the ninety so-called felonies i've been indicted on against the mythical peace and dignity of New York and New Jersey, all of them have been political and military in nature, even in cases where the charges have been dropped. The only time that i've been charged with offenses against working-class people who were not agents of the state was during a shootout with police where i commandeered a car, and while aiding an escape, when a man mistaken for a guard didn't follow instructions. It's been clear since i was forced underground while in the Panther Party that i have been a partisan on behalf of the liberation of Black people and in the ranks of Black resistance. The Secret Service wasn't issued a memo to detain, question, or at the very least monitor me in the event that i was in the same area as the president of the United States, might be because i might steal his watch, or because i ever voiced a threat; and the FBI hasn't put me in its National Index of Agitators to be arrested by them at any time on no charge because of molesting women or children, or selling drugs, or victimizing working-class people in any way. i am on the National Index of Agitators because i am a friend of liberty, an enemy of the state, and a

---

* While mention of the African National Congress and the Palestine Liberation Organization in this context may raise some eyebrows today, it should be remembered that in the 1980s both were considered legitimate national liberation organizations that at times faced severe government repression.

fighter in the ranks of the liberation army of New Afrikan people.

District Attorney Gribetz, Judge Ritter, and the state's propaganda arm, the establishment media, have sought to obviate this by calling me a defendant, as well as my comrade Sekou Odinga, as if we were American citizens negotiating an internal domestic legal system. We reject this, as well as the insistence on calling us, as well as Assata Shakur, Abdul Majid, and other POWs by slave names. We know that it is not just a case of racist arrogance or legality and note that Zayd Malik Shakur changed his name through the courts years before he was killed by State Troopers on the New Jersey Turnpike and was still called by the state and the media by his slave name. This is to propagate a colonial relationship.

i am tired of going through towns and cities, divided into sections where the houses are bigger and more fit for habitation in one section than the other, and the police protect one section and harass and terrorize the other, the one section enjoying better living conditions always white and the section most resembling hell nonwhite. i am tired of living in a land where the highest rank a Black man or woman can attain is a token appointment, and then hearing that crap that we are all Americans! i am tired of living the life of a colonial subject, while the hypocritical oppressors and exploiters of my people make pompous declarations about our democracy. America is racist, and by no twists and turns of semantics, by no evasions whatsoever, can a racist nation claim to be a democracy.

The media that carries stories about David Gilbert having a map of Orange County Jail while at Rockford County although no incident report was filed and the warden denied any knowledge of a map, first said to be a drawing, then a photo, ever being found. But besides justifying an incredible amount of security, this story was used as a motion to obtain a secret jury in a related federal RICO trial.* This court could not grant a motion to inves-

---

* This trial, the first political use of the anti-mafia RICO law, began April 4, 1983, the six defendants being Sekou Odinga, Bilal Sunni-Ali, Cecilio Ferguson, Jamal Josephs, Silvia Baraldini, and Iliana Robinson. Others, such as the then-fugitive Mutulu Shakur, were convicted in later trials.

tigate this through a hearing and a hearing to find out what traitor Samuel Brown* told state authorities. In another instance the
Rockland Journal reported that Julio Rosado was a FALN member
who visited Judy Clark and David Gilbert at Rockland, when it
is clear that Rosado is a public spokesperson of the Movimiento
de Liberacion National (MLN), and that the FALN is a clandestine revolutionary organization of fighters. A real investigative
reporter would have checked and found out readily that no visit
occurred, especially since the day it was reported to have happened, a Monday, is a day that freedom fighters don't receive
visits.

The media role in this case is to help the state build fascism
and is no more "neutral and detached" from the state than the
judge. The ruling that the jury be anonymous is a political ruling,
and we don't really care how it affects these individuals, because
the reality it communicates to everyone who knows of it is that
the state and supposedly "neutral" judge have reasons to believe
that we are of danger to people outside the state's repressive
apparatus, when it is clear that in no instance where a BLA member was on trial has a juror been harmed, threatened, or tampered
with in any way. We only engage the enemy in combat, and we
don't consider working-class people outside of law enforcement
enemies. The state's task is to make us appear to be everybody's
enemy—however, truth and history make it clear who is the real
enemy of the people.

In *Newsweek*, they had the nerve to state, "Nearly one half of
the 157 members of the United Nations hold political prisoners of
one sort or another: those of conscience, jailed for their beliefs or
those whose convictions have driven them to directly challenge
their governments. Some even accuse the United States of having
its own, though American tradition of democracy and due process make the charge seem more metaphysical than real." What
crap! In the U.S. political prisoners are called, among other things,
Grand jury resisters. They are brought before a grand jury and

* Samuel Brown was a member of the BLA arrested in relation to the
Brink's action who cracked and started cooperating with the police.

ordered to talk, and when they don't they are arrested and locked up for refusing to talk. Sometimes a judge orders them to answer a DA's question, and then, if they refuse to talk, they are tried with the aid of twelve people siding with the pigs under the guise of doing their civic duty and holding the fascist fabric of the state in place and can be convicted of contempt of court and can be sentenced to an undetermined sentence.

Aisha Buckner, Jerry Gaines, Fulani Sunni-Ali, Shaheem Jabbar, Richard Delaney, Yaasymyn Fula, Asha Thornton have been jailed for eighteen months or more; Julio Rosado, Andres Rosado, Ricardo Romero, Maria Cueto, and Steven Guerra have actually been sentenced — not for murder, not for arson or shoplifting or any alleged crimes — but for not submitting to an evil, alien, imperialistic power... the U.S. government. There have been at least seventy-five people jailed this way since 1970.... If these people were locked up in the Soviet Union, Poland, Grenada, or Cuba, they would be called "political prisoners." If they were in Zimbabwe or Libya, Kirkpatrick and Shultz* would call them prisoners of conscience. Lech Walesa† didn't do half the time that Jerry Gaines, Shaheeem Jabbar, Yaasmyn Fula, or Asha Thornton has, and they are still in, because America is a hypocritical empire. The [U.S.] propaganda machine moans each time Walesa is stopped by the [Polish] police, and when he admits to meeting with members of the underground, and then racistly and hypocritically ignores these people [grand jury resisters].

The *American Heritage Dictionary* defines a colony as a "group of emigrants settled in a distant land but subject to a parent country; 2. A territory thus settled; 3. Any region politically controlled by another country." But just as the hypocritical USA claims that it has no political prisoners, it claims it has no colonies.

Let's look at the word "genocide," same source. "1. The systematic annihilation of a racial, political or cultural group." The UN Convention on Genocide defines it as:

> A. Killing members of a group; B. Causing serious bodily or mental harm to members of a group; C. Deliberately inflicting on the members of the group conditions of life calculated to bring about its physical destruction

---

* During the Reagan administration Jeanne Kirkpatrick was U.S. ambassador to the United Nations and George P. Shultz was secretary of state.

† Leader of the anti-communist Solidarity trade union in Poland, which was at the time a satellite of the Soviet Union and was used as a constant example of human rights violations in the capitalist media.

in whole or in part; D. Imposing measures intended to prevent births within the group; E. Forcibly transferring children of the group to another group.

The American Bar Association objected to the Genocide Convention and the U.S. signing it through its special committee on Peace and Laws, because "Endless confusion in the dual system of the United States would be inevitable with the same crime being murder in state law and genocide in the federal and international fields. Race riots and lynchings being both local crime and genocide depending on the extent of participation."

Leader H. Perez, DA of Louisiana, stated, "All forms of homicide and personal injury cases would be brought under the broad mantle of genocide, and the mechanics of the thing would simply be that the United States Attorney would walk into state district court and move to transfer the case to federal courts. But what is still worse than the destruction of our constitutional setup and our framework of government in America is the overhanging threat that citizens of our states someday will have to face the international tribunal, where now they must face the state courts and a jury of their peers." *This constitutional setup has resulted in a white person never having been legally executed for the murder of a Black person in the history of the United States.* This is not by chance, this has been contrived, the genocide and hypocrisy have been elevated into civic virtue in the U.S. empire, while death rows across the U.S. are packed with Black prisoners.

The U.S. signed the Genocide Convention, with its government leaders knowing full well that they would not abide by it, just as it stated in the U.S. Constitution, Art. 6, para. 4: "The constitution and the laws of the United States shall be the supreme law of the land and the judges in every state shall be bound thereby."

They wrote these things out, real official, just as they wrote the Declaration of Independence, which said, "We hold these truths to be self-evident, that all men are created equal, that they are endowed by their creator with certain inalienable rights, that among these are life, liberty, and the pursuit of happiness. That to secure these rights, governments are instituted among men deriving their just powers from the consent of the governed. That whenever any form of government becomes destructive of these ends, it is the right of the people to alter or abolish it and to institute new government, laying its foundations on such principles and organizing its powers in such form, as to them shall seem most likely to effect their safety and happiness." These are noble words for slavers and rapists, and they go on to say, "but when a long train of abuses and usurpations pursuing invariably the same object evinces and designs to reduce them under absolute despotism, it is their right, it is their duty to throw off such government and to provide new guards for their future security."

They said this while kidnapping African people en masse from another continent three thousand miles away. Between 75 million and 110 million Africans were kidnapped, with less than 10 million surviving the Middle Passage to reach these shores. By the end of slavery there were only 4 million of us. Having endured every conceivable atrocity, including the forced separation and sale of family members, rape, murder, the raping and selling of children who were themselves the offspring of rape. Olmsted reported, "In the states of Maryland, Virginia, North Carolina, Kentucky, Tennessee and Missouri as much attention was paid to the breeding and growth of negroes, as to that of horses and mules."

J.E. Cairnes, the English economist, computed from reliable data that Virginia bred and exported no less than one hundred thousand slaves, which at five hundred dollars apiece (per head) yielded fifty million dollars. George Washington sold a slave to the West Indies for a hogshead of "best rum" and molasses and sweetmeats, and said it was because "this fellow is both a rogue and a runaway." Thomas Jefferson sold slaves on the open market. To refer to Washington, Jefferson, and the rest of those hypocrites as the fathers of *our* country is outright provocation.

Slavery was defended thusly: it was said, except for slavery, "The poor would occupy the position in society that the slaves do—as the poor in the North and in Europe do, for there must be a menial class in society and every civilized country on the globe, beside the confederate states, the poor are the inferiors and menials of the rich. Slavery was a greater blessing to the non-slave holding poor than to the owners of slaves, because it gave the poor a start in society that would take them generations to work out; they should thank god for it and fight and die for it as they would their own liberty and dearest birthright of freedom." This is the real justification for colonialism today.

Chattel slavery was an institution built on racism that built the USA, which for all practical purposes meant that the "owner" of a slave had complete control over the slave and also that any white person could order about any Black person. The slave patrols and militias were the predecessors of the fugitive squad, Red Squad, and the Joint Terrorist Task Force of today. The economy not only of the agrarian autocracy but of the whole south, through marshals, militias, breeders, auctioneers, overseers, slave drivers, and patrols looking for fugitives, was based on slavery, and there was much slavery in the North also: Maryland, Delaware, Washington, DC, New York, New Jersey, Pennsylvania, etc.

The Civil War that ended chattel slavery was carried out by the North not for that purpose but to stop the separation of the U.S. and to ensure industrial domination over agriculture. "The Negro became in the first year contraband of war: that is, property belonging to the enemy and valuable to the invader. And in addition to that, became as the South quickly saw, the key to the Southern resistance. Either these 4 million laborers remained quietly at work to raise food for the fighters, or the fighters starved. Simultaneously, when the dream of the North for manpower produced riots, the only additional troops that the North could depend on were 200,000 Negroes, for without them, Lincoln said, the North could not have won the war." (W.E.B. Du Bois, *Black Reconstruction*).

As the North began to secure victory over the rebellious states, the U.S. government with the Union Army and volunteer organizations established the Freedman's Bureau, which in conjunction with the treasury and newly freed slaves, lands throughout the confederacy were confiscated, and put into the hands of New Afrikans, who quickly proved they could support themselves even in the wake of war, as well as assist many people who had no land or provisions. Schools and universities were established and many New Afrikans attempted to become citizens of the United States.

On February 5, 1866, Senator Charles Sumner addressed the Senate and, among other things, said, "Our fathers futures and their sacred labor...and now the moment has come when the vows must be fulfilled to the letter. In securing the equal rights of the freedman and his participation in the government which he is taxed to support, we shall perform our early promise of the fathers, and at the same time the supplementary promises only recently made to freedmen as the condition of alliance and aid against the rebellion. A failure to perform these promises is political and moral bankruptcy."

The moment he spoke of has long passed, the promises have not been kept and the reason for this is inherent in the very nature of the U.S. empire. This was understood by nineteen out of twenty Black leaders of a delegation that met with General Sherman. When asked if they preferred to be part of the U.S. or live separately, nineteen said, "live by ourselves."

In short order, the U.S. government took back the bulk of the land confiscated from the Confederacy and handed it over to the New Afrikans who had been working on it. The Freedman's Bureau was dissolved, and President Grant urged removal of all political disabilities of former Confederates in December 1871. A bill was passed in the House to serve that purpose and was tied by Sumner to a Civil Rights Bill in the Senate. When it finally passed Congress in 1872, however, the civil rights feather was omitted.

Black federal troops were disbanded and removed from the South, at which point the militia searched Black dwellings for arms and took them away. The U.S. government, now consolidated, went back to playing the same role in regards to New Afrikan people as before the war—that of users. Carl Schurz, who was an adviser to President Johnson, observed: "The emancipation of the slaves is submitted to only insofar as chattel slavery in the old form could not be kept up. But although the freedman is no longer considered property of the individual master, he is considered the slave of society, and all independent state legislation will share the tendency to make him such. The ordinances abolishing slavery passed by the conventions under pressure of circumstance will not be looked upon as barring the establishment of a new form of servitude."

New Afrikan people could see this, and Henry Adams, testifying before the U.S. Senate Committee on Petitions on behalf of a petition by New Afrikans in Louisiana and Mississippi (two of the highest states in concentrations of New Afrikans) in 1874 said, "Well, in that petition, we appealed there if nothing could be done to stop the turmoil and strife, and give us our rights in the South, we appealed then at that time for a territory that could be set apart for us to live in peace and quiet." That's not asking for very much; however, the U.S. government rejected that petition. As it does now. The Fourteenth Amendment reads: "All persons born and naturalized in the United States, and subject to the jurisdiction thereof, are citizens of the United States and of the state in which they reside. No state shall make or enforce any law which shall abridge the privilege or immunity of citizens of the United States; nor shall any state deprive any person of life, liberty or property without due process of law nor deny to any person within its jurisdiction the equal protection of the laws."

Certainly, it can't be argued that New Afrikan people have ever received equal protection under the law, and besides being another official pompous lie, the Fourteenth Amendment "wrongfully and illegally precluded New Afrikans from exercising their options fully. New Afrikans were forced to accept the label of U.S. citizenship, and they had not been asked whether or not they wanted such citizenship or such a label. In 1856, 400,000 Afrikans had not been born in the U.S. These people could not be deemed to have been made citizens by any interpretation of the 14th amendment."

With a substantial portion of the New Afrikan people in the country legally unaffected by the Fourteenth Amendment and petitioners from two of the most populous states in regards to Black people noting that they were not receiving equal protection of the laws and asking for "territory set apart for us," what could

have possibly been the motives of the government of the United States of America outside of deceit, war, and colonization?

Between 1868 and 1871, there were 371 cases of violence, including 35 murders of Blacks in Alabama. Six churches and many school houses were burned before the election of 1870.

General Davis of the Freedman's Bureau reported 260 attacks, whippings, and murders of freedmen between January and November 1868 in Georgia.

In 1868, when Gov. Holden of North Carolina devised a plan to redistribute land and give ex-slaves a means to become self-sufficient, the Congressional Investigating Committee reported 260 outrages, including 7 murders and whippings of 72 whites and 141 Negroes.

A committee of the Constitutional Convention of 1868 on Partial Returns said that 1,035 men had been murdered in Texas (a part of Mexico that was invaded for the purpose of exploiting slavery) since the closure of the war, and the federal attorney said the number might have been 2,000.

Two thousand people were killed, wounded, or otherwise injured in Louisiana within a few weeks prior to the presidential election in November 1868. "Frightful conditions prevailed up the Red River around Shevreport in Caddo and Bossier Parishes, a trading center for Texas, Arkansas and the Indian nations. A United States army officer on duty in this place saw 2 or 3 men shot down in the streets in front of the store in which he sat. He picked up the bodies of 8 men who had been killed in 1 night. Never had he heard of anyone being punished for murder in that county." One hundred and twenty corpses were found in the woods or were taken out of the Red River after a "Negro hunt" in Bossier Parish.

"534 Negroes have been lynched by mobs in Mississippi between 1882 and 1950; 491 in Georgia; 352 in Texas; 335 in Louisiana; 299 in Alabama; 256 in Florida; 226 in Arkansas and 204 in Tennessee. Virtually no one has ever been punished for such a crime, because the courts and police collaborate with it." Three thousand four hundred and thirty-six Negroes are known to have been lynched between 1882 and 1950, thousands of us have been murdered without it even being recorded, throughout the USA. This is a war against New Afrikan people for the purpose of colonization and genocide. i could delay the proceedings indefinitely reciting instances of "legal" murders, such as countless rape frame-ups and executions, and instances where New Afrikans have been murdered, raped, assaulted, burnt out, or otherwise victimized, without any attempt to bring guilty persons to justice and for no other reason than national oppression. However, the objective of the imperialist war must be brought to light.

United States imperialism, which drains resources and profits from all parts of the world under its domination, has as its original base of this exploitation, and still largest source of super-exploitation, New Afrikan labor and talents, and this has been no less true with the shifting of the New Afrikan population.

Thus, in 1947, the median wage or salary of white wage earners was $1,980; of the nonwhite wage earners $863, or 43.6 percent as much, according to the U.S. Department of Commerce. In 1949, according to the United States Census Bureau reports, while 16,800,000 Americans in 4,700,000 families had an income of less than $1,000 a year, the income of white families was two times greater than that of New Afrikans.

Using the 1947 figure, this difference of more than $1,100 in normal earnings gives a measure of the amount of extra income, of superprofits, which employers derive from the average New Afrikan worker over and above the normal profits derived from the average white worker. Whites in 1939 who had a college education averaged $2,046 annually while New Afrikans with the same education had a median wage of $1,047. About the same disparity; so much for education.

Taken altogether, an appropriate answer might be gained by regarding as extra profits the $1,100 difference between the median Negro wage and the median white wage and multiplying the difference by the number of New Afrikan productive workers in agriculture and industry. Of the 6,000,000 New Afrikan gainful workers in 1947, approximately 3,500,000 were engaged in productive labor on farms or in industry, according to the U.S. Department of Commerce labor report. This number multiplied by $1,000 gives a total superprofit of almost $4 billion. More recent figures show a similar result for 1948 and 1949.

On top of this, the jobs with the highest percentage of New Afrikans include those least desired, due to working conditions, low pay, and risk of accident and disease, such as logging, sawmills, fertilizer plants, hospital workers, nursing home workers, U.S. armed forces enlistees (especially infantry, airborne, and armor), domestics, foundry workers, and farm and migrant laborers.

As of 1950, a single block in Harlem had a population of 3,871 people. At a comparable rate of concentration, concluded *Architectural Forum*, "The entire United States could be housed in half of New York City." Yet, due to redlining, being burnt out of places not permitted to us by a racist population, and a working conspiracy between banks, savings and loans associations, insurance companies, real estate corporations, police and fire departments, and other racist organizations, such as the original Southern Klans, Inc., Knights of the Ku Klux Klan of Florida, Inc., National Small Businessmen's Association, American Independent Keystone Society, Knights of the Kavaliers, Free White Americans, Inc., The Christian American, Inc., Order of American Patriots, Northern Klans, Inc., and other organizations who have state charters, corporate sanctions, tax exemption, and the right to establish subordinate lodges throughout the United States and its territories, we remain for the most part cooped up on Black reservations with rents 10 percent to 50 percent higher than comparable dwellings elsewhere.

That various states bestow these benefits of incorporation and tax exemption on these paramilitary racists is undeniable evidence of government conspiracy; that the Bureau of Internal Revenue, who harass ordinary working people, investigates who various presidents direct them to, and actually wreck homes, dig up yards, and confiscate small businesses, farms, and homes for nonpayment of relatively small sums to further this conspiracy by extending federal tax exemptions on the basis that these organizations are "nonprofit, benevolent, fraternal and educational" is outright war, hypocrisy, and deceit, second only to the U.S.

Department of Justice and the Defense Department that invades the Dominican Republic and other republics under any pretense and destabilizes popularly elected governments and commits real massacres in Chile, Indonesia, and Puerto Rico and supports and aids the Israeli government in its massacres of Palestinian people and the theft of their homeland—just as the euro-americans stole this land—and supports the invaders and nazis of South Africa, who not only exist on stolen land but exploit African labor and commit massacres and other atrocities like their racist imperialistic euro-american tutors.

In this period, called a recession and marked by inflated prices and high unemployment, we are still in the same position as regards to being economic cannon fodder in these United States. As of July 17, 1983, as reported in that edition of the *New*

York Times, the Center for the Study of Social Policy reports that the average Black college graduate's income is about the same as the average white high school graduate's income. Only 55 percent of Black men over the age of sixteen are employed today. Unemployment of Black men over the age of twenty-one is almost 50 percent; twenty-one years ago three out of every four Black men were employed. In 1981, the median income for Blacks was $13,266, while the median income for whites was $23,517. In other words, the Black median income is only 56 percent of the white. 54 percent of Black families are now at income levels below $15,000 a year, compared with 28 percent of white families.

As always, old age and survivors' insurance and unemployment compensation systems do not cover agricultural, domestic, service, and self-employed persons. Sixty-five percent of all Black workers fall into these categories, compared with 40 percent of white workers.

The Presidential Advisory Committee on Civil Disorders lists as the first level of grievance police practices, unemployment and underemployment, and inadequate housing.

Police in NYC have been involved in forty-nine racially motivated murders since 1979, and police throughout the country have murdered four hundred Third World people during the year.

- New York: December 22–24, 1980. Three Black males and one Hispanic male were fatally stabbed. Witnesses to at least two of the stabbings have described the assailant as a white male.

- New York: October 8–9, 1980—Buffalo, Cheektowanga, Niagara Falls. Three Black males and a Black teenager were shot and killed by sniper attacks or in shooting incidents. Witnesses have described the assailant as a white man.

- New York: August 8, 1979—Yonkers. The home of a Black family was firebombed. City officials describe the attack as racially motivated.

- Ohio: November 1, 1980—Youngstown. A Black teenager was shot and killed by a rifle fired from a pickup truck. Press accounts indicate a group of white youths in a pickup truck had been driving around shooting randomly at Black citizens.

- Oklahoma City: October 21, 1979. A Black male and a white female companion were shot and killed by a sniper attack. Police said the assailant was a white male.

- Johnstown, PA. A Black male and a white female companion were shot and killed by a sniper attack.

- Chattanooga, TN: October 24, 1980. A Black teenager was shot and wounded by two white males.

- Chattanooga, TN: April 19, 1980. Four Black women were shot and wounded by a shotgun fired from a car. A Ku Klux Klansman was convicted and two other Klansmen were acquitted.

- Salt Lake City: August 20, 1980. Two Black youths were shot and killed by a sniper attack as they were jogging with two white female companions.

- Bennington, UT: October 27, 1980. One of three [assailants] was sentenced to between three months and one year in jail for his role in the abduction and stabbing of a Black teenager.

- Contra Costa County, CA: November–December 1980. A series of attacks against Black families by white vandals occurred, including an attempted assault and shooting incident.

- Chico, CA: January 13, 1980. A deaf Black male was shot and killed by two white males and one white female. According to press reports, the assailants murdered their victim because they could not find any animals to shoot on their hunting trip.

- Manchester, CT: October 2, 1980. The home of a Black family was firebombed.

- Ft. Wayne, IN: May 29, 1980. Vernon Jordan, President of the National Urban League was shot and critically wounded by a sniper attack.

- Indianapolis, IN: January 1, 1980. A Black male was shot and killed by a sniper attack.

- Greensboro, NC: November 3, 1980. Demonstrations protesting the Ku Klux Klan clashed with Klansmen and Nazis. Five of the demonstrators, including three white males, one Black female, and one Hispanic male, were shot and killed. Six Klansmen and Nazis were later tried on state charges of murder and rioting. An all-white jury acquitted all of the defendants.

There have been recent lynchings of New Afrikans in rural Mississippi and Mobile, Alabama, and since Wayne Williams has been in custody, there have been twenty-five more killings of New Afrikans in Atlanta.* In April 1982, three young retarded Black men were found hanged and castrated in Atlanta. In the Greensboro, NC, killings of the anti-Klan demonstrators, FBI "informant" Ed Dawson rode in the lead car of a ten-car Klan and Nazi convoy; Agent Bernard Butkovich participated in the planning. The armed military assault by the Klan and Nazis against the demonstrators who were unarmed was shown on national television, the acquittals were announced. What was this, if it wasn't a case of propaganda by the deed? What did this communicate to the murderers of Willie Turks in Brooklyn? What did the five-year sentence of Bova communicate? What did the acquittal of Paul Mormando, after he admitted to taking part in the beating that led to Turks's death by actually pulling a man who was trying to run from a fight out of his car?† Well, the answer to that was duly reported in the next day's paper: a gang of white armed males attacked a Black teenager in Queens, with at least one knife and one baseball bat, with no arrests made.

But that's only part of what is communicated. Not only are these actions announcing over and over that in the United States, Black life is cheap, and that any white racist armed with a weapon or crowd of other racists, which aren't hard to find, can attack

---

* In the 1980s, Atlanta was hit by a wave of serial killings of New Afrikan children. Under immense public pressure, the Atlanta police arrested and convicted Wayne Williams, a young Black music producer who had no previous criminal record. The evidence was largely circumstantial, and many people have believed Williams to be the victim of a coverup to protect a white cop child molester.

† On June 22, 1982, Willie Turks, a thirty-four-year-old city transit worker, was one of three Black transit employees driving home after work through Brooklyn when their car was attacked by a white mob. Turks was savagely beaten to death and his coworkers injured. Of the approximately twenty white men in the mob, the police and prosecutors indicted only six, and none were ever convicted of murder. One had his charges dropped, one died before his trial, the others received terms of five, three, three, and two years, and served less than that—Paul Mormando, who was only convicted of assault and sentenced to two years, was released after only nine months.

and even kill Blacks with little or no consequence, but that the American legal system has no problems finding jurors able to overlook words, pictures, or whatever they have to accept a racist tradition.

At Camp Fuller, on the Texas Gulf Coast, CIA-rained mercenaries, national guardsmen, and army reserve personnel train Klansmen and women. At Dekker Lake, a marine recruit is in charge of training Klansmen. There's Klan training camps in Connecticut, New York, California, Alabama, and Georgia as well, and not only is there no effort to stop them from being armed — this government of the United States supplies them. There's no shortage of police, jailers, or U.S. GIs in the Klan, and there's no shortage of federal agents. In North Carolina alone, forty-one chapters were maintained by the FBI. You tell me the difference between the Germans in World War II and the euro-americans, except that euro-americans have killed more people within its confines than the followers of Hitler who were inspired by euro-americans to commit their slaughter and have been and are very often harbored and protected since by the U.S. government. Where and when in the history of this earth have there been a bigger bunch of murderers, liars, and hypocrites than the USA, and yet the war machine hasn't satisfied the state. Twenty-four percent of Black women have been sterilized by the state; Black infant mortality rate is 23.1 percent, while white infant mortality rate is 12 percent;* Black life expectancy is nine years less.

The U.S., with the aid of Turkish and other UN forces, were set back in Korea and thus lost a market to exploit. They wanted a puppet government over the whole of Korea and had to settle for half. They make "fashion jeans" over there for wages people over here wouldn't work for, and i am certain you've heard some of the stories by GIs returning from South Korea after the so-called

* This sentence is as it appears in the New Jersey ABC edition of Balagoon's Opening Statement. While accurate regarding sterilizations, Balagoon's infant mortality statistics may have been the result of a typo as the correct statistics for 1980 are roughly 23.1 *per thousand* (Black infant mortality) and 12 *per thousand* (white infant mortality), not per hundred.

police action. The U.S. lost markets in Southeast Asia. This unde-clared war was not an adventure gone astray or an attempt to aid the people of South Vietnam by propping up a fascist puppet, who had a difficult time leaving after his defeat because of the weight of the gold on his plane. The Vietnam episode was a clas-sic imperialist war, from the rubber on its plantations once under French rule, oil on its offshore—which Standard Oil had sur-veyed and had begun negotiations for with both the U.S.-backed government and the democratic Republic of Vietnam—and the poppy fields that provided most of the heroin during that war, for the chemical warfare against and enslavement of much of the Black and other Third World youth within the U.S. colonies, and provided extra funds for the Central Intelligence Agency.

The U.S. imperialists have lost Somoza's grip on Nicaragua,* and the U.S. puppets in El Salvador and Guatemala stand on shaky ground. Imperialism must expand or die; the recession is due to lack of expansion and new supplies of raw materials, in an economy whose growth is in video games for diversion, comput-ers for taking people out of work and storing information against them, "security" to guard the rich and intimidate the poor, and pornography and provocative violence against women and chil-dren, is the cause of this crisis.

In 1968, the Republic of New Afrika petitioned the U.S. in pursuit of secession; the Nation of Islam under the leadership of Elijah Muhammed had demanded land for a Black Nation since 1940. In the 1930s, Marcus Garvey and the Universal Negro Improvement Association organized five million people of African descent in an effort to return to Africa. The U.S. govern-ment charged this man, who bought a ship line and land in Africa and mobilized five million people into industrious self-sufficiency and one purpose and one aim, with mail fraud and deported him to the hands of the British who kept him in jail until his death

---

* Anastasio Somoza's brutal dictatorship in Nicaragua was overthrown by a popular left-wing revolution in 1979. Balagoon was writing at a time when Nicaragua was ruled by the left-wing Sandinistas and was the victim of military attacks by the CIA-backed Contras.

(after confiscation of the ship line and rubber plantation in Liberia and selling them to Firestone, B.F. Goodrich, etc.) The Nation of Islam was dubbed by the press as "Black Muslims" to the point where few people, comparably, knew their real title. They were persecuted and special oppressive conditions and denial of their rights to religion occurred when members were imprisoned, often on framed-up charges, and yet they were accused of teaching hate. At least part of this was because their program called for land and for the building of a nation of and for Black people. Twenty-one Black Panthers were indicted on thirty-six criminal conspiracy charges in 1969; twelve of us who were captured were held in isolation in county jails, because we had established housing, medical, and food programs and had in our political program a call for a vote conducted by the UN to ascertain the number of Black people in the U.S. who want to live in a separate nation of Black people. After over two years, a jury acquitted all brought before them after ninety minutes of deliberation. But for two years, twenty-one people who were key organizers had to sit in jail or go underground. Some are still underground, as flight to avoid persecution is a "criminal" charge.

The Republic of New Afrika presented the U.S. State Department with a petition for land for the New Afrikan nation and has been hounded by the federal and state police ever since. The federal and state police attacked New Bethel Baptist Church while a public meeting was in progress, attended by 142 men, women, and children in Detroit. The New Afrikan Provisional Government was having a meeting, and although they were surrounded and surprised, the participants, including Mtayari Shabaka Sundiata and Mutulu Shakur, gave a good account of themselves, and the police got one of their own killed and another wounded for their efforts. This was a clear case of self-defense, and no New Afrikans were imprisoned with this shootout used as justification, and, of course, none of the federal or state police who had fired over four hundred shots into the church were charged with anything.

On August 18, 1971, in Jackson, Mississippi, the Mississippi State Police and the FBI attacked the headquarters of the Provisional Government of the Republic of New Afrika and got a few holes in their hides for their efforts. In fact, the head of the Jackson Police Intelligence Squad, Louis Skinner, was killed and two other euro-americans in that lily-white death squad were wounded.

Eighty years before that, Thomas Fortune and the National Afro-American League championed the cause of a separate nation for New Afrikan People. A hundred years before, New Afrikan people in Mississippi and Louisiana petitioned Congress for a separate territory. The first permanent inhabitants after the Native Americans in what is now the United States were slaves that rebelled against Spanish enslavers and colonizers and joined the Native Americans in what is now South Carolina, in the year 1526.

So understand this demand is no fad, that this struggle for land and independence is a legitimate aspiration that has been within the national will of the New Afrikan people since we first stepped onto these shores. We are a colonized people who have a common language, culture, and history of oppression.

If the United States was a democracy it would set a date for a UN plebiscite, hold elections with no interference, and abide by the outcome. If the United States had been "forthright" in its dealings with us it would be doubtful if thirty million people would decide to move and begin anew, rather than choose what they know and have experienced, but you know and the American government knows it has not been anything but hideous.

This "criminal" trial will not settle the question, there will be a war until justice is served. Some New Afrikans feel that once America sees that it comes out cheaper to leave us alone we will achieve independence. i feel that independence will come after total revolution, when the government no longer exists or simply hasn't the power to extend its authority over us. That there is something in the psychology of Americans that permits the continuation of the marines in Guantanamo Bay in Cuba, even though it is clear that neither the Cuban government nor the Cuban people want them there.

i don't know how many generations of migrant workers will pick through the same groves year after year, or how many children will grow hungry or worse, cynical, packed up in sub-human dwellings. i don't know how long people will speak of officers like O'Grady and Brown* as if they were saints and accept photos of warriors like Mtayari lying dead under the caption "Death to Terrorists" in papers like the *Daily News*.

How can people talk of survivors, the wives and children of cops, and their grief as if revolutionaries come from Mars and don't have families, when our families and loved ones are harassed and attacked? Sundiata's wife was literally driven insane, and police went to the mental hospital to obtain a statement nevertheless. The answer must be the same as why Americans can say right off the bat that fifty-seven thousand "Americans" died in the Vietnam War without caring as to how many Southeast Asians were killed. This kind of disregard comes with the territory of being a freedom fighter in a racist, imperialist, fascist empire, but it comes, for the most part, with being Black.

Throughout slavery there were numerous rebellions and conspiracies to rebel, and laws were enacted against it, defining rebellion as criminal. Nat Turner, Cinque, Denmark Vesey led revolts and conspiracies, there were over 250 slave revolts during these three hundred years of slavery and countless cases of arson and poisonings. Just as there were slaves and jerks like Crispus Attucks who fought with the Americans against the British, there were ex-slaves who fought with the British and after the British gave up, these ex-slaves became Maroons and continued to fight. Evidence of at least fifty such communities (of Maroons) in various places and at various times, from 1672 to 1864, has been found. Today from the backlands of New Jersey through Appalachia, southward into Texas, and even across the Mexican border, the descendants of many of these Maroons who chose to cast their lots with the Native Americans can still be found, largely forgotten and often desperately poor. New Afrikans fought alongside the Seminoles against the Americans, 1,500 white soldiers

---

* Waverly Brown was the only Black cop on the Nyack police force and Edward O'Grady was his white sergeant in the NPD. Both were killed at the roadblock during the Brink's action.

and twenty million dollars. U.S. history doesn't record our loss of life. In September 1850, three hundred Florida Maroons took flight from their abode in present Oklahoma to Mexico. This was accomplished after driving off Creek nationals sent to expose their exodus. On October 30, 1851, 1,500 former American slaves were aiding the Comanche Indians of Mexico in their fighting.

In *The Conclusion of the President's Commission on Civil Disorders*, Dr. Kenneth B. Clark commented, "I read the report of the 1919 riot in Chicago, and it is as if I were reading the report of the investigating committee on the Harlem riot of '43, the report of the McCone Commission on the Watts riot. I must again in candor say to you members of this Commission—it is a kind of Alice in Wonderland—with the same picture reshown over and over again, the same analysis, the same recommendations and the same inaction."

Black people have attempted to be recognized as human beings in this country despite its history of murder through non-violent marches, sit-ins, etc., appealing to America's moral conscience, and only got more oppression for this. They couldn't speak the right language; tell me the difference in the fates of Martin Luther King, El Hajj Malik Shabazz, and Mark Essex?*

Expropriation is an act of war carried out by every revolutionary army in history. The have-nots must take from the haves to support their war. Washington, even though he had slaves and was aided by the French, crossed the Delaware to raid the British. Stalin was expropriating from banks at the age of fifteen. Carlos Marighella expropriated from the North American imperialist banks in Brazil, as the Tupamaros did likewise in Uruguay. During the Spanish resistance to fascism, the banks were necessarily targets of *Nosotros* and *los pistoleros* and other guerrillas.

---

* Martin Luther King was assassinated on April 4, 1968, in Memphis, Tennessee. El Hajj Malik Shabazz is better known by the name Malcolm X and was assassinated on February 1, 1965, in the Audubon Ballroom in New York City. Mark Essex was a Black revolutionary in New Orleans who got fed up, armed himself, and started shooting cops. He was killed after a day-long siege on January 7, 1973.

Anyone not funded by an outside power must engage in acts of expropriation or collect "revolutionary compulsory tax" to carry on revolution. No member of the BLA has ever opened fire during an expropriation unless forced by a fool. Actually, we'd prefer not to fire a shot, because the purpose of an expropriation is to get funds and not to execute guards or police, as a retaliating action might be for, but also because shots are signals. The ideal expropriation is carried out without anyone outside of the action being any the wiser. When the BLA has assassinated police officers on purpose and by design we've issued communiqués explaining why and leaving no questions.

My comrade Sekou Odinga has been rejected from this case and indicted in a federal case, charged with racketeering, justified by the same incidents that leave me charged with murder and robbery, so that the New Afrikan position can be hopefully put out of focus by the state, by having one New Afrikan defending against the same criminal charges as two white anti-imperialists. i am defending the revolution, the state's arrangements are of no consequence. It does not matter what the legal outcome will be. Our fates are not in the hands of the state, but in the hands of the masses of New Afrikan people. In revolution, one either wins or dies. This case awaits a bigger jury.

In regards to the death of the money courier and the two police officers, i am insulted that it's thought of as such a horrendous act by the media and a population that doesn't conclude that twenty-five murders of New Afrikan children in Atlanta since the incarceration of Wayne Williams or the drowning of a crowded boat of Haitians under the eyes of the United States Coast Guard is a big deal.

But that's the system. Like Public Law 831-81 Congress, Title II, Sections 102, 103, 104, otherwise known as the McCarran Act, which authorizes Concentration (Detention) Camps should the president declare an Internal Security Emergency. Security is the word. The U.S. Army has 350 record centers containing substantial information on civilian political activists. The pentagon has twenty-five million cards on individuals and 760 thousand on organizations held by the defense Central Index of Investigations alone, and this information includes political, sociological, and psychological profiles of twenty-five million people in the U.S.

There are special prisons in the U.S. Army Reserve's 300th Military Police POW Command at Kivonia, Michigan. Other "emergency detention centers" are at Allenwood, PA; Mill Point, West Virginia; Maxwell Air Force Base, Montgomery, Alabama; Avon Park, Florida; and Elmendorf at Eilson Air Force Base in Alaska. The Air Force has one of the largest police departments in the so-called free world.

The introduction to the King Alfred Plan,* a plan to be utilized by the U.S. Defense and Justice Departments in the event of rebellion, reads: "Even before 1954, when the Supreme Court of the United States of America declared unconstitutional separate educational and recreational facilities, racial unrest has become very nearly a part of the American way of life. But that way of life was repugnant to most Americans. Since 1954, however, that unrest and discord have broken into widespread violence which increasingly has placed the peace and stability of this nation in dire jeopardy. This violence has resulted in loss of life and limb and property, and has cost the taxpayers of this country billions of dollars. And the end is not in sight. This same violence has raised the tremendously grave question as to whether the 2 races can ever live in peace with each other."

The U.S. doesn't intend to make fundamental changes, it intends to bully New Afrikans forever and maintain this colonial relationship based on coercion, or worse, a "final solution." This means that some New Afrikan soldiers like myself must make our stand clear and encourage New Afrikan people to prepare to defend themselves from genocide by the American nazis — study our mistakes; build a political program based on land and

---

* The "King Alfred Plan" was detailed in a radical Sixties novel, *The Man Who Cried I Am* by John Williams. It involved using the army to physically exterminate the entire Black population of the U.S. It was published in the *Black Panther* newspaper as if it were fact, and was widely discussed in radical circles and believed by many (including Balagoon) to be an actual existing government plan. Nevertheless, it was a work of fiction.

independence; a counterintelligence program to ferret out traitors the likes of Tyrone Rison, Sam Brown, and Peter Middleton;* and be ready to fight and fight and organize our people to resist on every level. My duty as a revolutionary in this matter is to tell the truth, disrespect this court, and make it clear that the greatest consequence would be failing to step forward.

i have thrown my lot in with the revolution and only regret that due to personal shortcomings on my part, failure to accept collective responsibility, and bureaucratic, hierarchical tendencies within the BLA, i haven't been able to contribute as much as i should or build a better defense against my capture due to denial of fuse. i am confident that my comrades still at large will correct their thinking and practice thorough criticism/self-criticism and begin to strike consistent blows at the U.S. imperialist. i wish i could inspire more people, especially New Afrikan people, to take the road to liberation and adequately express my contempt for the U.S. ruling class and its government. Other than that, i have nothing else to say.

Demonstration in Support of October 20th Freedom Fighters on opening day of pre-trial hearings. New City Courthouse, New York. September 13th.

---

* New Afrikans arrested in connection to the Brink's expropriation who flipped and cooperated with the police and prosecution.

Anthony Accurso

Brink's Trial Closing Statement
September 13, 1983

For the record, i'll say right now, that this place is an armed camp. It has the trappings and props of a court. A state-issued clone in a black robe, an ambitious state-issued clone at the state table, a fenced off area, and a section for spectators with a smaller section for members of the press, who can listen to an opening statement, and between them not one mentions anything i said about America being an imperialist empire that among other things holds New Afrikan people in subjection, or that the U.S. government, while hypocritically speaking of human rights in places like Poland, never mentions the political prisoners it holds and calls grand jury resisters. The state-issued prosecutor objects, the state-issued court sustains, and the media that pats itself on the back and hypocritically calls itself free erase whatever notes they might have taken automatically and take their places beside the state-issued court and prosecutor. Although i think the press is capable of following instructions, the ruling that politics have nothing to do with this case is enough. A reporter, Van Sickle, describes the opening as a list of grievances. That New Afrikan people are subjected to living in reservations administered by an occupation force calling itself police and being systematically beaten out of wages, liberties, and our very lives is not news, and that the media is just so many state-issued clones is not news either. Their job all along has been to present the state in a false light and instill fear in the population, so that people will find fascism acceptable. And call it democracy. Under no stretch of the imagination, twist or turn, summations or evaluations can a racist, imperialist country call itself a democracy, without its victims, its enemies, calling it anything more than a hypocracy.

Taking up a couple of other rows in the court are the pistol-packing, armor-plated plainclothes cops paid to keep an eye on

things. On the roofs and in the surrounding areas there's more
and a herd of hastily deputized armed clones in gas station attendant uniforms, as well as German shepherds, and of course the
usual guards. There's a lot of iron in here, state-issued iron. And
in the hallway leading to this theater there's more state-issued
clones with state-issued iron and metal detectors to make sure
that all the iron that enters these state domains, this imperialist
theater, is state-issued. They wish to have us believe or act as if
we believe that war is peace—as the press apparently believes
that ignorance is strength.

Other than that are the people who braved searches, having
their pictures taken and filed away by the fascist, to come here
to actually be as they are designated, supporters and spectators.
And one group of people that stinks of the trappings of this court
is designated a jury, among them some wear sunglasses while in
our midst—another has children who have Black friends whose
homes they visit but who never visit them at home, and who has
Black friends himself who never drop by. Another who thinks we
are so ugly she turns and looks at the wall while we ride by in
police cars. None of these people are racist or have any prejudice,
and we know this because the court asked them, and they said
they didn't, all of them. None of the potential jurors were racist or
infected by racial prejudice, and showed this to the satisfaction of
a racist court.

Had i not taken the position that no court in the imperialist U.S. empire had the right to try me as a criminal, i would have demanded that this case be tried in Rockland County. One cannot hold both positions. However, i believe that the people of Rockland County and elsewhere deserve an explanation of the event, the expropriation and related actions that took place on October 20, 1981. Not a mere criminal defense in relation to it, that type of legal mumbo jumbo could have matters more confused than ever. An explanation on the other hand, by someone who might have given them directions on the subway in New York City or sweated through a basketball game with them or shared a dance floor should make things clear factually, as well as let people in Rockland who are not already our friends and everyday people throughout the confines of the U.S. know for sure that it is not the people but the United States government and its oppressive apparatus that we are at war against.

The media said that on two separate occasions members of the Black Liberation Army jumped out of vehicles shooting randomly in incidents where one guard and two policemen were killed. On the face of it, it doesn't appear random at all according to that line. Either the guerrillas and the people around not participating were lucky; the armed money courier and the two policemen were very unlucky; or the guerrillas were armed with guided bullets. Obviously, none of this was so, but it was broadcast far and wide for a long time to taint not only people who might be jurors but everybody in a land where a war is going on between oppressed peoples and the oppressors. It's clear the guerrillas intended to shoot police and that's who they shot. They shot the enemy.

Expropriation raids are a method used in every revolution by those who have got to get resources from the haves to carry on armed struggle. When George Washington and company crossed the Delaware, it was to raid the British, to take money, supplies, and arms, even though he was financed by the French and owned slaves. Joseph Stalin robbed banks when he was fifteen to support revolutionary struggle. The Sabate brothers in Spain were obliged to empty the tills of banks to resist Franco during the Spanish Civil War. When Carlos Marighella in Brazil or the Tupamaros in Uruguay expropriated from banks to finance their struggles, it was clear to the press that they were revolutionaries; this government sent counterinsurgency specialists to help the juntas and dictators they resisted and expropriated from, just as they've done in regards to Argentina. But here in the U.S., the government doesn't acknowledge the collection of revolutionary compulsory tax as the work of revolutionaries, just as the British do not acknowledge the IRA, just as Israel doesn't acknowledge the PLO, and just as the South Africans do not acknowledge the ANC. It's too close. The British called Washington a criminal and issued a reward for him dead or alive, just as the Americans put a price on the head of Twyman Myers. The state must deny revolution and call revolutionary acts and revolutionaries something else, anything else — bandits, terrorists. The state must suppress revolution and say they are doing something else. Rather than argue that there's no need for revolution and be confronted with Harlem, the South Bronx, Bedford Stuyvesant, Newark's Central Ward, North Philadelphia, etc. They say there is simply not a revolution, as if there is no reason for sweeping the oppressors from power. Revolution is always illegal and revolutionaries are always slandered.

There are clearly more than a few points that the state has pushed for reasons beyond that of legal that clearly go past the objective of getting convictions. The first lie is that Peter Paige, the Brink's guard and money courier, was gunned down without a chance to defend himself or surrender. In order to portray the Black Liberation Army as cowardly and cold-blooded, bloodthirsty.

The BLA is an organization that takes credit for preplanned assassinations. In our history there are numerous instances of ambushed police where credit was clearly taken, where communiqués were issued to the media who do not broadcast them completely, if at all, because the government has directed them not to. These ambushes have always been retaliations for terrorist acts against Black people — these acts have always been responses to murders, brutalizations, and threatening against Black people,

Third World people, or their forces of resistance. Never has a guard or a bank teller been shot down as part of a plan; no unit of the BLA has ever done this, including the unit involved in the expropriation of October 20, 1981. Our war is not a license and the BLA reserves assassinations for those who are combatants in opposition to the revolution and those who direct them. Money couriers are safe so long as they do not put their bodies and weapons in between someone else's money or try to shoot their way out of a source of embarrassment or into a promotion or an early grave.

This is because the goal of an expropriation is to collect revolutionary compulsory tax and not casualties. A unit is no better off with a guard killed. Shots are signals that alert more police more quickly and directly than an onlooker's phone call. Guerrillas prefer to take the weapons from the holsters of guards or pick them up after they've been dropped and complete the action without anyone except guards and guerrillas being any the wiser. Had Peter Paige not acted the fool, he would've lived and his coworker would not have been injured.

War is expensive, you know that; you don't pay taxes once. And no matter how much money a unit may get from an expropriation, that unit as well as others will have to engage in other expropriations in the course of a protracted war. The BLA doesn't want a situation where guards believe they will be shot whether they comply or not, because then there would always be shootouts. Dead guards don't bring us a step closer to land and independence and don't add a cent to a war chest. At the same time, the BLA doesn't want guards to believe for an instant that they have any reasonable alternatives outside of compliance.

The only parties that benefit from a bloody shootout during an expropriation are the bankers, the bosses of the armored car corporations, and career counterinsurgency experts. The first two put their money, or what they label their money, before the lives of guerrillas, as well as their employees; the third, without New Afrikan, Puerto Rican, or Mexican fugitives to justify raids in those colonies, could find themselves in fatigues in the wilds of the Dakotas laying siege to Native American colonies. Paige died for his bosses not for himself, his family, or his fellow workers.

State clone Michael Koch issued another slanderous attack for the state. At one point in his testimony he says that one of the combatants says in regards to Kathy Boudin, "Fuck her, leave her." On one episode of *Today's FBI*, a band of "terrorists" takes a truck of 1.6 million dollars and purposely leave one of their comrades. On one episode of *Hill Street Blues*, a radical band gets 1.6 million dollars from another truck. In the FBI fiction the radicals mow down the guards as a matter of course; in the *Hill Street Blues* fiction, the beautiful white girl when faced with life in prison serves up her comrades for a deal that sounded not unlike a slave auction, with time being the medium, rather than money. Koch meanwhile hasn't gotten a contract as a writer or an actor—i tell you, there is no justice in this world.

There's no record of the BLA leaving comrades in hostile areas on purpose. When comrades are wounded, attempts are made to carry them. The state contends that Marilyn Buck* was wounded and taken to Mount Vernon with the unit in question. The state wants to have it both ways.

The BLA doesn't work that way. We have a saying: "The lowest circles in hell are reserved for those who desert their comrades." The BLA has a history of aiding the escapes of comrades from prisons and other detention centers. The state-issued lie that any of us said anything to the effect to leave anyone who had

---

* Marilyn Buck was a white political prisoner. During the 1960s, as an anti-racist activist in California, she was convicted of helping former Black Panthers. Federal prosecutors often referred to her as "the only white member of the Black Liberation Army." After years in prison, she escaped but was later recaptured and convicted of helping to free Assata Shakur and other revolutionary acts. *Update to 2019 edition:* In 2008 Marilyn was granted a parole date in February 2011, then won an advance to August 8, 2010. With less than twelve months left to serve, she was diagnosed with a rare and very aggressive uterine cancer. Despite surgery and chemotherapy, treatment came too late to save her life. She was granted an early release on July 15, 2010. She paroled to Brooklyn, New York, where for the next twenty days she savored every moment of her freedom.

participated in any action with us is designed to portray us as users and racist. For the state to project that piece of propaganda at the same time that it lines the roofs with rifle-toting clowns, posts guards at each block and intersection, and transports us in armed convoys without red lights is not only an insult to us but an insult to anybody outside the state who hears it. Every day we come to court there are scores of fat middle-aged cops crouching behind trees, phone poles, and cars, guns at the ready. This is not because they think we can break out of handcuffs, waist chains, and leg chains, and then dive out of closed car windows and sprint to the next county before anyone notices what is going on. They do this because the BLA does not forfeit comrades into the hands of the enemy and does not forfeit those who struggle beside us into the hands of the enemy. There are enough instances of aided escapes, attempts at escapes, and fierce battles to avoid capture to make it clear how we feel and how we deal.

They say that veteran police officers responding to an incident where one guard was mortally wounded were convinced to put a shotgun away by Boudin, but Waverly Brown didn't have a shotgun. They say he was the first to go in any event, that O'Grady was loading his weapon when someone ran up to him shooting, but didn't he have six shells in his weapon when he responded? And if he was reloading, doesn't that mean he fired six times and, for all practical purposes, missed. Lennon says he watched O'Grady get shot but didn't Lennon have a pistol that was loaded, as well as a shotgun? Why didn't he shoot the man who ran up and shot O'Grady? Why was Keenan so far away from the action? And didn't hit no one? Why is it that so many police officers converged on the scene so soon after the battle?

Once they got a couple of suspects who had surrendered, who were outnumbered, handcuffed, they got tough at the action, but i suggest that they lost heart! That the odds were too even, that Koch has been spinning his yarn to his coworkers for two years, took a circular approach to the roadblock, because the shortest distance between two points is a straight line. Do you believe that he [lost] an opportunity to shoot someone who had been shooting at other cops because some lady's scream broke his concentration? Or that another cop, John McCord, missed his opportunity to shoot Marilyn Buck, because just as she drove up he dropped a shell and by the time he reached down to pick it up, she zoomed right past him? What was so important about that particular shell, outside of it being a catalyst for a fish story? Why would an experienced cop and bodyguard like O'Grady try to load every shell into his revolver when someone is running up to him to kill him? Why does the state insist that we swallow all of this?

How did those cars that had been spotted and noted get out of the area? Well, i'll tell you why; it was because the cops who got paid so much a week wanted backup in a big way. This was discernable war. One group of soldiers in opposition to another group of soldiers. One group of soldiers who ate and slept at the front and another who may not have witnessed colonialism contested so aggressively before. i don't know. The state says there were six people coming out of the back of the truck, with pistols and an automatic rifle, and counting Koch there were five cops with revolvers and two shotguns. The insurgents left one pistol at the scene of the expropriation, one pistol and one shotgun at the scene of the roadblock. i don't think there were any supermen or saints around that day battling it out on Route 59, or Mad Dog Killers or Cowboys, i think there were only men, mortals, one group called niggers and the other group called pigs. Lennon during his hypnotic session, when he described a Black man running up to O'Grady shooting, didn't describe that Black man as a "terrorist" or "robber," he called that man a nigger, "a big nigger." He'd taken his mask off while in the car weathering the storm, and he had to push a dead nigger away from the door to get out of the car.

[District Attorney] Gribetz, the perfect representative of the United States, a pimple of a man, has tons of evidence that has been labelled, marked, and stored for two years. He has two Browning 9mms, the doberman pinscher of pistols, no prints on them, no bullets from them in bodies, but it's important. He has a shotgun, or a picture of one, also, and shell casings that can't be placed on anyone, but it's important too, because niggers are only supposed to have spears. He's got expert witnesses giving expert testimony and opinions on prints and glass. Ms. Clark* had five kinds of glass on her, two, in the "expert's" opinion "consistent" with Brink's brand glass and Honda glass, and three other kinds of glass. They mention two pistols and a shotgun of mine, which had a part missing, by the way, as if it's evidence. When the fact is that i should have had a bomb or at least a grenade. He's got a witness who remembers — when he asks, "Did you happen to see a white male with brown hair, a brown beard, and a big nose." He's got lots of witnesses. He's got clothes, pieces of bullets, pictures of bullets, pictures of cars, trucks, and everything but our masks.

He has ski masks, and he has his own public official mask, his civil servant mask. But he doesn't have ours, we've thrown them away. We are not going to act like wayward citizens in a democratic society before a just court with the duty of administering justice. We act like ourselves. New Afrikans and anti-imperialist freedom fighters in an imperialist empire that colonizes and commits genocide against New Afrikan, Native American, Puerto Rican, and Mexicano people, before an impostor in an armed camp.

In an effort to deny the issue of New Afrikan Independence that is part and parcel of the October 20, 1981, action, the state has presented its politics that we are to be confronted with. The politics of imperialism, based in their myth of justice in their colonial courts, whose function somehow should be participated in by its victims, as if this whole scheme of things is in the interests of the oppressed. It's legal to oppress and illegal to resist.

At the helm of this myth are the police, who *are* the government after six o'clock p.m., are of a species above that of mortals. Whose racism is less than the general society's, whose competence and heroism is beyond us all and is the apex of all culture. When, in fact, police are at best only human and are tools of the state who are employed to maintain an unjust, exploitative, oppressive system that holds New Afrikan and other Third World peoples under subjection and in a colonial relationship.

---

* Judy Clark, another of Balagoon's white codefendants in the Brink's case.

When i was growing up, the bulk of programs on TV were Westerns, where the heroes shot down endless rows of Native Americans, while calling them Indians, Redskins, and what not. There were other Westerns too, like *Gunsmoke*. Marshal Dillon shot fifty-two people a year and was the central character in Dodge City. i never remember seeing the mayor, preacher, or schoolteacher, only Dillon and his friends—Doc, Chester, and Miss Kitty—and i thought they were my friends too.

Now, Matt Dillon is Chief McCain, on the cop show *McCain's Law*, and even Captain Kirk is a cop! Westerns have been replaced by cop shows. There are twenty-nine hours of cop shows on TV each week. There are more cop shows on during prime time and all the other times on TV on any week than any other type of program. There is not a single program on TV other than comedies where a Black is the central character. We are portrayed as sidekicks of cops, snitches, and sources of humor, without exception.

This is all in the interest of images. Pictures say a thousand words; they say what seems to be a fact over and over in ways that can't be countered by reasonable argument, without investigating reality. White racism does not for the most part care what really goes on inside New Afrikan colonies, or even recognize that we do indeed live in colonies. But because white racism is politically and morally bankrupt, it is concerned about its image. That's why people familiar with Newburgh, Harlem, and Overtown can ignore the issue of colonialism, even while Reagan speaks of free enterprise zones, *Bantustans*!* That is why the U.S. with jaw-shaking righteousness can say that it doesn't have colonies, while planning to turn the beautiful island of Puerto Rico into an industrial park.

These people who judge us should take a city bus or a cab through the South Bronx, the Central Ward of Newark, North Philadelphia, the Northwest section of the District of Columbia, or any Third World reservation and see if they can note a robbery in progress. See if they recognize the murder of innocent people.

---

* The name given by the South African government of the day for the reservations that Blacks were confined to under apartheid.

This is the issue, the myth that the imperialists should not be confronted and cannot be beaten is eroding fast, and we stand here ready to do whatever to make the myth erode even faster, and to say for the record that not only will the imperialist U.S. lose, but that it should lose.

i am not going to tell you that the Black Liberation Army's ranks are made up of saints; it is clear that there have been impostors among us who have sold out and are worse than the enemies history has pitted us against. And i am not going to tell you that there's no virtue among money couriers or policemen. However, i will tell you now and forever that New Afrikan people have a right to self-determination and that that is more important than the lives of Paige, Brown, and O'Grady or Balagoon, Gilbert, and Clark. And it's gonna cost more lives and be worth every life it costs, because the destiny of over thirty million people and the coming generation's rights to land and independence is priceless.

Brink's Trial Sentencing Statement
October 6, 1983

The ruling class of the United States and its government colonizes the New Afrikan people; that is, Black people held within the confines of the present borders of the U.S. i've been brought here to be sentenced by the state partly because all New Afrikans, notwithstanding a Black astronaut and Miss America, have been sentenced to an indefinite term of colonialization and partly because of my response to genocide, exploitation, oppression, degradation, and all the elements that make up this process of colonialization.

The bulk of New Afrikan people are restricted to living in certain areas, restricted to certain areas of employment; we, as well as other Third World peoples of color in the confines of the U.S., make up the caste of captive nations within this empire who perform the menial tasks far out of proportion to our numbers in relation to whites. Although the ruling class exploits all workers, they exploit New Afrikan and other Third World people at a higher rate. Our infant mortality rate is higher, our life expectancy shorter, our unemployment rates double, and none of this is by chance. This is contrived by the enemies of my people, our colonizers, the American imperialist, and this is enforced by force of arms.

Historically and universally the counter to imperialist armies are liberation armies, the counter to colonial wars are wars of liberation, the counter to reactionary violence, revolutionary violence. As a New Afrikan prisoner of war, i have no more respect for a sentence by the colonializers than i have for hypocritical legislative rituals leading to it or the enslavement apparatus of a corrupt order that commits genocide against entire peoples and threatens the entire biosphere or the pompous proclaimers of democracy and free enterprise in a country of racists, where less than 2 percent of the population own more than 30 percent of the wealth in a pyramid whose base is made up of 50 percent of the population earning less than 9 percent of the wealth.

The United States imperialist government colonializes New Afrikan people in every sense of the word, and every New Afrikan who investigates that fact and all that it means comes face to face with a dilemma: to deal with the condition on a personal basis and do the best they can under a circumstance that's dictated by what is in fact the enemy and leave the decision with others and perhaps to another generation, or to join with those of us committed to overturning conditions for the entire New Afrikan nation and make war with those who historically and presently make war against us for however long it takes.

When the oppressed bear with it, accept colonialization for the most part, or at least don't get so upset about it as to entertain the idea of war, things are okay by pig logic. [District Attorney] Gribetz wishes out loud that there were a death penalty, but the fact that there has never been a white executed for the rape or murder of a Black in the entire history of the United States doesn't provoke any wishes for a need for change. Not one in all of the fifty states or colonies before them during four hundred years is an incredible statistic. But although he rants and raves, he doesn't challenge the truth of that statement or the recent murder of a Black man in Manhattan for writing graffiti on the subway or murder of a Black man in Boston or of the two in Chicago or a child in California, all by police; or the fourteen Black women murdered in Boston,* twenty-five Black children murdered in Atlanta since the arrest of Wayne Williams, or the beating death of Willie Turks. These crimes don't call for the death penalty, if any penalty at all, all this is okay by pig logic: that kind of killing helps to keep the colonies in check.

When Somoza passed out the best land in Nicaragua to members of his family, sent his henchmen out to kill whoever disagreed and subjected the rest of the population to poverty, illiteracy, poor sanitation, and hunger and printed the face of an American ambassador on Nicaraguan money, everything was

---

* Victims of a serial killer.

okay, there was no need to arm anyone to overthrow or "destabilize" that situation or bring a naval blockade to bear or talk about some other people's nation being America's backyard. But when the people of Nicaragua resolved to change their conditions for the better and remove all obstacles in their way, then it was time for "dirty tricks," a War Powers Act, and reactivation of the draft.

As long as the people of El Salvador suffered their best land given to the United Fruit Company (or whatever name it goes by now) and lived clearly under the heel of American imperialism, by pig logic everything was okay. But once people said enough and really contested it, well, it was time to fortify the puppet regime's army and send advisers,* and when a Salvadoran patriot blew one of those advisers away, by pig logic it was a shame before God.

When the reactionaries killed journalists and nuns, it was cause for concern;† when the reactionaries killed peasants and other colonial subjects, that was unfortunate, their names or even numbers were not noted. Just so many niggers. But when a career soldier, trained and armed to kill and direct intelligence for the purpose of more killings so that large corporations could continue to drink Salvadoran blood, gets killed, the culprit must be found right away.‡

When a cop gets killed, by pig logic it's different than when an old lady or a teenager or almost anyone else gets killed. Especially if that anyone else is nonwhite. When Mtayari Shabaka

---

* In the 1980s and early 1990s, a popular left-wing guerrilla force, the FMLN, was active in El Salvador. With U.S. aid in the form of military "advisers," mercenaries, and arms, the Salvadoran military and paramilitary death squads carried out a scorched earth policy against the entire peasant population and those suspected of left-wing sympathies.

† A Salvadoran death squad raped and murdered three American nuns and a female religious worker in 1980; in 1982 a death squad killed four Dutch journalists who had written articles critical of the government.

‡ While less than two dozen U.S. "advisers" were killed during the Salvadoran dirty war (1980–1993), the army and paramilitaries killed some fifty thousand people, the vast majority of them peasants.

Sundiata was killed, they put a picture of his corpse on the front page of the *Daily News*, and then in the centerfold under the caption "Death to the Terrorist." They did this because he opposed the colonialization of New Afrikan people, and they make a big deal out of the deaths of the cops and money courier, because they impose colonialization and this is war.

Legal rituals have no effect on the historic process of armed struggle by oppressed nations. The war will continue and intensify, and as for me, i'd rather be in jail or in the grave than do anything other than fight the oppressor of my people. The New Afrikan Nation, as well as the Native American Nations, are colonialized within the present confines of the United States, as the Puerto Rican and Mexicano Nations are colonialized within, as well as outside, the present confines of the United States. We have a right to resist, to expropriate money and arms, to kill the enemy of our people, to bomb, and do whatever else aids us in winning, and we will win.

The foundation of the revolution must rest upon the bones of the oppressors.

Destroy All Traitors

Sekou Odinga, Kuwasi Balagoon,
Judy Clark, David Gilbert, Silvia Baraldini

The government is bringing forward its dirty snitches and traitors in the current RICO trial. Dealing with traitors has been a paramount issue for all revolutionary movements: from Vietnam to Che's group in the mountains of Bolivia; from the traitorous assassination of Amilcar Cabral to the guerrilla war in El Salvador today; from the streets of Belfast to occupied Palestine. In the four hundred–year struggle of New Afrikans for self-determination and human rights, traitors have always been a key weapon for the rulers to smash righteous rebellions by the oppressed. Traitors have been a cancerous presence in the proletarian and anti-imperialist movements within the oppressor nation.

Traitors and snitches are universally hated and vilified in all people's cultures because of the harm they do and their total violation of all standards of human decency. For example, look at Tyrone Rison. Here is a person who turned on the movement that gave him dignity and life. He readily betrays the ideals and aspirations that he once loudly proclaimed. He has become a willing tool for the government that—as he so often stated—is responsible for the murders of Black children in Atlanta. He works to destroy the movement that provides the only promise for self-respect and liberty for his children, for his children who now face the legacy of a father who turned traitor. This man has become a bootlicker and a base liar without a shred of morality.

The government's purposes in displaying and promoting

This joint statement appeared in *Let your motto be...Resistance* (No.4) July 1982, published by the Coalition to Defend the October 20th Freedom Fighters.

such despicable characters go beyond the effort to convict specific individuals in particular court cases. Their main purpose is to discredit and dehumanize the New Afrikan Independence Movement. In particular, they want to destroy the armed movements by piercing the shield of clandestinity, attacking the morale of freedom fighters, and creating fear that anyone who joins the ranks could be betrayed. This is the reason for their lie that Rison was a leader. They also want to drive a wedge between the masses of people and the revolutionary movements; the emergence of traitors and the line they project are designed to produce cynicism and distrust towards revolution.

The government is also trying to create a culture of snitches, create a situation where traitors are seen as commonplace and it becomes acceptable to large sectors of the population. It is a way to make people accept and participate in their own oppression. By far the greatest damage of traitors is how they are used to undermine the very spirit and fiber of the movements.

Traitors are a product not only of the power of the state but also of the penetration and internalization of imperialism's values. The traitor displays the worst forms of individualism, corruption,

Samuel Brown and Judge Ritter

and contempt for oppressed people. The proliferation of traitors exposes serious political weaknesses within the ranks which must be corrected.

Our goals in dealing with traitors go beyond legalism and the needs of individuals. The paramount issue is the character and integrity of the movements we are building. We must confront, vilify, and destroy traitors at every opportunity; deal with them as the dehumanized vipers that they are; instill "the greater fear." The political terms must always be clear: discredit and destroy all traitors.

To minimize the development of traitors we must build movements based on clear principles, deep politicization, a strong commitment to oppressed and exploited peoples. We must struggle for collectivity and show that there is a scientific strategy to defeat imperialism. Would-be traitors should know that they will be destroyed. We must teach that the state is our implacable enemy and fight for total noncollaboration as a basic principle. Such movements can also spearhead a broader people's culture that reviles traitors and snitches and that builds on strong principles, human values, and collective commitment.

Tyron Rison and prosecutor Robert S. Litt

Statement to New Afrikan Freedom Fighters Day July 18, 1983

Revolutionary Greetings Brothers and Sisters:
On the third anniversary of New Afrikan Freedom Fighters Day i'd like to extend my feelings of comradeship and optimism.

That the government of the United States or any government has the right to control the lives of New Afrikan People is absurd and has no basis in principled reason or justice or common decency. Only New Afrikan people should govern New Afrikan people, in the manner that we collectively as a people deem correct.

This being so, and that on top of forcing us to live as a colonialized people, the government of the United States has been and is practicing genocide against us, it is our right, duty, and natural inclination to defend ourselves and provide for the safety and well-being of our people. As Marcus Garvey stated: We cannot leave the fate of our people to chance.

The necessity of building a people's army to carry our armed struggle and a mass movement to build the infrastructure for the superseding society must be explained to the masses of our people. We must organize this, our army and our total revolution, along principled lines that will deliver us as a people to land ample enough to support our population in order to obtain our self-determination. It is either liberation and self-determination for us as a people or more colonial degradation and genocide. These are the choices.

If we choose to live, we must carry on a revolutionary struggle to completion, guard against corruption and liberalism in our ranks, and be consistent in building not only the means of cutting ourselves free of America but of securing our survival and self-determination by building the superseding society to provide for the needs of our people. As a better organized, more politicized, and security conscious approach must be developed in building our army, a more grassroots basic approach must be developed to deal not only with the political mobilization of the masses but the needs surrounding our day-to-day survival. We must build a revolutionary political platform and a universal network of survival programs, along with the army.

Imperialism must expand or die, and even as the pigs escalate their military and political offensive, they have lost their grip increasingly throughout this world, despite their wolf tickets, because the peoples of Cuba, Zimbabwe, Mozambique, Libya, Angola, Tanzania, Vietnam, Cambodia, Nicaragua, Grenada, and other lands have put their heads and hearts together to devise no nonsense methods to drive the Americans out.

If we do the same, we will obtain the same results. In fact, we will obtain greater results, because our liberation would mean a greater decline to imperialism than any of the previous people's victory and reaction would be weakened to a corresponding extent.

There is no way for us as a people or any of us individually to correspond our conditions to those we desire, we have *never* known freedom—however, we will know freedom. We will win.

Anarchy Can't Fight Alone

Of all ideologies, anarchy is the one that addresses liberty and equalitarian relations in a realistic and ultimate fashion. It is consistent with each individual having an opportunity to live a complete and total life. With anarchy, the society as a whole not only maintains itself at an equal expense to all but progresses in a creative process unhindered by any class, caste, or party. This is because the goals of anarchy don't include replacing one ruling class with another, neither in the guise of a fairer boss or as a party. This is key because this is what separates anarchist revolutionaries from Maoist, socialist, and nationalist revolutionaries, who from the onset do not embrace complete revolution. They cannot envision a truly free and equalitarian society and must to some extent embrace the socialization process that makes exploitation and oppression possible and prevalent in the first place.

When i first became a revolutionary and accepted the doctrine of nationalism as a response to genocide practiced by the United States government, i knew, as i do now, that the only way to end the evil practices of the U.S. was to crush the government and the ruling class that shielded itself through that government through protracted guerrilla warfare.

Armed with that knowledge, i sat out the initial organizing of the Black Panther Party until the state's escalation of the war against Black people that was begun with the invasion of Africa to capture slaves made it clear to me that to survive and contribute i would have to go underground and literally fight.

Once captured for armed robbery, i had the opportunity to see the weakness of the movement and put the state's offensive in perspective. First, the state rounded up all the organizers pointed out to it by agents who had infiltrated the party as soon as it had begun organizing in New York. It charged these people with conspiracy and demanded bails so high that the party turned away from its purposes of liberation of the Black colony to fund-raising. At that point, leadership was imported, rather than developed locally, and the situation deteriorated quickly and sharply. Those who were bailed out were those chosen by the leadership, regardless of the wishes of the rank and file or fellow prisoners of war, or regardless of the relatively low bail of at least one proven comrade.*

Under their leadership, "political consequences" (attacks) against occupation forces ceased altogether. Only a fraction of the money collected for the purpose of bail went towards bail. The leaders began to live high off the hog, while the rank and file sold papers, were filtered out leaving behind so many robots who wouldn't challenge policy, until those in jail publicly denounced the leadership.

How could a few jerks divert so much purpose and energy for so long? How could they neutralize the courage and intellect of the cadre? The answers to these questions are that the cadre accepted their leadership and accepted their command, regardless of what their intellect had or had not made clear to them. The true democratic process which they were willing to die for, for the sake of their children, they would not claim for themselves.

These are the same reasons that the People's Republic of China supported UNITA and the reactionary South African government in Angola;† that the war continued in Southeast Asia after the Americans had done the bird; why the Soviet Union, the product of the first socialist revolution, is not providing the argument that it should and could through being a model.

This is not to say that the people of the Soviet Union, the People's Republic of China, Zimbabwe, or Cuba aren't better off because of the struggles they endured. It is to say that the only way to make a dictatorship of the proletariat is to elevate everyone to being proletariat and deflate all the advantages of power

---

* This was the case of the New York Panther 21.

† UNITA was an anti-communist army controlled by the South African apartheid regime that worked to destabilize the Marxist Angolan government in the 1970s and 80s.

that translate into the will of a few dictating to the majority. The possibility must be prevented of any individual or group of individuals being able to enforce their will over any other individual's private life or to extract social consequences for behavior preferences or ideas.

Only an anarchist revolution has on its agenda to deal with these goals. This would seem to galvanize the working class, déclassé intellectuals, colonized Third World nations, and some members of the petty bourgeoisie and alright bourgeoisie. But this is not the case.

That China, North Korea, Vietnam, and Mozambique would build round a Marxist ideology to drive out invaders and rebuild feudal economies in the midst of Western imperialism's designs and efforts to reinvade and recolonize is a point that can be argued in the light of the international situation. It is one thing that they don't back the will of the people as much as they choose allies in the East-West wars fought on the ground of the nonwhite colonies. It is another thing that anarchy ceases to inflame or take the lead in combating fascism and imperialism here in North America, with the history of the Wobblies, the Western Federation of Miners, and other groups who have made their mark on history. It is a denial of our historic task, the betrayal of anarchists who died resisting tyranny in the past, malingering in the face of horrible conditions. It is the theft of an option to the next generation and forfeiture of our own lives through faint hearts.

We permit people of other ideologies to define anarchy rather than bring our views to the masses and provide models to show the contrary. We permit corporations to not only lay off workers and to threaten the balance of workers while cutting their salaries but to poison the air and water to boot. We permit the police, Klan, and Nazis to terrorize whatever sector of the population they wish without paying them back in any kind. In short, by not engaging in mass organizing and delivering war to the oppressors we become anarchists in name only.

Because Marxists and nationalists ain't doing this to a large extent doesn't make it any less a shame. Our inactivity creates a void that this police state, with its reactionary press and definite goals, is filling. The parts of people's lives supposedly touched by mass organizing and revolutionary inspiration that sheds a light that encourages them to unveil a new day, instead are being manipulated by conditions of which apathy is no less a part than poisonous uncontested reactionary propaganda. To those who believe in a centralized party with a program for the masses this might mean whatever their subjective analysis permits. But to us who truly believe in the masses and believe that they should have their lives in their hands and know that freedom is a habit, this can only mean that we have far to go.

In the aftermath of the Overtown rebellion, the Cuban community conceded as lost souls by Castro came out clearly in one instance in support of the Black colony. And predictably the Ku Klux Klan, through an honorary FBI agent, Bill Wilkinson, made no bones about supporting the rights of businesses and the business of imperialism. Third World colonies throughout the United States face genocide, and it is time for anarchists to join the oppressed combat against the oppressors. We must support in words and actions self-determination and self-defense for Third World peoples.

It is beside the point whether Black, Puerto Rican, Native American, and Chicano-Mexicano people endorse nationalism as a vehicle for self-determination or agree with anarchism as being the only road to self-determination. As revolutionaries we must support the will of the masses. It is not only racism but compliance with the enemy to stand outside of the social arena and permit America to continue to practice genocide against the Third World captive colonies because, although they resist, they don't agree with us. If we truly know that anarchy is the best way of life for all people, we must promote it, defend it, and know that the people who are as smart as we are will accept it. To expect people to accept this, while they are being wiped out as a nation, without allies ready to put out on the line what they already have on the line, is crazy.

Where we live and work, we must not only escalate discussion and study groups, we must also organize on the ground level. The landlords must be contested through rent strikes, and rather than develop strategies to pay the rent, we should develop strategies to take the buildings. We must not only recognize the squatters' movement for what it is but support and embrace it. Set up communes in abandoned buildings. Sell scrap cars and aluminum cans. Turn vacant lots into gardens. When our children grow out of clothes, we should have places where we can take them, clearly marked anarchist clothing exchanges, and have no bones about looking for clothing there first. And, of course, we should relearn how to preserve food. We must learn construction and ways to take back our lives, help each other move, and stay in shape.

Let's keep the American and Canadian flags flying at half-mast.... i refuse to believe that Direct Action has been captured.

The Continuing Appeal of Anti-Imperialism

Great works measure up, inspire higher standards of intellectual and moral honesty, and, when appreciated for what they are, serve as a guide for those among us who intend a transformation of reality. *Settlers: The Mythology of the White Proletariat* caused quite a stir in the anti-imperialist white left and among nationalists of the Third World nations within the confines of the U.S. empire, as well as anarchists and Muslims of this hemisphere. In short, among all of us who are ready and willing to smash or dismantle the empire, for whatever reasons and whatever reasoning. This is in spite of the fact that it is a Marxist work, because it isn't out of the stale, sterile, static, mechanical mode of the vulgar sap rap that has carried that label.

Its historical recounting of the sequence of horrors perpetrated against nonwhite people, from the beginning of Babylon to the recent past, has not been discounted publicly, to my knowledge, by anyone, including the cheap-shot artist who offered an underhanded review of it in the *Fifth Estate* called "The Continuing Appeal of Nationalism."* *Mythology* should serve as a reminder (to anyone who needs one) of the genocidal tendencies of the empire, the traitorous interplay between settler-capitalist, settler-nondescript, and colonial flunkies. The flaws and shortcomings of the IWW, which marked the highest point of revolutionary conscientiousness among whites here, the fraud carried on by the Communist Party USA, and assorted other persistent offenders of common sense and common decency. To my amazement, a couple of white anti-imperialists i know had started the book without finishing, complaining that it was old hat, but i've heard nothing

---

* The essay Kuwasi is referring to here, *The Continuing Appeal of Nationalism*, was written by the late Fredy Perlman and is available as a pamphlet from Black and Red Press.

particularly new from them, and i suggest that they take special note of detail, and i'll remind them that this work is so accurate as to be able to serve as files on people who will say anything to support a position that doesn't support real action.

Not being one to take figures verbatim without crosschecking and believing that class struggle or war within the white oppressor nation would be a prerequisite for complete victory of the captive New Afrikan, Mexicano, Native, and Puerto Rican nations, i decided to crosscheck with the most authoritative work available to me and perhaps anyone, *The Rich and the Super Rich* by Ferdinand Lundberg. This was necessary, i felt, in order to get a clear picture of the material conditions of white folks. This in order to investigate white Americans' interest in revolution. Professor Lundberg used two graphs to illustrate his point: "Most Americans—citizens of the wealthiest, most powerful and most ideal-swathed country in the world—by a very wide margin own nothing more than their twin household goods, a few glittering gadgets such as automobiles and television sets (usually purchased on installment plans, many at second hand), and the clothes on their backs. A horde, if not a majority, of Americans live in shacks, cabins, hovels, shanties, hand-me-down Victorian eyesores, rickety tenements, and flaky apartment buildings."

The second and third tables help us to make things out a bit clearer; it shows that 25.8 percent of households had less than one thousand dollars to their collective names and the third showing us that 28 percent of all consumer units had a net under or less than one hundred dollars. With 11 percent with a deficit and 5 percent holding at zero, a total

The true story of the White Nation

SETTLERS

THE MYTHOLOGY OF THE WHITE PROLETARIAT

by J. Sakai   8.95

of 16 percent. This goes on to show that 35 percent of all households had a net worth of less than five thousand dollars. Is this affluence?

It certainly looks like a good case for classic class struggle, with the evidence that Lundberg gives us. Sakai warns us, however, "most typically, the revisionist lumps together the U.S. oppressor nation with the various Third World oppressed nations and national minorities as one society."

In this light, the figures check out. New Afrikan income, which today averages 56 percent of white income and stood at about the same or less in 1953, makes up a disproportion of the deficit, zero, under-a-thousand, and under-five-thousand dollar consumer units. Definitely more than 10 percent of them, which was our percentage of the population. If we could make a sensible judgment, we'd have to say that the combined captive nations— New Afrikan, Mexicano, Puerto Rican, and Native, or about one sixth of the population as of 1981—all make up a disproportionate amount of the consumer units with deficits and below five thousand dollars. This forms a cushion for the white population.

Sakai points out that "the median Euro-American family income in 1981 was $23,517," and "that between 1960 and 1979 the percentage of settler families earning over $25,000 per year (in constant 1979 dollars) doubled, making up 40 percent of the settler population." We may have had a general idea from neighborhood walks, but Sakai gives us an idea of the extent.

This extent, and the "conspicuous concentration of state services—parks, garbage collections, swimming pools, better schools, medical facilities and so on" and the fact that "to the settlers' garrison goes the first pick of whatever is available—homes, jobs, schools, food, health care, governmental services and so on," not to mention racism within settlers puts to rest an idea of a multiracial class struggle that includes whites. "Nation is the dominant factor, modifying class relations."

Lundberg, who overlooked the national factor in the economic tables he based his argument on, notes that "in the rare cases where policy is uppermost in the mind of the electorate it is usually a destructive policy, as toward Negroes in the South and elsewhere. Policies promising to be injurious to minority groups such as Negroes, Catholics, foreigners, Jews, Mexicans, Chinese, intellectuals and in fact, all deviants from fixed philistinish norms, usually attract a larger-than-usual supporting vote," or mandate, if you will.

"Approximately 10% of the European-American population has been living in poverty by government statistics. This minority is not a cohesive, proletarian stratum, but a miscellaneous fringe of the unlucky and the outcast: older workers trapped by fading industries, retired poor, physically and emotionally disabled, and such families supported by single women." (Sakai)

How many of this group of whites will side with the revolution, how many whites will come to view their interests with the long-term interest of those of us who prefer to live on a living planet, and how many will fail to equate their quality of life with fifty billion hamburgers is anyone's guess.

However, it's a small wonder why white anti-imperialists have been giving me blank stares whenever i've mentioned class struggle to them.

The left in this country is very small, whatever way you might want to look at it. If you define left as those of us who stand for a decentralization of wealth and power — taking the question completely out of the realm of bourgeois civil rights and rightfully include the independence of captured nations, which is part and parcel of the decentralization of wealth and power — the left is microscopic.

We are left with ourselves. Left in homes that police drop bombs on from helicopters, and without any shared sense of outrage. We are left where murders by police and other racists are commonplace and for the most part celebrated. Left in the ghettos, barrios, and other reservations.

Let's not forget that New Afrika has a class problem. That not only do police but politicians, poverty hustlers, and representatives from the established Black publishers and churches move up in the world when they join the ranks of the oppressors. The oppressors never have a problem finding Black leaders to condemn their blatant disregard for life, like that which took place in Philly.* We only have established leaders to draw us into the ranks of a Democratic Party, without being able to introduce as much as one Black plank into a white platform. Leaders who beget other leaders like Mayor Goode.†

Where i differ with Sakai is the assertion that "building mass institutions and movements of a specific national character under the leadership of a communist party are absolute necessities for the oppressed." What communist party is he talking about? i feel that we must build revolutionary institutions that buttress on survival through collectives, which in turn should form federations. Grassroots collective-building can begin immediately.

In an epoch where New Afrikan nationalists and Marxists have voluntarily taken the defensive, without even a fraction of a blueprint of a party or consistent practices in the colony, it's incredible that people outside the ranks and currents of those who believe in magic words aren't encouraged to collectively take matters in their own hands, to build the collective institutions and superstructure of a superseding society. We must begin where we are, with each other and the time we don't waste.

i think that the building of revolutionary collectives and forming of federations of collectives is the most practical and righteously rewarding process of preserving and enhancing life and developing the character of all nations. We can change ourselves and the world.

---

* On May 13, 1985, Philadelphia police bombed a home belonging to the radical group MOVE, while eleven Black people, including four children, were trapped inside. All but two, Ramona and Birdie Africa, were killed in the police attack.
† Wilson Goode was the first Black mayor of Philadelphia and, as such, presided over the MOVE bombing.

Why Isn't the Whole World Dancin'?

The first time i experienced terror and was able to keep my wits enough to examine it, i was in the notorious Vroom building, watching the goon squad proceed with a shakedown and waiting for them to get to my cell, which was the last on the opposite end of the tier from where they had started.

As soon as i saw them in their bloused boots, overalls, helmets with plexiglass visors, flak jackets, and extra-long clubs, i was frightened and curious as to what all they were up to. i as well as the brother who locked next to me, got up to see just what was to happen. "What's all this shit. Look at those punks.... It takes thirty of those motherfuckers to deal with one man?" It didn't take long to see just what they were up to as the first man was ordered to strip, place his hands behind his head "Vietnam style" and back out of his cell. The brother next to me said something, but i said nothing, being intent on seeing what was happening, so as to have some idea what to expect. Next, the guy being searched was told to run his fingers through his hair, open his mouth, lift his balls, slowly turn around, lift his left foot, his right foot, and bend over and spread his cheeks.

The brother next to me said something else, to which i replied that he should be cool. More instructions followed: "Walk to the wall and sit on the floor cross-legged, without taking your hands from your head." This is a pretty involved maneuver and if you don't believe me, try it. i began to worry even more, as i'd been placed in the Incorrigible Unit of the Vroom building for interrupting a funeral, pistol whipping a "corrections officer," shooting at another, and aiding an escape. It became clear that something extra could be in store for me. After five or so renditions of the routine described above, without them actually vamping on anyone, i began to feel a bit at ease, and at the same time felt they might be "saving the best for last."

It was too much to think about, so i went and sat on my bed. Only to watch a pig named Sudal come down to the cell next to mine and spray mace on the brother, after he had stepped from the door and laid down on his bed. "Punk motherfucker!" he shouted through the bars. "Don't get yourself fucked up now," Sudal replied. The expedition was getting closer, and i tried to decide whether to come out with my clothes on or just start swinging, stay in the cell, and mess up as many as i could as they entered, after of course being soaked with mace, or coming out like everybody else and hardly being in any position to fight.

As i sat on the bed, looking out, they arrived at my neighbor's cell and began repeating: "Strip, put your hands behind your head, back out your cell...," etc., as the door opened. He did as he was told. "Open your mouth!" a pig instructed. When he did, the pig slapped him, causing him to stumble off to one side, as another pig punched him, saying, "Stand still!" They had tasted blood now and started getting better grips on their clubs, as one pig hit him on the arm with a stick. By now i was thoroughly terrorized; there was no fight in the brother. Their jokes about "the German army," as they referred to themselves, just entangled in a massive knot inside my head.

i began to look at the faces. There was an Italian jailer who had caught a few good shots some time ago by the look on his face. He had never given me any trouble personally but had been assigned to escort me, standing at the ready. He was one of the guys they counted on. Another jailer who was running the show and had initiated knocking the brother around, told a rookie cop, "What do you expect?" There was a couple of Black pigs in the gang as well, which never fails to strike me strange.

My door opened. i'd decided to come out naked and follow instructions unless i got hit, in which case i would go on at least one of them who had something exposed, as the ninety-degree heat had coaxed a couple of visors up. It was a puny resolve, as i felt that an attack would spell the end, and that fear is a great source of power. The issue was decided as much as it could be. "Run your fingers through your hair, open your mouth, lift your balls, turn around, lift your left foot, lift your right foot, spread your cheeks, turn around to your right, walk to the wall, sit down cross-legged without moving your hands."

Somehow i assumed the position and listened to the fascist chatter behind me. "That's Harris's partner," i heard Sudal instigate. i'd heard they had vamped on him already. Trotman, the pig who was actually in charge of the goon squad, tapped the bandage on my back with his club. "Shouldn't pistol whip correctional officers!" i heard a couple of more remarks about "getting more practice at the range." i couldn't help but picture one of those creeps hitting me in the head while i was sitting in that ridiculous position and had thought for an instant that the tap was a signal to get up. i started to, but decided to wait until told, while listening to stuff being thrown around in my cell.

Finally, i heard, "Ok, get up and go back into your cell." The squad had begun leaving. When i got to the door a jailer named Wise, a Jewish fascist who hates "jews and niggers," and who was later charged and acquitted of beating a prisoner, jumped in front of me and struck me in the stomach, holding the stick in both hands in the vertical butt stroke taught to Infantry. But it had no effect. Although my stomach looked out of shape since i had not been able to do sit-ups for a couple of months, it was stronger than it looked, as i'd done sit-ups and leg-raisers for years. Every muscle in my body was like a spring. As the stick rebounded off my gut and i looked him in the eye, i couldn't help but smile. He responded by panicking: "Turn around, face the wall of your cell!"

i looked at the wall until i knew they had all left, found a cigarette, and sat down to smoke before even putting on my clothes. Later when recounting this to a prisoner who went through the same thing at the same time, i could see the recognition in his eyes. So this is state terror. The most terrifying part being watching what was happening to my neighbor, hearing what could happen to me... not what actually did.

This was terror. Done for the purpose of producing terror as the search was, in fact, a justification and had anything been found considered contraband, it indeed would have been incidental and only by chance of ridiculous proportions. Just as the "shakedowns" taking place at Marion now, after that prison has been locked down for nine months, have nothing to do with finding contraband and everything to do with attempts by the state at "behavior modification." With making prisoners so fearful for so long that their personalities change to that of wimps who will accept whatever the state has in mind without resistance or retaliation. They are looking for hearts, and they believe their slogan: "When you got them by the balls, their hearts and minds will follow."

Of course, the *New York Times* has not carried an article on terrorism at Marion. Nor has any of its partners in Newspeak, such as the *Post, Daily News, Village Voice, Rolling Stone*, publications of the Hearst empire, or any of the other establishment papers. They are not really interested in "terrorism." What they are interested in is changing the definition of terrorism from (*American Heritage Dictionary*) "the political use of terror and intimidation" to "armed acts carried out by political partisans on behalf of captive nations."

. The Klan, whose violence at the voting booths is all but too well documented, are often accused of committing racial violence, but they are never accused of terrorism. Nor are the Jewish Defense League (JDL), American Nazis, or any of their people. The CIA imports losers from fallen fascist regimes. Iranian students used to wear masks while demonstrating against the shah, but SAVAK (the Iranian secret police) was never accused of terrorism, nor was Alpha 66, though they, among many other reasons, were brought here to attack the Puerto Rican Independence Movement and to kill Orlando Letelier. He was exiled from Chile after the CIA- and ITT-sponsored coup took the lives of thousands and placed thousands more in concentration camps, where they suffered cruel tortures.

These people, who have a license and a free hand to kill in this empire, are never called terrorist nor are they accused of terrorizing anyone. At the same time, if members of the Black Liberation [Army] kill a couple of cops who are, by whatever your politics, armed men or women trained to do battle against lawlessness — and revolution is against the law — this is defined by the media and blasted until the senses are bombarded as an act of "terrorism" by their definitions. The endless raids of apartment buildings and vehicles supposedly for suspects is not terrorism. The bombing of police headquarters is "terrorism," but the arrest of people who have nothing to say to the FBI or to the federal and state grand juries is not.

Nothing that the right wing, the establishment, the people who "got it" already do is terrorism — the political use of terror and intimidation — and likewise nothing that their lackeys do is terrorism. By that logic, the only Black people victimized by terrorism are those Fosters and Browns who join police departments to do Black folk a good turn! There is nothing terroristic about being burned out of your home that you bought in the wrong community. There is nothing terroristic about the murders of Neville Johnson,* Michael Stewart,† or any Black victims of the police; or what about the deaths of Willie Turks or the murder of Sundiata and the photo of his corpse under the caption "Death to the Terrorist" in the center of the *Daily News*; or the twenty-five children (at last count) killed in Atlanta since the arrest of Wayne Williams; or any of the murders across the U.S. of New Afrikans, Natives, Chicanos, Puerto Ricans, or Asians. These things have no effect on us. We feel safe in our communities within alien communities and have no inhibitions in regards to securing our human rights. All this murder of Black and other Third World peoples is just human nature. We kill a cracker, its terrorism.

Klanners and Nazis gun down five unarmed people on national TV, and it is just one of those things. SLA members are surrounded and their dwelling is torched on national TV, and again it is just one of those things.‡ Thirty fires in a couple of months in the women's dormitory at the University of Massachusetts, and the FBI comes to investigate links with the women's community and the "Brink's suspects." This is not terrorism either because the state and the state's media defines terrorism as any attempt by the oppressed and exploited nations and allies to pry loose the grip of imperialism. (By the way, the FBI arrested a New Afrikan woman and charged her with arson.)

---

* Neville Johnson was a 20-year-old Black man, shot through the head and killed by a Miami police officer while playing a video game in an arcade, on December 28, 1982. *(Note to 2019 edition.)*

† Michael Stewart was a 25-year-old Black man arrested on September 15, 1983, for spraypainting graffiti in a New York City subway station; he was beaten while in custody, went into a coma, and died of his injuries thirteen days later. *(Note to 2019 edition.)*

‡ The Symbionese Liberation Army was an armed group active in California in the 1970s. It carried out assassinations and bank robberies, and was made famous through the kidnapping of heiress Patty Hearst. On May 16, 1974, police surrounded and attacked the group's safehouse in Los Angeles. The house caught fire; six guerrillas were killed, either by the fire, or shot by police as they attempted to flee or surrender. *(Note to 2019 edition.)*

South Africa, which has just signed treaties with Angola and Mozambique after years of invading these countries, is not called "terrorist." But the South Africans have killed and maimed civilians in these attacks by cutting off their ears, a habit the Americans practiced in Vietnam. And they have killed scores of thousands of Azanians* in the territory they presently occupy. But the SWAPO guerrillas who detonated a bomb in Namibia, which is occupied illegally by South Africa, that killed two South African Intelligence officers and an American military attaché are called terrorist loud and clear — as is the African National Congress. But what on earth is the domination and superexploitation of 80 percent of the population based on? One would be hard-pressed to find a regime as repressive as South Africa, but it is the indigenous peoples who resist tyranny who are branded terrorist.

The difference between Steve Biko's death on Robben Island† and George Jackson's death in San Quentin's Special Housing Unit is simply that the South Africans are not as hypocritical as the Americans. It is clear that Robben Island is for holding political prisoners and prisoners of war who resist or are suspected of resisting the settler regime. Americans are not so clear as to the purpose of their Special Housing Units, Incorrigible Units, and maxi-maxis. The United States is no less a settler regime, just more genocidal. Instead of maintaining apartheid (segregation) as the South Africans do — who got their ideas about reserves (Bantustans) from the American Indian reservations — the Americans systematically reduced the population of original inhabitants from 50 million to 1.6 million. With the sterilization of half of Native women and living conditions designed to bring

---

* Azania was the name given to what is still today the country of South Africa by the radical anti-integrationist wing of the anti-apartheid liberation movement of the time.

† Steve Biko of the Black Consciousness Movement in South Africa, was in fact murdered by police while being interrogated in Port Elizabeth. Kuwasi mistakenly situates his death in Robben Island, the notorious maximum security prison that housed many anti-apartheid political prisoners in South Africa. (Note to 2019 edition.)

about the destruction of Native peoples, the policy is still intact.

We all know the criminalization of the Native American Warriors, who were branded as "savages" by the euro-american press for defending their peoples, and most of us know that Crazy Horse was murdered in prison. But who recognizes the struggles of Native peoples as anti-imperialist? The policies developed in the genocidal campaigns against the Native Americans—wars against the entire population forcing the Natives into small, scattered, confined areas—has been repeated in Vietnam in the infamous Phoenix program brought to light by the Pentagon Papers. Similarly, the criminalization of the defenders of the people by the press and the military and justice system was repeated by the FBI's Cointelpro program, as brought out in the Freedom of Information Act files from the 1978 secret conference in Puerto Rico against the left in general.

One doesn't have to be a political scientist to see the parallels in imperialism's war against the Palestinian people: the robbing of the land, the branding of those who resist the tyranny of the Israelis as terrorists, the forcing of people into ghettos (the West Bank) or reservations (refugee camps), the massacre of unarmed civilians, the special confinement of political prisoners and prisoners of war. The fact that all of Palestine has been overrun doesn't make the Palestinians any less of a colonized people any more than the fact that North America has been overrun makes Native Americans any less colonized, or the New Afrikans brought here to replace the Native population and enrich the euro-american oligarchy with free identifiable labor.

However, the pigs will argue that time and persistence okays any wrongdoing. "Israel exists," they argue, "the white man is here to stay, and as soon as the Palestinians or Indians realize it, the better off they'll be." Well that's not acceptable; when the victims accept the victimizers and cease to resist, how can the victims be better off? How can anyone be better off, other than the victimizers? History shows that the Greeds are never satisfied.

In the U.S., white anti-imperialists have supported the right to self-determination of captive nations, and it is clear by the use of grand juries and sham trials that they indeed have political prisoners in their ranks. A look at the Canadian left since the capture of the Vancouver Five* and the means employed to suppress it draws many parallels with the recent RICO trials in Manhattan. Two of the biggest differences: there were no traitors on the stand, and the actions of the Five established the right of citizens in Canada to stand up against tyranny, just as a colonial subject or an ally of the armed forces of a captive nation have the same right here. As citizens of oppressor nations stand up against tyranny on their own behalf, the state's definition of terrorism will expand as it has already. But as in other state definitions, the expansion of the definition is in the other direction.

In closing, i'd like to address the question of the Soviet Union in Afghanistan, which reactionaries like to throw in when someone of my political bent addresses American imperialism. i resent this a bit, because i haven't been advocating Russian foreign policy and certainly don't share the relation to Russia that i do with the Americans. They kidnapped my foreparents for the purpose of enslavement and rape and continue to colonize, oppress, and exploit New Afrikan people and insist that we celebrate their sadism.

The Soviet Union, by invading Afghanistan, is of course carrying on imperialist aggression, since it is an internal conflict to which the Russians were invited. It is no less so than the American presence in South Korea, the Philippines, West Germany, Panama, Haiti, the Congo, Thailand, Grenada, Puerto Rico, Guanatanamo Bay, or any other place an oppressed nationalist may have missed whose mind may have been dulled by weight training and running around in the same damn circles in the yard.

As my people of my nation are colonized by the Americans, it is not an academic question to be balanced out by someone who

---

* In 1981 and 1982, bombings against a hydro substation and an arms manufacturer were carried out in Canada by a group called Direct Action, while a sister organization known as the Wimmin's Fire Brigade firebombed several video stores specializing in pornography. When five members of the Vancouver anarchist scene were arrested in relation to these actions they became known as the Vancouver Five.

intends to do nothing about it. This colonization is a challenge and an affront, taken personally and politically. As i am not suffering the effects of the Russian but American imperialism, which incidentally is more rampant, i oppose the American ruling class and puppets to whatever extent i can. That bullshit about "land of the free and home of the brave" provokes me a bit.

A Letter to *Overthrow* Newspaper

Back in—on or about 1971, after the jailhouse rock rebellion in NYC, where every house of detention was taken over by prisoners who had not been disarmed of their sense of outrage, a few of us were transferred from Branch Queens House of Detention to Riker's island and placed in the segregation unit, where Sekou Odinga sits sharpening his sword now. Among us were some brothers who—indicted in the famous, or infamous, New York Panther 21 case, along with thirty-one other brothers—simply refused to surrender and submit to the systematic beatings and torture that pigs with baseball bats, ax handles, and night sticks issued, as the brothers who surrendered stepped out offering no resistance. Those of us who didn't give up were not made to kneel on the ground with our hands cuffed behind our backs while the state-issued robots struck us. Among us was the brother Dr. Curtis Powell.

One night when we went to "sick call," Doc and I happened into this state prisoner he'd met earlier in his incarceration, who had recounted when he had first met Doc he took for granted that the brother was insane, because he had listed his occupation as a physician. He was really amazed to discover that "by golly," Powell was indeed a doctor after all. After telling us that story, he asked Doc how he was doing—or something to that effect. Doc replied, "We are being railroaded .... I am on the train." The practitioner's brows arched and lost for a moment, he turned to find relief in the face of a "correctional officer" who had just entered that section of the hallway. After speaking, the state practitioner asked the jailer, "Do you know Powell here? The doctor?" the jailer answered, looking at Doc, "Weren't you in C-76?" To which the Doc answered, "I'm in 1-a." To which the state practitioner

From *Overthrow* 6, no. 4 (December 1984–January 1985).

replied, "He doesn't know where he is, he thinks he is on a train."

We all had a good laugh at that, the practitioner at the irony of a member of his profession being a crazy nigger after all. Doc and I had a good laugh, because it shows just how an interpretation sticks; he was crazy when he tried to convince the interpreter that he was in fact a doctor of medicine. And now that that fact was confirmed, he was crazy because he thought he was on a train. A lot of such interpretations have resulted in trips to the mental wards, shock therapy, thorazine, and psychosurgery performed by real psychos, and under a dominant alien culture there is bound to be misinterpretations. The fact that one group of people are to be a society's menial class and be subjected to institutional put-downs and sanctioned to violence is a misinterpretation of common decency, or, better put, a misinterpretation of acceptability, for sure.

There is not one social topic that can be discussed free of the stench of racism. Social problems such as housing summon visions of our colonies called ghettos. Unemployment raises the specter of what the media terms "discrimination." Health care brings to mind that infant mortality among New Afrikans is double that of Americans, that 50 percent of Native American women have been sterilized; not by one Ronald Reagan running from one reservation to the next with a knife but by thousands of dedicated practitioners who were at work under the regime previous to what has been termed a mandate, and have sterilized over 20 percent of New Afrikan and Puerto Rican women as well. How can we address crime in a land where there has never been a white executed in the murder or rape of a Black? How can a victim of Diana Ross concert mugging or a rape or a mob attack see such an experience in the light of historical conditioning, and how can the sheepish mob behind the crimes of Hiroshima, Korea, Vietnam, Nicaragua, and South Africa not take responsibility for these crimes and not take responsibility for stopping them? Who can believe that this condition can go on indefinitely?

The United States was founded on the genocide of Native Americans, which continues. Out of the 50 million who inhabited this land only 1.6 million remain. The economic structure based on the subjection of a caste continues. The colonization of our brothers and sisters and neighbors to the south and barefaced denials, the innumerable invasions and occupations with the same shameless justifications, continue.

Pick up an almanac and read the short historical sketches of Puerto Rico, Santo Domingo, Guatemala, Mexico, El Salvador, Nicaragua, and other nations in that region while the synopsis are still in print and it will be clear what the invasion of Grenada, Harlem, El Barrio, and Wounded Knee continue to be, with the approval and aid of duped citizens and colonial subjects alike.

The highly polished "news" shows, the ruling class presses, the airwaves guarded by the FCC manipulate our cultures into commercials, filter out much of that which challenges them, and flood our senses with subliminal attacks to maintain racism. Rock reflects progressive and liberating tendencies, as well as backward and fascist tendencies. It has challenged our thinking and that of those around us, sensitizing us to our doings, and it has packaged subtle and rank racism which are untitled. Anybody who believes they have rights over others is part of the problem. Anyone who believes they have the rights to use and abuse and attributes these rights to simply being born a particular species or gender and not on these beliefs or promotes them must be contested, as there is no trait worse, save accepting evil nonsense of that type.

This progress, which has devoured entire peoples and poisoned the biosphere of those of us remaining, must be attacked spiritually and culturally, as well as fought physically and resolutely in all its aspects, if we are to maintain our sovereignty as human beings rather than parts of the machine. Self-determination, the freedom to be ourselves, only conflicts with the interests of a tiny percent of the population that controls.

So Rock Against Racism, imperialism, and sexism. It's a good sign that the new age art form, indigenous and ingenious, can be acknowledged piercing the net of commercialism and clearly out of the use of the state's arsenal.

Let the good times roll, and let the chips roll where they may.

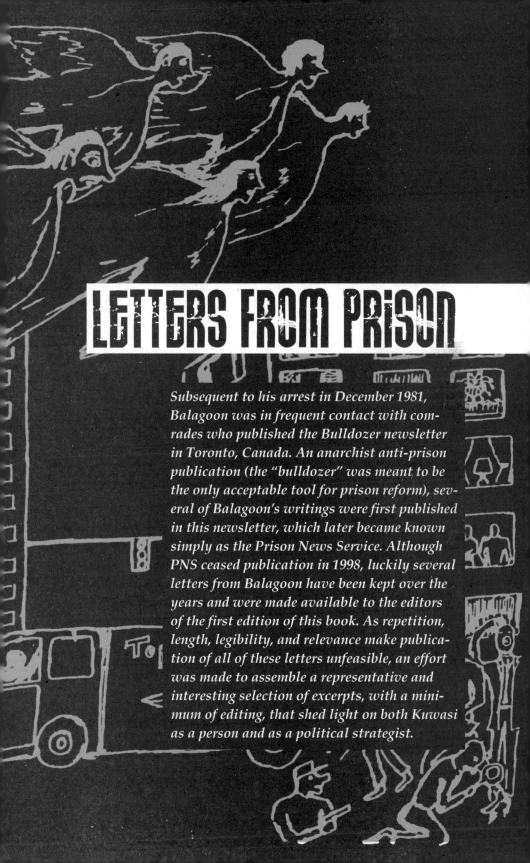

LETTERS FROM PRISON

Subsequent to his arrest in December 1981, Balagoon was in frequent contact with comrades who published the Bulldozer newsletter in Toronto, Canada. An anarchist anti-prison publication (the "bulldozer" was meant to be the only acceptable tool for prison reform), several of Balagoon's writings were first published in this newsletter, which later became known simply as the Prison News Service. Although PNS ceased publication in 1998, luckily several letters from Balagoon have been kept over the years and were made available to the editors of the first edition of this book. As repetition, length, legibility, and relevance make publication of all of these letters unfeasible, an effort was made to assemble a representative and interesting selection of excerpts, with a minimum of editing, that shed light on both Kuwasi as a person and as a political strategist.

SUPPORT NEW AFRIKAN FREEDOM FIG[HT]

Its

WE
NEED
AN ARMY!

National Committee to Defend New Afrikan Freedom Fighters

The Trial

April 12, 1983

We've been dealing with the public movements so much with explaining our stance and perceptions that it has twisted me to the point where i've written very little suitable for publication for *Bulldozer*. Having to unify with M-L [Marxist-Leninist, ed.] and Nationalist and to defend the rights to nationalist aspirations have pulled me a bit out of line with my predilections.

December 9, 1983

That bullshit about seventy-five years wasn't designed to affect me, i had been sentenced to twenty-five to thirty before. December 22, i'll be thirty-seven years old. That sentence was to affect others, to frighten others into giving up their lives altogether without fighting for real control of their lives. But if i worked thirty years at the post office and went bowling on Thursdays or doing anything but opposing the U.S. i'd be worse off, it would be like making a rope so my children and myself could be tied up.

January 25, 1984

The federal trial ended with the five most politico people taking the most principled position getting convicted of conspiracy, two others convicted basically for not turning their backs on their friends once they were wanted (aiding and abetting), and two acquitted altogether, one which all they had was a traitor cocaine fiend's word on, the other who had two traitors words against him—and had fled to Belize (British Honduras) and was extradited back. So people called it a victory—but i really don't think so; the government didn't get all they wanted, but four out of six? and the two most politico getting the highest convictions?

The line i put forth is that the question of if it's a victory lies with how many people are mobilized by it, the same with our portion of it. i am glad for the people who are home now, by legally didn't that much happen, simple math. Politically, i feel a bit disappointed, but at the same time i know that the weight of what went down and what we said, etc. should grow, people will get better at explaining it, that just our defiance in the face of what the state says is life, will have more impact as life progresses.

The Left

May 31, 1983

We had to hassle with the *Guardian** to git one article counter-
ing some reactionary shit they were saying, and the rest of the
"left" has disassociated themselves from us like most of the left
in Canada disassociates themselves from the Vancouver Five.
We took Prisoner of War positions to forfeit the illusion of the
state being able to judge enemies of the state. In the first place,
most of the left didn't even speak to it, the "establishment" press
mentioned it first, and a lot of the folks who protest U.S. involvement in Central America condemn us for, git this, shooting three
working-class people. You know who they are talking about, a
sweat hog guard and two outright pigs.

Two papers especially, the *Village Voice* and the *Rolling Stone*,
are mistaken for left because they cover antinuke rallies, and etc.,
had it in for us from the beginning. They would print accounts by
police and creeps nowhere near the underground and at the same
time refuse to print anything any of us had to say. It's still their
policy. The *Voice* demanded the inside scoop on one person's sex
life after they sent in a political article; the *Rolling Stone* wrote a
series on the Weatherpeople at about the same time the national
news agencies were doing a number on us, dripping with sexual
accounts, even a picture (a drawing).

May 31, 1983

i think we tend to use the term "left" too loosely; everybody left
of Reagan ain't left. Basic self-determination, the means of production being in the hands of the workers, should be the criteria
of recognizing an ideology as left. Just because someone doesn't
want some fool in Washington to blow the world to pieces doesn't
make them left. Everybody who protests the curtailing of civil

---

* *The Guardian* was the historic main weekly newspaper of the U.S. socialist
left. Started in the 1940s to provide a broader voice for pro-Moscow independent socialists, it became a voice of the 1960s New Left, and then pro-
Maoist before its final collapse.

liberties that affect them ain't left. And we make a mistake when we assume that they are, and they let us know we made mistakes when the basic issues arise.

May 31, 1983
When a gay group protests lack of police protection by making an alliance with police to form a gay task force, they ain't making a stand against the system, they are joining it. Putting more power in the hands of those who attack them for being what they are in the first place. Those women's organizations with members with underpaid Black, Puerto Rican, and Mexican maids who decided to vote differently when the Equal Rights Amendment* was defeated can't be called left, just as Blacks mobilizing to field a presidential candidate ain't left. Left is the land and means of production in the hands of the masses, and right is land and the means of production in the hands of a few pigs.

As i am writing this it occurs to me that it sounds rigid, but dealing with land and the means of production in a different manner calls for a different system. This is not to say that we should sabotage antinuke... organizations that call themselves "left." ... but we should keep the basics constantly in debates, and we should establish the working definition.

Xmas Night 1983?
The point is that there are only a few people in the "left" about armed struggle and self-determination, so although i personally think they are ideological imperialists, i will work with them as i do with nationalists, even though they are hierarchical, and righteous Muslims, even though i am antireligion. i think it's okay as long as you don't get lost in the sauce, so to speak—that is abandon anarchist principles and the objective of building anarchist organizations.

---

* The Equal Rights Amendment would have made sex discrimination unconstitutional in the United States. It was defeated in a referendum in 1982, largely as a result of the New Right's first major political mobilization.

Xmas Night 1983?

It's a very dangerous period we have been going through; the state is quickly consolidating fascism, on the one hand, and, on the other hand, there's no mass movement. All kinds of laws are being passed with no debate, and people are looking to Jesse Jackson to change the focus of things, and not only is he electoral (which goes without saying) but he's reactionary. He stands up in front of rallies and says things like "If we (got that we, that tells you he's an Uncle Tom right away) can't have enough marines in Lebanon to do the job, we should bring the Americans home. Bring our boys back." Well, if we have any boys in the marines, then obviously our boys have gone astray. What in the fuck are they doing over there in the first place? Why are there so many ads in Black magazines and in the commercials at basketball and football games and boxing matches with Blacks and the phrase "Be all that you can be" for the U.S. Armed Forces? There's nobody Black addressing that.

Xmas Night, 1983?

Not since the Western Federation of Miners and the Wobblies in the '30s, have workers been struggling for actual control and in fact ownership, but in the past couple of years Greyhound Bus Company, National Baseball League, and some other unions have been kicking it around. At the same time all the public movements — since they are too elitist to even want to organize the working class, and they fear them like the plague because the public movements are largely petty bourgeois, college students, white-collar workers, etc. — have been debating each other in a vacuum, instead of really going out to work.

Xmas Night 1983?

After that ass-kicking in Southeast Asia, you can bet your life they went through a lot of mass psychological preparation before going to Lebanon* or invading Grenada,† but their calculations proved true. There has been no real response from the Black colony here — and culturally and historically the Grenadians are so similar to us that its incredible. They've been able to do all of this because there's been no real mass movement and so many outright reactionaries like Jackson, who has the blessings of all the egghead, pencilneck, armchair Marxist and Black copout artist posing as progressive. The only high points occur when the United Freedom Front or United Fighting Group‡ or FALN strikes, which at least has been happening fairly consistently.

---

* The Reagan Administration had sent eight hundred marines into Lebanon in 1982 to support the pro-U.S. Lebanese Army and Israeli armed forces that were fighting against pro-Palestinian groups. The marines stayed until 1984.

† In 1983 the U.S. invaded the Caribbean island of Grenada to suppress its Marxist government and establish a pro-American regime.

‡ United Freedom Front and United Fighting Group were names used in bombing communiqués by anti-imperialist underground groups.

January 22, 1984
It's a small circle of revolutionaries in this hemisphere or in the northern half of it, we can't just deal within the same small circle, at some point new recruits must be won over, youth must be ignited: all the rallies have got basically the same people showing year after year. i ask: Do these activists talk to people outside the movement? Obviously they don't talk to people about the movement—we got to build a movement of activists who…address people who are already committed as well as people who are into other things. "The revolutionary war is a war of the masses: it can be waged only by mobilizing the masses and relying on them."

January 25, 1984
[T]he sad thing is those white M-Ls who are really few in number—when it comes to supporting armed struggle, have no foothold in the white working class, and being mostly of a petty bourgeois background, not only don't know where to begin but are contemptuous of the working class—even though the petty bourgeoisie as a class is at least as reactionary. Plus, they are just beginning to be clear as to the fact that New Afrikans are indeed colonized and what that means and just beginning to accept their role in the struggle to initiate the overthrow of the bourgeoisie and the establishment of a dictatorship of the proletariat—they ain't really Marxist and morality has been their line, rather than the nuts and bolts of what is really going on. That in itself wouldn't be so bad but the fact is the nationalist on this coast, where the [Brink's] trial actually took place, simply refuses to organize in the Black community, no survival programs which New Afrikans need, no challenging the neocolonial Uncle Toms, like Jackson, Washington, etc., no showing up at police brutality hearings to declare that the issue is not a few mad-dog cowboy cops, but a mad-dog cowboy empire, no going to the New Afrikan colonies at all. To them, it is enough to tell people what is happening with us, which is ridiculous when people are starving, freezing, and getting shot themselves, but they believe in magic words.

May 2, 1984

There's a lot of Islamic influences in our movement now—there always have been—but now more than ever. i am flooded with Islamic propaganda through the mails that i pass on to Muslims, and at the same time i am a bit shook up about it, but rather than counter this, i intend to cooperate when it's principled, continue to argue when points of difference arise, and busy myself with what i am up to my neck with, and let the people decide.

January 9, 1985

i hope this finds you in the best of health and spirits, as it leaves me feeling okay, considering everything. At least except for the last round of busts nothing of consequence has happened, and at the same time there's been a lot of busts. Supposedly support is growing, people from other movements have been shook up by the indictments for thought crime, and there has certainly been enough grand jury subpoenas to constitute a witch hunt (twenty-eight this far, to my count) and the Black colony is stirring behind it, but i don't know what the movement is doing inside the colony. i've heard they have vowed to do more grassroots organizing, and i hope so, because people are upset about the pigs who've really been getting away with the grossest murders, as well. In one case they tortured a guy to death for allegedly writing on the subway walls, and in another they shot a sixty-year-old woman while evicting her. So any retaliation action should have the nod.

January 9, 1985

[T]he part of the "left" that has no interest in what is happening to prisoners and prisoners of war is not left. If the difference is that we believe in the decentralization of wealth, the redistribution of land, and armed struggle — and those of the right believe in amassing more wealth, building empire, and repression — then these are the lines by which we should define "left" and "right." We can't go by other people's definitions — even their definitions of themselves — suppose Rev. Sun Myung Moon* declares he's left, against the establishment, and has been victimized by racism. The left here is small in proportion to the population no matter how you define it — but when you talk about redistribution, freeing the colonies, etc., its micro, and when you talk doing and actually do something — people look at you as if you're from Mars — *rare species*. You put that same measure to Canada, i'd bet its micro too. So if we limit our propaganda to people in the left and *Bulldozer* reaches a small percent of that, people who are down already — Martians.

---

* The Reverend Moon is the head of the far-right Unification Church ("the Moonies"). In the 1980s, he was briefly jailed for income tax fraud.

Revolution

May 31, 1983

When a principled conscientious public movement is developed there's no problem finding soldiers, and in terms of being as best as you can, figure what the revolution needs: there's a lot you can do that can't be taken for granted. The speech you make at the rally would be impossible to give if you were underground, and you would have to hope that someone else would. All of us who agree would have to hope also. Meanwhile by the time the public movement gits built to the point where you know those things will be said, and there's comrades out organizing people to take their lives into their own hands, there will be an army to play its historic role.

i never was happy with the amount of input i could contribute when i was in the underground. There's little chance to debate with people doing aboveground organizing, and if you don't agree with how they are going about things, there's not much you can do. That problem is not unavoidable, but it is a problem.

May 2, 1984

And although there's been a lot of bombings, i think that the hierarchy embedded in the consciousness of the movement prevents the type of attacks we used to stage with the sole purpose of punishing pigs with death. There's not enough real [punishment] for them kind — translated into a body count, that registers in the population — that these creatures can indeed be dealt with, and the way i see it retaliation will have to be commonplace for a long time before people are really prepared to support revolution. With all kinds of things happening to revolutionaries and people who just mind their own business and nothing happening to the pigs and very little happening to turds like [Samuel] Brown — just doesn't seem to be a balanced and attractive occupation.

July 28, 1984

Reaction has been moving on a grassroots level uncontested. Here the Klan says that illegal aliens take jobs, while Ford, IBM, and so many other corporations move plants to South Africa, England, Korea, etc. There's plants operating in Mexico, where U.S. corporations ship parts to be assembled and shipped back to the U.S. — why don't the corporations git blamed for stealing jobs? What's the difference, except that the corporations pocket the difference in wages? The Klan, Nazis, etc. spread their crap uncontested as champions of the white workers, when it's clear that they are dupes of the ruling class. If we really adopt the preamble to the wobblies' constitution, that the working class and the ruling class have absolutely no common interest, we will beat them on the ground level, we will out-organize them — and as they are tools of the empire, we will begin to be out-organizing the empire. Once the fragments of the working class are united in hostilities against reaction instead of each other — the tide will begin to shift.

An anarchist underground will develop in turn, with the only connection to the aboveground being anarchist ideology, which is enough. The relatively simple tasks the pigs have now of peeking into the visible and exposed sections of the movement to aim their gadgetry for suspects will be fruitless with really widespread mass mobilizations. With a federated army of collectives, striking at whatever is opportune in the area of monopoly capital, imperialism, and repression, we will be settled down in a long protracted people's war that can't be nipped at the bud, until the governments simply cannot exist and authority and economies collapse. To, of course, be replaced by one built around collectives, rather than capitalism or state capitalism. All railroads, ship lines, airlines, phone companies, oil, gas, and electric companies will be socialized, all trucking will be put into the collective ownership of drivers, all overseas possessions left to sink, all textile mills collectivized, all military industries and arms manufacturers taken over by militias. A people's referendum is set for Native, New Afrikan, Chicano, and Puerto Rican nationals in the mainland to decide on autonomy with 1.7 acres set aside in a common area for all that vote for nationhood. As well as a referendum for whites who wish to live separately. The chemical companies, banks, etc. and other capitalist residue being the province of the will of the people who live in certain areas.

If we don't already have an established territory, and perhaps if we do, we set another people's referendum for those of us who want no government. A federation of collectives would conduct the referendum. The local militias would mop up the reactionary residue. With no public capital in private hands there wouldn't be any ruling class to suppress in the anarchist areas; where people choose state socialism, there would be no interference from us. Just what i envision, but the idea of doing away with money — just arranging things so that everyone who wants gets necessities, food, clothing, housing, education — knocks me out. If we needed a transitional period, we determine that reefer is currency.

Anti-Imperialism, Nationhood, and National Liberation

May 2, 1984
The Native American struggle is against imperialist occupation. Because the present movement doesn't know how to deal with this doesn't make it any less so. That's just a shortcoming of the movement, but a second's thought would have to tell us that Native Americans were indeed the first victims of imperialism in this hemisphere, and if we are to be anarchist in the here and now, and thus be anti-imperialist, as one cannot be an anarchist and not be against imperialism, we got to accept the Native struggle as our own. If the Greeds had not put the Natives in their position, none of us would be in the position we are in.

May 2, 1984
It's clear to anyone that Native peoples are repressed more so than anyone else, that genocide has been practiced against them more so than any people who still exist as a people. Well that means we got to defend them — fight alongside of them, just like they fought alongside of the slaves. People shouldn't be able to forget for a moment that this land was under the guardianship of Native Americans for centuries before anyone else arrived. Anyway, the way to start is by recognizing if you're supporting

land and liberation for Native Americans, you're anti-imperialist and should be in a movement that recognizes and includes that, and if there's no movement—well, you got to build one.

May 2, 1984
[T]o me it's the ultimate meddling...for a white person supposedly for the revolution to oppose tendencies for Third World people confined to various reservations in the present U.S. It seems rather clear to me how our history here would kind of inhibit us from wanting to continue to be outnumbered and surrounded by whites.

July 28, 1984
This is the place to begin erasing borders, not only because the U.S. uses up 40 percent of the world's resources and the bottom 50 percent of the population controls only 8.2 percent of the economy (nationally), but on top of it, 5 percent of the population controls 70 percent of the land. Peoples from the South whose land and resources have gone into this empire are coming to get it and are entitled to it just as the West Indians and East Indians are entitled to the portions of the British Empire they were forced to donate as colonial subjects. Anti-imperialist struggle grows out of anti-capitalist (class) struggle, just as imperialism is a development of capitalism.

January 9, 1985
Right now, i am into a slight struggle with a comrade who put forth the proposition of whites supporting national liberation, as i (especially after reading *Mythology of the White Proletariat*) believe in parallel development, complete movements engaged in national liberation and class struggle civil war inside the oppressor nations. The fact that this is now only beginning to happen, that whites are striking blows at the colonial apparatus is one thing—but colonial subjects should be free to attack monopoly capital...phone companies rip everyone off, but these policies in the Black community are really different; when i lived in a predominantly white neighborhood i never was pressured to pay

like friends living in the colonies, and whereas the defense industrial complex may rip everyone in the confines, it murders us.

i've read the *Mythology of the White Proletariat* and know what i would write in a book review now ... its enlightening, but i would hope that it wasn't used as an excuse by a lot of whites to not attempt to organize inside the oppressor nation.

Anarchism

April 12, 1983
i hope this letter finds you in good health and high spirits, as it leaves me none the worse for wear and really happy to hear from you, as *Bulldozer* is my favorite political publication. i really hope we can work well together and promise to make a sustained effort in keeping the lines out and open and working, as although i share a lot of feelings and principles with the Nationalist and Anti-Imperialist movements i am an Anarchist and feel rather isolated ideologically and low for not pushing my politics as much as i should. This has mostly been due to a lack of connection with the anarchist movement due again for my being on the lam and working with who i could readily see were opposing the state.

Xmas Night 1983?
i think that throughout this hemisphere we should unite with real get down anarchists first, and then others, and recognize that the so-called left doesn't really represent a lot of people. The politics of the so-called left hasn't reached a lot of people, and their elitist airs are actually turnoffs — there's not much mention of "serving the people." If we start putting things together that actually do serve people the day when anarchy is seen as a viable way of life rather than chaos will not be far away, because most people when they stop and think of it have to admit that the empire sucks.

January 22, 1984

Tonight, i am up eating peanut butter sandwiches, just putting the stale bread over steaming water, when for years i automatically threw it out and fed it to the birds (this being one of the few times the birds might be better off for it). i think that waste and bourgeois thinking really affects how we operate, both in terms of perceiving strong points and weak points and effectiveness, when it comes to acting after we make our observations. In Vietnam, GIs had to burn, bury, and grind the stuff they sent to the dumps, because the Cong would use the tin cans, wire, bottles, and whatever else against them. They can't do that here because they're always encouraging people to consume more and make more waste.

On the other end, i think that making the most of everything is exemplified pretty well by working in a collective setting and living in a co-op, and it seems like it would be an easy thing to found an anarchist food co-op somewhere in Toronto. As time goes on, anti-imperialist anarchism will prove to be the only anarchism, since others will need to make alterations. We should push the idea of collectives and federations, while continuing to support anti-imperialist struggle with the aim of not merely building a real movement that really supports armed struggle but an actual infrastructure.

January 22, 1984

[T]he idea of collectives was alien to the Panther Party. We had different survival programs, and people were involved to be part of them, to donate time, afford to git things/stuff [from] businesses operating inside the community, to use the space of institutions such as churches. But the Party, being a hierarchy, simply could not simply initiate alternatives — it felt it had to lead them — it was to be, in its mind and words, not just the leading party but the sole representative of the Black colony. So there was not any organized effort to take space in the colony and to actually produce (only to distribute) or to provide transport or a militia. It was miles away from all of that, because it was a hierarchy. To fully take on the power structure in a given area, you got to not only provide alternatives but institutions that render the old ones useless. Just completely take their place, that provide the [goods] itself, so it's not a question of a merchant giving material aide to our operation or being boycotted but a mechanism where one by one the outlets become collective, because the economy evolves to the point where the corporate fingers just cannot pull the strings. You don't call a Checker cab when an outlaw gypsy cab service will take you where you want to go cheaper, you don't shop at Safeway if you can buy what you want cheaper at a co-op. People are putting all kinds of co-ops together — the trick is to form a federation that takes care of the needs of its members and invites more. That teaches self-reliance and demonstrates it. That supports and practices anti-imperialism and demonstrates that you don't have to be a party to it and that imperialism is not necessary, because capitalism is not necessary, rather than necessary evils, they are just evils. This sounds like preaching, but without examples how would you expect it to sound.

January 25, 1984
Why ain't an anti-imperialist anarchist organization — that's pro-armed struggle + self-determination for oppressed nations + socialism and liberty and complete egalitarianism — been formed? With collectives in areas wherever there's enough individuals to put one together and an international hemispheric program? A "Committee to Promote Anarchy." That way at least people who think similar to us would at least have a unified voice inside and outside the prisons. The network for all its looseness does cover a lot of territory — rather than debut with the anarchist who ain't about what we are about or compromise with M-Ls and nationalists, we should start building something to take directly to the masses. That doesn't mean everybody who thinks similar to us isolating themselves the way i am, not dealing with M-Ls, nationalists, and anarchists, or even trying to ignite reformists — but it means putting something of our own on the ground.

May 2, 1984

What's as bad is that public movements can't grow into mass movements, not because of the apathy that they claim everyone else has but because of a fantastic elitism. If they organize a mass movement, they'll lose their identities. They won't be so much smarter than the people they're supposed to be organizing and providing models for. Of course, there's other real reasons too: the almighty media and state floods people's minds with the centuries of chauvinism and diversions, coupled with an economy that makes rent too much to think about. But the main thing that affects people is that they know no other way and have no access to a living breathing ideology or a movement that does things differently. But there's no public movement that recognizes this, and i think that that is partly because the next step would be doing things differently … at the same time what you do shapes how you think, so it's a vicious cycle.

Anarchy is the ideal way to break out of it, but since it's been defined as chaos by every other proponent of every other ideology, on one hand, and defined by too many people who define themselves as anarchist as "whatever," it is simply not being presented for people's inspection. A collective is not only (for lack of a better word) a propaganda organ because its members may say or print certain things, it's a propaganda unit…. If a collective chooses to recycle and accumulate capital for a co-op of sorts, people will see people working together … they will see a process that can be duplicated…. With eggheads sitting around spinning yarns and isms, you have something that can be duplicated, but for what? The masses are smart not to get involved in any more bullshit.

July 28, 1984

The crazy thing is that there are no anti-imperialist organizations with a class analysis or program. Of the "communists" who speak of (their only support of) strikes, none of them really make a stand for self-determination of oppressed and superexploited colonies, of the anti-imperialist organizations who do support self-determination, there are none that explain the exploitation of the working class in terms of its relation to imperialism.

If an anti-imperialist anarchist organization establishes itself and calls for an end to imperialism abroad and within the borders of this hemisphere and supports self-determination for oppressed nations and supports the working-class struggle against the same monopoly capitalists who reap the lion's share of superprofits from the colonies, it will be the only organization with a complete ideology. If this same organization begins modest programs in the most depressed areas, centered around survival, turning waste into capital, taking over spaces and occupying them for the good of the community, offering services denied to the communities, like food co-ops, clothing exchanges, and book exchanges, and then extends this into taxis and a militia to deal with the Klan and other predators, but on top of this supports autoworkers, hospital workers, etc. when they are on strike, etc. and reports and explains why, we will soon have an international community-based organization that people will support. They will not only buy a paper that could expand into an international paper with its own distribution system but cultural activities, because they will see what's happening with their support and more importantly they will have access to a new way of living.

July 28, 1984
Maybe i've been sitting around thinking of the same shit too long, but it seems to me that anarchy would have to be anti-imperialist, that there's no other ideology that refuses to recognize borders. Every communist regime has degenerated into a narrow nationalist state capitalism, almost as if, and i tend to think that, they couldn't help it. Stalin might have been a bastard, but he wasn't corrupt, or Mao for that matter. The masses were certainly willing to make sacrifices, but what do we have now, the very first communist state invading another country "to protect its borders," and the second making a treaty with the U.S.

The Enemy

August 18, 1983
[A] physical propaganda offensive has been escalated against supporters and other aboveground legal people. About a month ago two sisters and three children, one only two years old, came to visit. At first the cops gave them a runaround about how they dressed, which was bullshit, and then they gave them a run-around about ID. Their ID works out okay when they visit other jails, but after being held up and insulted by pigs with no name tags or badge numbers, they were told to leave. When they went back to their car and drove off, they were stopped by a pig who went through their papers and mumbled some sap rap and let them go. This made them really paranoid, and they drove way under the speed limit, which saved their lives, because a wheel started to wobble. Once they wobbled into a gas station and had it checked out, they discovered that the bolts between the wheel and the axle had been loosened. Had they driven on the highway at fifty-five miles an hour, they would have had an accident and with five people in the car, three of them children, there's no telling how bad it would have been.

One accident occurred like that after the John Brown conference in Chicago last year and another at a conference in Texas a bit before that; you would think by now people would automatically check wheels. About two weeks after that, one of the sisters, _____, after going to court, where her old man is on trial, went shopping, and then caught a subway not far from her home. When she got off and decided to catch a bus to git closer, two white guys stepped in and asked her for directions. When she took her attention off them, one of them started punching her while the other acted as a lookout. The one punching her knocked her down, continued to punch her, took her pocket book with rent and bill money, and then kept on punching her in the face, while sitting on her. Just before he stopped and left, he said, "Your husband can't help you now."

There's been the usual break-ins and women running into guys they find out later are cops. Right-wing underground harassment (so far, it seems) groups have been stepping up their activities. So that's the general tone of things.

Xmas Night 1983?
There's a conservative wave sweeping the U.S., lots of mob attacks on Third World people, lots of police killings; one cracker in Detroit got two years' probation because he beat a Chinese guy to death, and the judge said the punishment should "fit the criminal, not the crime." Vietnamese in Boston and Texas are being attacked at random. In Western Massachusetts, the feds were called in to investigate attacks on women and started investigating the women's links with "terrorists." At the same time there's been thirty fires in a women's dorm, and they've arrested a Black woman who lived there and kicked her out of the school; a white guy who is charged with rape still goes. The local pigs have raided the projects (public housing) with slug hammers twice under different pretenses that didn't pan out. The feds did security for the United Technologies Corporation, which has been having a secret conference there—as if those turds can't afford to hire Pinkerton. And ROTC, the young Republicans, SHUN (Stop Homosexual Unity Now), and every other type of Nazi is running rabid, and that's just one town. And, as i said, there's a wave of conservatism.

Xmas Night 1983?
i think that you got to stop thinking in terms of the U.S. and Canada as separate and literally in terms of the hemisphere as far as organization goes—which the network is definitely right in doing—and i think politically we should attack the whole of imperialism, that is, not only dealing with a particular government force that's involved in, say, El Salvador but any ruling class power involved in imperialism. This means not only noting South African involvement with IBM and ITT's involvement in Chile but every link in the Fortune 500.

May 2, 1984

Here, some new laws have been passed that make support for "terrorists" a crime, and to change the feds into a more clearly military outfit. There was an even more outrageous murder in NYC, a brother was beaten to death, supposedly for putting graffiti on a subway car. Not a murder where a guy gits hit on top the head one too many times and dies but torture and overkill. There's been forty Blacks murdered this year and a general upswing throughout the country. No retaliation, though, no pigs caught up and filled full of holes.

July 28, 1984

i think that we simply have to be clear about the fact that the media is part of the state's arsenal, they never contradict the state. They universally and totally miss the point of the matters that pertain to the opposition of the state. For instance, the Watergate shit that happened here a few years ago made the press look good, but there was never any print about all the lawyers' offices that were broken into when left-wing clients were involved. They never talk about the things that DINA or Alpha 66* have gotten away with. They covered our case without mentioning colonialism one time, even though our position was/is that New Afrikans are colonized and have a right to defend against colonial oppression. [Associated Press] quoted a statement by me, after i handed it to them, as i did every paper that covered the trial, but nobody thought it newsworthy to make a clear statement about our position. So it's not just a thing about a press ban on the proceedings involving the Armenians. The press knows their job, and they know it's not to do our propaganda for us. The *New York Times* couldn't address U.S. corruption in Quebec when the separatist

---

* DINA was the Chilean secret police during the right-wing Pinochet dictatorship, and Alpha 66 is a paramilitary Cuban exile organization sponsored by the CIA. Both were involved in violent attacks against their opponents internationally, the most infamous in North America probably being the assassination of former Chilean ambassador Orlando Letellier in Washington, DC, in 1976.

was clearly challenging the ruling class of the entire hemisphere! A guy with a trench coat doesn't meet with all the reporters over-night to tell them what to write or their editors what to print. These caffeine crazed patriots censor themselves.

Prison Life

August 18, 1983
Meanwhile, i am freer to write and will be writing _____ this week for sure—the only thing that will hold me up is a lack of stamps if i can't work out some kind of deal with the commissary guy tomorrow. The food is so bad here that when the order blanks come around i don't think of anything besides getting enough to eat. However, my discipline shall improve.

December 9, 1983
As to the seventy-five years i am not really worried, not only because i am in the habit of not completing sentences or waiting on parole or any of that nonsense, but also because the state sim-ply isn't going to last seventy-five, or even fifty, years. If there's not a revolution in thirty years—in which case i really don't care to live anyways, or an atomic war, the environment will for all

practical purposes resemble the aftermath of an atomic war. The jerks in charge now are not only committing genocide but destroying the biosphere.

Xmas Night 1983?

There's nothing to be amazed of as far as continuing to struggle in jail, what else can you do? The struggle continues, and if you don't, if you give up, you die, you are damned, because it takes effort just to be in contact, and when they put you in isolation, fuck with your mail, etc., you have all the proof you need that whatever it was you did, it was of consequence. "As long as you fight, the decision is still up in the air," Ruchell Magee.* They only win when we are convinced to let them have their way.

Xmas Night 1983?

[W]hereas i would be up writing at night, i am going to the movies; they had *Flashdance* and *Raiders of the Lost Ark*. i've been telling myself that it's impossible to know what's been affecting the masses if you don't check out what they have—nothing superfragalistic has been revealed to me—but i figure as long as i ain't betting football games or some nonsense like that, a little diversion doesn't hurt.

January 22, 1984

Well, due to the storm we've been locked in for two days, which in and of itself wouldn't be such a big deal, but i am locked beside one motherfucker who plays oldies twenty-four/seven, and on the other side is a Cuban who Castro kicked out of the country for singing. He starts right after breakfast most mornings and continues each time he comes back to the cell until he falls out sometime around eleven, so last night i kept him up a bit longer with some of my singing.

---

* The sole survivor of Jonathan Jackson's raid on the Marin County Courthouse on August 7, 1970, Ruchell "Cinque" Magee remains in prison today. He is one of the longest-held political prisoners in the world.

July 28, 1984

i've meant to write you for a long time, but i guess a combination of factors have slowed me down in correspondence; for one thing the pace of writing two or three letters a night and feeling like i've been sentenced to writing has kinda worn me out. Then of course, i am still going to trial. Since '82 there's been some kind of bullshit with legality. i am tired of it but must pay attention to what's happening in court, cause no matter what we must preserve the position that the state simply has no right to try us. At the same time, these bastards got over sixty suspects in this case, including every busted BLA member, a statement by a traitor that they want to act as if they never had, and a hundred thousand dollar reward. Its outright disgusting how people were turning in ex-employees, drinking partners, and etc. So it's an ideal opportunity to show in detail how the pigs are trying to change New Afrikan culture into a snitch culture ready to support fascism.

But every time i go to court i really fall behind in letters; last time they moved me six times in six days, cuffed and shackled. It was impossible to git visits, because i was never at a jail during a time when visiting was allowed: a third to half of the time in bullpens or in a van. The few letters i did write are just getting where they were addressed. Added to the court time is the trip we go through once we return. It's a week before you git any addresses or even legal papers, another week confined to the cell. Last time i went to the hole for a day, because there wasn't any empty cells, and for some reason i always git the same cell, which isn't for anyone else, and it's pretty possible that the whole thing will be happening again before the 31st. So in letters i'll be even further behind.

July 28, 1984

Over the weekend a pig shot a brother down in the yard. The official version is that he was swinging a baseball bat at another prisoner and some pigs and to protect lives the pig in the tower had to shoot. Of course, that's bullshit, there was no one close to the guy when he got shot; he had gotten stabbed just before and the pigs broke camp. Prisoners had to pick him up and carry him to the door and demand he receive medical care for the M15 wound, which you know is difficult because the bullet tumbles to make wounds large and break bones, to make more missiles inside the body to penetrate more organs. Anyway, after the shooting, 180 men refused to lock in—you got to be literally mad to see someone shot and risk your lives just to make a point. Meanwhile the pigs have everyone who witnessed the crap firsthand locked down.

November 29, 1985
Friday they told me to go back to the block (and i immediately thought transfer). When i got back to my block they said i was to be kept locked. When i said, "For what?" they said, "Investigation," then within a half hour or so, this pig comes to tell me i am being transferred. Then i was brought here, kept in lockup until yesterday at noon, and released into population. But that has just meant another day with the same underwear, only one blanket, and asking over and over about my stuff. i got a chance to talk to one of my comrades personally, and in the process of doing some chin-ups some turkey lifted my coat, so i couldn't go out tonight and am basically in limbo. Tomorrow night there's no yard or opportunity to use the phones in the yard. So basically i'll be stuck with whatever i have after wading through bullshit in broad daylight. i can't remember a similar situation, but it kinda feels like sitting around a dusty empty apartment waiting for the landlord to put the heat on—walkin' to the pay phone, never catchin' him, looking forward to next to nothing.

Love, Power Peace by Piece

Kunitsi

KUWASI REMEMBERED

The following memories and poems appeared in the 1999 first edition of A Soldier's Story.

Kuwasi and David

In Memory of Kuwasi Balagoon, New Afrikan Freedom Fighter

David Gilbert, December 15, 1986

When i think of Kuwasi, i think of the word "heart." No, i got that backwards. When the term "heart" comes up i think of Kuwasi, because he epitomized it so beautifully—but of course he also lived and expressed many other fine qualities. "Heart" has two distinct meanings: one is great courage; the other is great generosity. Kuwasi was an outstanding example of both.

People at this commemoration* are aware of Kuwasi's core identity as a New Afrikan Freedom Fighter. His political activity began as a tenant organizer in Harlem. (He was, incidentally, also part of the Harlem contingent who, bringing food and water, broke the right-wing blockade around we students who were holding buildings during the Columbia Strike of 1968.) Kuwasi was part of the landmark New York Panther 21 case of 1969. In the same period, he was imprisoned for expropriations in New Jersey; he escaped a few years later.

It takes both daring and creativity to escape from prison. Kuwasi did that and a whole lot more: three and a half months later, and on very short notice, he went to free a comrade being taken to a funeral under armed guard. Kuwasi was hit by a bullet, yet kept moving, and he almost made it too. With a little more time for planning and preparation, he would have been successful. His second escape, about five years later, from a maximum security prison was even more impressive. That time he stayed free and active until his capture subsequent to the Nyack expropriation of October 20, 1981.

---

* The New Afrikan People's Organization December 21, 1986, memorial for Kuwasi Balagoon, held in Harlem.

After each of these prison escapes in the '70s, he was able to quickly establish himself in a secure and comfortable personal situation. He didn't go back for his comrade or reconnect with that unit of the BLA out of any personal desperation. It was purely a commitment to the struggle, to New Afrikan liberation, to freedom for all oppressed people.

When one hears of such courage and sacrifice (and here we have mentioned only a small portion of his deeds) the stereotyped image is of a stern or fierce character, perhaps with an inclination for martyrdom. But nothing could be further from Kuwasi Balagoon the person. Actually, he had an affecting ebullience, a zest for the pleasures of life, a keen appreciation for the culture and creativity of the people who lived in the ghettos and barrios. Politically he placed great stress on the need for his movement (and other revolutionary movements, as well) to respond directly to the concrete needs of the people in the communities: he opposed anything he saw as hierarchy that stifled initiative from below.

Kuwasi was a poet; or, to put it better, he was a revolutionary who wrote fine poetry. He had read his poetry in the same clubs as the "Last Poets" way back when they were forming, and he continued to write poems in prison. Here at Auburn, he worked on drawings late at night and listened to tapes of both punk rock and jazz with great enthusiasm.

Being in prison population with Kuwasi for this past year, i got to see an additional dimension of his humanity. Prison can be depressing, especially in a period of low political consciousness. Kuwasi had a truly unique ability to make people laugh and to create a sense of community. Most jailhouse humor is either bleak or sexist. Kuwasi was able to create a healthier community humor where we'd be laughing at the authorities or at our own foibles and pretensions. Sometimes in the yard, i could hear his whole workout crew in uproarious laughter from fifty yards away. His great spirit is not just my personal observation. Something like one hundred guys have come up to tell me about it in the two days since Kuwasi died.

When a guy comes into prison with such a high-powered case and reputation—well, often the terms are what favors other prisoners can do for him. With Kuwasi it was just the opposite. i've never seen anybody do so much for other people. i actually felt that he was accommodating to a fault. We couldn't have a half hour political discussion in the yard without about ten or fifteen guys coming up to him to ask him for some help or favor. He always used his day off from work—even when he should have been catching up on rest—to do "personal baking," which he gave away to innumerable persons over the many weeks; he shared his commissary purchase with whomever asked. Kuwasi ran a very substantial and worthwhile political education class for several months.

Kuwasi Balagoon, a bold New Afrikan Warrior with a giant heart: while we all mourn together there is something particular about the situation here at Auburn prison that puts the meaning of his life in sharp relief. The prison guards, who never had the courage to face him straight up in his life, have been obviously gloating over his death. Meanwhile, literally hundreds of prisoners are mourning him (particularly prisoners of his nation, but also a wide range of prisoners who are stand-up against state authority). Both sets of reactions, in their opposite ways, are tributes to Kuwasi and how he led his life. The loss is immeasurable; what he gave us is even more.

New Afrikan People's Organization Memorial Statement

Black revolutionary soldier Kuwasi Balagoon died on December 13 [1986], at the Erica County Medical Center in upstate New York. He had been moved there from the New York State penitentiary at Auburn, where he was incarcerated for his political-military work on behalf of Black Liberation.

Balagoon was born Donald Weems on December 22, 1946, in Lakeland, Maryland, the youngest of three children of Mary and James Weems. His parents and two sisters, Diane Weems Ligon and Mary Day Hollomand, still reside in Maryland. Kuwasi attended Fairmont Heights High School.

At seventeen, as an enlisted man in the U.S. Army, Kuwasi witnessed racism and discrimination in the treatment of Black soldiers. At this young age he began to realize that Black people had no reason to be fighting in Vietnam or anywhere else on behalf of a racist "Amerikkka," where Black people's survival remained threatened by capitalist economic policies and a white dominated political system. He left the u.s. military and moved to New York, where he became a tenant organizer and, in 1968, a member of the Black Panther Party.

When the u.s. government's repression campaign against the Black Liberation Movement known as Cointelpro took aim on the Black Panthers, he was among twenty-one men and women named in a federal conspiracy rap to bomb shopping centers and police stations. It was in the intense atmosphere of an eighteen-state alarm to pick up these twenty-one Panthers and vicious FBI and police attacks against Panthers throughout the empire that Brother Kuwasi would elude arrest and go underground. All twenty-one defendants would be found not guilty on all counts. His latest arrest (he escaped from prison two times) would occur in December 1981, when he was arrested and charged with participation in the Brink's armored car expropriation attempt of October of that year in Nyack, New York.

In the show trial on charges arising from the Brink's action, Balagoon would uphold a Prisoner-of-War position and refused to participate in the trial. He openly acknowledged that he was a soldier in the New Afrikan Freedom Fighters Unit of the Black Liberation Army (BLA), a political-military clandestine organization formed in 1971 to defend Black people and to fight for Black people's liberation. This unit is said to be responsible for the liberation of Assata Shakur.*

Balagoon was also a contributing author of the book *Look for Me in the Whirlwind* and has written many poems, short stories, and political articles published in several Black, U.S., and Canadian journals and newspapers.

Balagoon was loved and respected by many as a dedicated fighter for freedom. His spirit will live in the people's struggle for a new and better world.

Free the land!

---

* BLA member Assata Shakur was liberated from a New Jersey prison in November 1979. She now lives as a political refugee in Cuba.

The Following Statement Was Signed by 117 Prisoners at Auburn and Sent to the December 21, 1986 NAPO Tribute

We mourn deeply the loss of Kuwasi Balagoon. We knew him here as a man of great courage and principles, warm generosity, and vibrant spirit. The death of such a person is heavier than a mountain; what he gave us all in his life is even greater.

A Soldier's Story
The Making of a Revolutionary New Afrikan Freedom Fighter

A MEMORIAL TRIBUTE
to
KUWASI BALAGOON
Revolutionary New Afrikan Freedom Fighter
Dec. 22, 1946 - Dec.13, 1986

December 21, 1986
Harlem, New York

A Eulogy

Sundiata Acoli, December 16, 1986

Kuwasi Balagoon was a revolutionary, a rebel, a poet, and he was faithful to his calling. Once he stepped upon the revolutionary path, he remained true to the struggle for the rest of his life, fighting the good fight, staying in shape, writing poetry, and helping fallen comrades at a moment's notice, never stopping to count the cost.

He was a natural rebel, couldn't stand conformity or authority, especially an illegitimate one. And he had the heart of a gunfighter, which he was—using all his tools in the service of Black people all his adult life.

If you ever read or heard his poem "I'm A Wild Man," you knew him, because it described him to a T—and he was wild. He knew it, we knew it, and we loved him for it, because it was his nature…and the nature of the times, in the late '60s, when Black folk needed wild men; and still do today.

But now Kuwasi's gone, and the beat goes on, and we who knew and loved him can only eulogize him—and constantly scan the horizon wondering how long, how long will it be, before another giant such as he comes along again.

Born on Sunday*

David Gilbert, December 31, 1986

Oh that Saturday, that Saturday —
why can't we make it go away?
Don't want to believe it — though
It's all too real
Where did our warrior go?

Born on Sunday; died on Saturday;
struggled the whole week through.
Gave "24/7" and more.

As bad as Death is ...
no way it could take Kuwasi head on.
No one took Kuwasi head on.
He'd dodged a couple of bullets,
caught a couple too,
always kept moving.
No, Death must have snuck up on him,
to take our warrior away.

Born on Sunday; died on Saturday;
struggled the whole time in between;
Struggled and loved, danced to the beat, laughed,
and then struggled even harder —
whole life through, struggled for his people
to be free.

---

* Kuwasi means "Born on Sunday"; Balagoon means "Warlord."
Kuwasi died at Auburn prison on Saturday, December 13, 1986.

Gentle Warrior—
writing poems, cooking oxtail stew, tussling with
kids (when he could)—
gentle warrior, valor in action.
No, he didn't like violence,
not even a little bit,
just hated oppression a whole lot more.
So he fought and fought and fought
and never looked back.

Born on Sunday; died on Saturday;
created the poetry of struggle all week long;
said New Afrika had to be free.

Our warrior, revolution personified,
and mainly, well mainly he just loved people.
Not only "the people" in the abstract,
but people,
his people,
common people,
and all kinds of individuals
with their faults and foibles, soul and creativity.

Said New Afrika would be free;
said all forms of oppression must be overturned;
said let the human spirit flourish!

Born on Sunday; died on Saturday—
how could we lose him so soon?
Death snuck up and snatched him.
Yet his life is much greater than death:
Can still hear Kuwasi's giant laugh,
ringing across the other side.

Died on Saturday; Born on Sunday,
wherever people struggle to be free.

In Memory of Kuwasi Balagoon

Marilyn Buck, December 13, 1986

Dear brother you spoke so plain
      children listened to your song of freedom
      played in games, stories and life

brother you danced so lightly
      you whistled as you soared
      over prison walls and tombs

dear brother your spirit sings
      songs of freedom
      wrenched from slaver's cruelty

you leave us your tunes
      swinging blues
      rocking rap
      brass staccatos
      peace by piece
      a revolution riff

Some Reflections on an Unpublished Poem

Meg Starr

I met Kuwasi Balagoon when I was in my early twenties and very new to the movement. As a political prisoner and former member of the New York Black Panther 21 he was up on several pedestals in my mind. I was petrified by my first visit with him and completely unprepared for him to leap off the damn pedestals and meet me as a human being!

This was in the early 1980s, when the movement was very sectarian, defensive, and hierarchical. The "problem of racism" was "solved"— at least according to my sector of the left—by allowing white leaders to meet with Black leaders, while we white followers had almost no direct contact with the Black movement. I only saw Kuwasi because I ran a white anti-imperialist kid's organization. Paradoxically, all children were allowed to have contact with the Freedom Fighters.

In our children's group was a young Black girl with a single white mom. In a nationalist-oriented movement, they fell through the cracks, until Kuwasi adopted the little girl. He gave her as much of a Black role model as any locked down dad can do. He was warm and uncontainable.

I never knew him that well, so my stories about him are these little ones. He chatted with me about the punk music scene and writing poetry. Punk was frowned upon in my part of the movement as "white music," but I was a young punk and the only person visiting Kuwasi who listened to the Gang of Four and knew the clubs on the Lower East Side. He sent me poems he was working on and talked about music. Looking back now through his letters, it seems he was always in "isolation"—waiting to get back into prison general population and have a radio.

He was closeted. I wish I had known as a young lesbian that the woman in his poems was probably his transgendered lover of many years. I wish I'd asked him more questions about his anarchism then, about his bisexuality. But my interest in anarchism and my own coming out as bi came later.

What else can I say? I remember his memorial in New York, where neither his lover nor his full politics were acknowledged. I remember his sister saying at the time that she could hardly believe he was dead, because every time his family was at their most worried about him in the past, he'd pop up and say he was fine and ask how they were taking everything.

Life is short, knock down the pedestals, be human, resist. As Kuwasi ended every letter: Peace by Piece.

An Unpublished Poem

Today
in reach of the wind
i thought of the bridge of one of Baby Washington's songs
and thought about my ex
pictured her walking down the street
in her jeans and mod heals
the way other men see her

And last night
while standing in the rain
thinking about a future party and rum bout
to someone through a window
who doesn't touch the stuff
i thought about a party we went to
as i did all during that day, really

And the day before that
i really don't remember what was on my mind
tho i think she may have visited me in a dream
i don't know …
All the days look the same sometimes

Kunasi Jaw— 24-1984

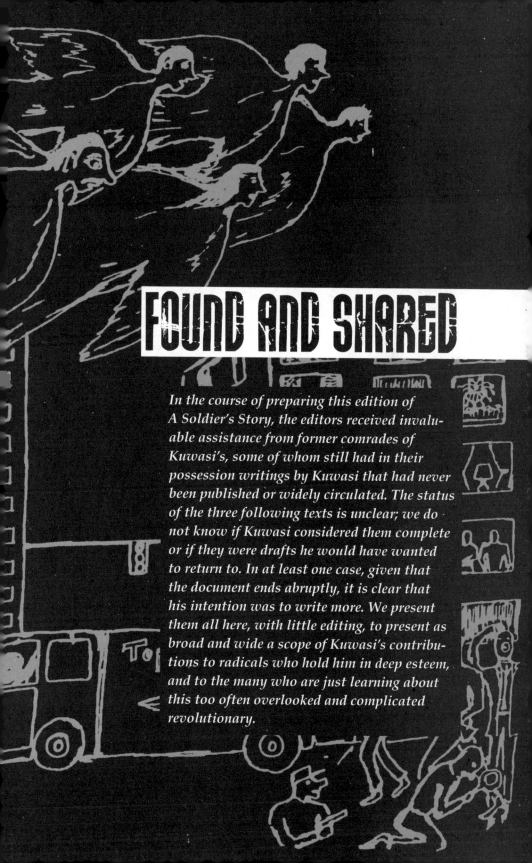

FOUND AND SHARED

In the course of preparing this edition of
A Soldier's Story, the editors received invaluable assistance from former comrades of
Kuwasi's, some of whom still had in their
possession writings by Kuwasi that had never
been published or widely circulated. The status
of the three following texts is unclear; we do
not know if Kuwasi considered them complete
or if they were drafts he would have wanted
to return to. In at least one case, given that
the document ends abruptly, it is clear that
his intention was to write more. We present
them all here, with little editing, to present as
broad and wide a scope of Kuwasi's contributions to radicals who hold him in deep esteem,
and to the many who are just learning about
this too often overlooked and complicated
revolutionary.

1. WHERE DO WE GO FROM HERE?

"Where do we go from Here?" is first and foremost a strategy for building collectives from the material basis of will. It is an attempt to point out a path of thinking and action that leads from one stage to another or one position to another, by cultivating the collective process within any small determined group of three or more people and making the best use of time, space, and whatever specific available resources to influence others to join the process, contribute, and exercise a measure of control consistent with their participation immediately. The basis of this process is agreement, and since collectives are guided by popular one person, one vote, the strategy is an anarchist strategy and this work is an anarchist organizing manual.

The collective process is more important than a large treasury, cache of arms, or throngs of people shouting your name, because to do anything in the social arena that determines the conditions for liberty and wealth, the spending and the investing of wealth must be organized. If it does nothing but sit it does no good, if one person or a few spend it as those few decide, while it was in fact the fruits of the labor of many, it only reinforces the existing structures that are responsible already for the genocide of entire peoples and the literal murder of the biosphere, and if it's spent pell mell it will only bring temporary and partial relief and problems. A large cache of arms in the hands of a few doesn't translate into much more than a weapon apiece unless it can be sold to someone who can be counted on to at the very least not use the arms to take back the money, and, of course, there's problems attendant with security with both money and arms. It wouldn't be wise to simply pass out arms to everyone who's been kicked in the ass, because one traitor fearful of being kicked out of existence or glad of pleasing his or her masters or to receive awards would immediately put you and all you had armed in peril. To carry on a war, many people united in purpose and organized into small manageable units must be present. While simply arming those who wish to and deserve to be armed would indeed be a service in a giant step towards self and community defense, it must be borne in mind that the enemy has an inexhaustible supply of both arms and ammunition and is continually on the attack, and so in order for people to really practice defense, they must practice offense, if only to force the enemy to have to be on guard.

Masses of people who believe in the cause is the greatest asset a movement can have, and even that doesn't bring you and them "out of the woods." Sympathy is not support. Actions must be channeled and coordinated with other actions that interrelate and translate into offensives that cannot be stopped. To do this people must attend to practical matters in measurable groups to ensure that there are in fact enough people to complete tasks, and that things that must be done at different places can be dealt with at the maximum efficiency and the least amount of time, effort, and resources being wasted or idle.

Who will lead these collectives? Who is the most qualified? Those are questions for the collectives to decide. All that can be decided on a one person, one vote basis should be decided that way. At the same time, at different points, on different matters, particular individuals will clearly be more knowledgeable than others, but this too should be decided collectively. Obviously, a mechanic in a collective garage would know more about what tools should be bought first, how to obtain the best at the best rates, and the approximate amount of time that may be required for certain work and would therefore practically be a leader. However, at the same time a collective shouldn't establish a garage if there's not at least enough mechanics to do a large portion of collective transportation work, and it is the collective who decides if, when, and where. Additionally, an auto repair collective would have other members, based in some aspects of auto repair and maintenance, such as changing tires, batteries, jump starts, etc. and would be required to learn more through on the job training.

Besides this, there are other things attendant to operating a collective garage or any other collective project. The obtaining and stocking of supplies and parts, the allocation of funds for light and heat, propaganda, the national procuring of office supplies and lunch, maintenance of the building, scheduling of shifts, classes and meetings, security, services, and interactions with the community.

On the ideology front, who is to decide what is to be studied in each collective which is also a study group? Who is to determine the mass line and be certain that it's consistent with the organizational line? There is simply no single person qualified. No individual knows what's best collectively. Only the collective can solve its ideological needs through collective participation and it's the collective who has to take responsibility for its propaganda, cultivation, and etc.

But how can a maze of separate collectives connect into a mass organization? Firstly, by aligning with other collectives whose purposes and rules are in alignment. Further, once a number of collectives of the same collectives agree to work together, they simply call a congress to further coordinate their efforts. The propaganda at that point is decided by that congress. Rather than a group of fifteen people struggling to put out a paper, a portion of the federation of collectives is channeled into that end, while the remainder do collective work that now translates into a larger organizational work.

Should a collective be concerned fundamentally with establishing anarchy where it is, it groups with other collectives, reorganizing its organizational efforts. Should a collective be concerned with liberation of a territory to achieve independence for colonialized nationals, it should group with other collectives, reorganizing its organizational efforts. Three or more collectives become a federation. A neighborhood organized becomes a community, a commune or federation of communes. Because armed struggle and mass propaganda alone will not develop into mass movements and significant irregular and regular forces necessary to overthrow the USA, mass organizing must be the main focus of a revolutionary program. If these federations of collectives and communes choose to institute a republic and this is the mandate of the masses (that is determined through referendum), then it is the task of the organization to aid in translating the will of the people into reality. If at the same time the federation of collectives and communes chooses to continue anarchy on a national territory, and this is the mandate of the masses, determined through referendum, then it is the task of the organization to translate that will into reality.

It must be borne in mind that all the suggestions as to enterprises, etc. do not beg to be followed and that many times it may be opportune to attempt objectives in the later phases, and perhaps come back to others or omit them altogether, it depends on particular conditions and predilections. Many would shun all elections as a matter of course, and many would deal with mass organizing alone, more than likely the bulk of collectives will, and since that is in fact what is needed most that should prove more than enough. The line between open work and clandestine work should be respected, because to proclaim a cause in the open and then do military work is overly risky, you become too easy to be found. The state will watch public organizations while looking for clandestine organizations, and it is best that they have to start with no idea as to participants in military acts.

At the same time, an underground movement simply cannot wait until mass movements complete their tasks before building itself and beginning its program of action. People applying for federal firearm licenses should not be identifiable as movement figures, and at the same time they should belong to a collective and consequently to a study group. Not aligned with the public movement, visibly, and prepared to buy weapons wholesale and in bulk transfer them, distribute them, and join an underground military collective, with the training and preparation necessary to be a class-one people's soldier.

Collectives who infiltrate comrades into correctional departments, security firms, police departments, and the armed forces should be as careful to not align with public movements. Build a treasury, procure weapons, and establish and maintain communications with at least but not necessarily more than one underground formation through a representative of a collective or a representative of a federation. This representative should have no police record and should have no direct involvement with the underground or public organizations, and coordinating in that line should have a straight nonsensitive job and the appearance of a regular worker.

These people should be well studied, disciplined, and known and checked out. For instance, if a comrade can't make meetings for a year and participate in a study group, they shouldn't be approached to take on the tasks of revolutionary spies or ordinance personnel. Except in instances where a regular group operating underground picks members with straight jobs and records for one of these tasks, the procedure should be initiated by collectives who choose that task, are not yet public, and choose as well to develop a military collective. That way only those responsible pay for mistakes and shoddy security.

The regular army is the immediate army that carries on irregular actions while the mass movement is being built and militias are being formed. This army is also made up of collectives formed in prisons, the u.s. armed forces, and anywhere that a collective of people come together and decide that that is what they want to do. Like every other collective, it is a study group as well, and like ordinance and spy collectives, security is of the utmost importance. Aside from meetings and study sessions, the underground must conduct security checks, obtain electronic detection devices, weapons, explosives, apartments, lofts and warehouses for hospitals, presses, and fronts, [and] among other things, carry on armed actions, such as bombings, arson, assassinations, expropriations, and kidnappings. To do this an underground military collective must establish a people's academy where books on these subjects can be studied and where training and testing can be given, along with ideological cultivation. It must develop the means to supply identification to all members and develop codes and procedures to change addresses and locations quickly when a member knowledgeable of them is captured, as well as devise objective methods of detecting weaknesses in members that could eventually be used against members of the army, as well as supporters.

Boastful, vice-ridden, vindictive, petty, and weak-willed people, as well as "rug eaters," people who storm out of meetings when they cannot have their way, should be eliminated before they are suspected of going over to the side of the enemy, just as bullies and people who talk of violence and are overly fearful. Character, strength of will, clear thinking, and physical fitness, along with truly democratic selfless principles are the elements a guerrilla must pit against superior mobility, firepower, methodological intelligence, and the principle of command and/or coercion that the police employ to enlist the cooperation of citizens and colonial subjects. If a member of a military collective finds at any point the traits needed [wanting], in his or herself or any other member, it is time to make new arrangements. At the same time when and if a guerrilla discovers that he or she can't make scate, they should be able to say so and should be allowed to leave the collective and be respected for their honesty.

With all the fundamentals in check, a collective should consist of two teams, with from five to seven members in each team. Have two drivers armed with sidearms, one automatic rifleman or woman or shotgunner also armed with a sidearm, and other members with sidearms. As soon as possible these arms should be minimized and all members should obtain bulletproof vests and grenades, either manufactured or homemade. Likewise, each group should have electronic detection equipment, and any member should be able to call a strip search to check for wires at any meeting. Additionally, each group should employ sniper rifles, bombs, in providing weapons and fires as they see fit to monopoly capital, defense industrial complex targets, police stations, businesses that contribute to rewards, and any opportune enemy targets that can be reconned, studied, and ascertained to present the least risk. The key is to consistently be on the attack when not preparing to attack, and remaining victorious, even when the victories are small, like a small police station, sporting goods shop, an unarmed government agency, armored car, a bank, landlord or marshal's office, electric, gas, or phone monopoly billing offices. After each action, the group should hold a critique, keeping in mind that simply because no problems were encountered or problems were overcome, those facts do not indicate that either the plan or execution was flawless; it only indicates that the plan and execution was passable under the particular set of conditions present.

The most important tasks will be the assassinations of clear enemies such as police, traitors, landlords, and the liberation of captured guerrillas; ofttimes this will take no more expertise or execution than an expropriation. All actions should be considered not only on the basis of value but also in terms of ability to do. A continuous thoroughly developed reconnaissance program will make clear weak spots in the enemy's defense area, where small portions of them are isolated, exposed, and vulnerable. Likewise, links with captured guerrillas who are not celebrated but are in fact dedicated soldiers should yield easier escapes than known revolutionaries held under extra-deep extra-tight security. Again, every action should take into account the risks involved in order to minimize them, as we have no soldiers to hand over or trade, and small victories that incur no losses are indeed victories nevertheless. It is the insurgents who choose when and where.

The first and hardest task of any revolutionary army is to avoid getting "nipped at the bud" and to become established in the minds of the people as a force that will not be stopped. The second task is to grow and develop into a force that is responsible for consistent military political acts, that establishes in the mind of the people that a war is clearly in progress. The values of the revolutionaries must be reflected through the conduct and propaganda of the revolutionaries. When the masses of people conscientiously choose revolutionary values over reactionary values, to the point where they support revolution and refuse to collaborate in any way with reaction, the balance of power will shift (all people is truly of the people).

Once the movement perceives that a balance of power has in fact evolved, the final offensive begins. The "regular" people's army units become commando irregular units attached to the people's militias, who are in and therefore within the consensus of the mass party. Destruction of monopoly capital begins in earnest, with the occupation of territories and public executions of those who profit from exploitation and oppression.

GENERAL STATE OF THINGS

Perceptions — Experiencing and Building an Experience Rather Than Allowing the Media to Describe Our Lives

When we examine, where do we go from Here? it is clear from the onset that to discuss or address that question we have to talk about Here. Where this particular Here is in relation to everywhere else. In terms of our health and living conditions. Socially, in terms of how other people are doing and where they are. Our dealings with other people individually and in terms of whatever institutions they have built to serve their purposes, and of course mentally, how we experience things and what we recall about the events or processes that brought us or made us decide to come Here.

"We" is plural, meaning more than one. Appropriate because as individuals we interact with other individuals and, regardless of our designs, do not live in a vacuum. Since that is the case, who we are with is part of the answer to where we are, and the answer to what we are doing with who we are with is part of the answer to where we are going. Where we might be at a particular time and who we may be with at a particular time can be answered without the resulting illumination lighting the way very far. For instance, one can leave here for work, get on a train and ask oneself that question, and it is obvious that you are going to work. If you were in a desert aided by a map which showed a water hole that you were standing near, that would be part of the answer to where you were. If you were there with others and it appears either that there was enough water for all or that there wasn't enough for all to drink their fill or for all to take rations of it to sustain them until they got out of the desert or to another water hole, then that would enter into the question of where you were.

So it would serve us better to ask that question in regards to where we live. We can agree that we live on a planet called Earth, and go on to say in the northern hemisphere, and for some of our purposes what is presently the United States.

When we advance further on that question in relation to where we live, we may examine ourselves in regards to our health. Investigate how we feel at the moment and most of the time. What does our diet consist of? Are our dwellings safe? Do we share these dwellings with others? Who are they? Who is in the immediate area? Who occupies the surrounding areas? How do we feel about this, as well as the people closest to us?

If everything appears to be satisfactory and what you do every day insures you satisfaction, then this manual and suggested agenda will only serve as a poor diversion. If, on the other hand, you are not satisfied with things, are trying to decide what to do or if you should leave wherever you are and take your chances elsewhere, this will hopefully aid you and those who come in contact with you.

If you feel that the house you live in is not safe or not worth the time you spend in it and that it's not worth the money you pay to live there. If you feel that those who inhabit your surroundings are in a similar condition, that the money you pay for food and clothing takes up too great a portion of what you make even after budgeting, that what you do each day, how you are employed, does nothing to change these matters, perhaps it is time to consider another course.

If on top of this you perceive decisions that shape these and other aspects of your life are out of your hands and influence, as well as out of the hands and influence of those in the environment you share, then it is time to sit down and talk with your neighbors; if not all of them, then some of them.

Out of the issues that affect you and them directly, discussion can disclose new insights and confirmations. Where the basics of living are the issue, they should be dealt with and listed first. If stretching money or getting money in the first place are problems, living in a suitable domain of your own, abuse from law enforcement personnel, landlords, and other community criminals are a problem, then a program must be built and maintained to change this situation or eradicate these problems.

There is no one act an individual can perform that can change these things in an instant and nothing that a small group of people can do except begin to create ways of defending themselves and, more importantly, organize and initiate organizing of large groups of people in the neighborhood and area; as in all the neighborhoods and areas.

The main thing is to focus on your lives collectively, rather than accept the definitions and descriptions of others. The things that you can confirm through your experiences must be more creditable than those things that you cannot. If you cannot make hide or hair of what the government's economic forecasters issue you, you can disregard it. At the same time, there is no book that will liberate anyone. A book may give ideas, but it takes people to apply, adapt, and if they don't work disregard and develop and find new ones.

A Revolutionary Agenda

At the point where a group of people find themselves agreeing to the fact that they have the same problems, where their decisions hold no weight, as well as any influence they may have on the government in charge, the question is then to decide if the government is the source of the problem, or a source. When this is perceived to be so, then the solutions ultimately will be changing that government, overthrowing that government and replacing it with a new one; overthrowing the government and replacing it with anarchy; seceding from the government, and in the waging of a war of liberation by colonized people, that [is to say] people exploited for their land and labor and controlled by a separate nation of people.

Organizing—Collectivizing and Revolutionizing Our Lives

None of these solutions can be brought about by decree or by simply deciding on the part of a small group of people or even a large group. The society and, in fact, the world is organized a certain way that results in people having problems basic to living and, of course, have to be organized another way, to rearrange the situation in a real way.

Before the revolution is organized a movement must be organized, and before a movement can be organized a revolutionary organization must be organized that will empower people to distribute power and wealth in a free egalitizing manner.

Before revolutionary organizations can be built; people who know in their hearts that only a drastic change will be suitable must cultivate their thinking and actions into the thoughts and actions that bring about the changes they seek.

They must accept the consequences of their actions in the event the state and the establishment forces prevail and know in their hearts that these forces must be contested, in any event, for a worthwhile change/revolution to be established, and yet never make a needless sacrifice. That is, a revolutionary must strive to minimize the possibility of defeats, and yet act in accordance with the game plan that will lead to the overthrow of the government and the retaking of power by a revolutionized mass organization that can set matters right. In this regard a revolutionary's private life cannot run contrary to collective responsibility, and the desire for this change within one's self should stem from love of people and the desire to aid the evolution of society where people can live completely with both bread and liberty. The more our lives fit into this revolutionary context, the more revolutionary we become, to the point that we do simply what we conclude the revolution requires, cognizant of what that means and clear as to why.

Across these United States, in every large city, there are New Afrikan colonies, as well as in towns too numerous to name. In the middle of the night when the streets are deserted one can still see that these are the areas where New Afrikan people live. The actual real estate belongs to someone outside the colony. The services that are a matter of course elsewhere are withheld, apartment buildings and public buildings from schools to storefronts are boarded up. In the light of day unemployment is admittedly 50 percent according to the U.S. government. Police patrol and harass but do not protect residents—they shoot residents; any day's reading of a newspaper will recount an incident where a New Afrikan man, woman, or child was killed or brutalized. At the same time these conditions that are ripe for rebellion have not been organized into a revolutionary mass movement.

Hispanic colonies that are often bordering New Afrikan colonies suffer the same conditions. Puerto Rican, Mexicano, and New Afrikan migrant workers pick the bulk at America's tables and are only paid enough to live to produce new generations of migrant workers. While Native Americans are isolated on reservations and oppressed in cities and get the same range of work that other Third World people get; hospital workers, nursing home workers, factory workers, and employment that make of them a menial class and castes, and employment that brings less salary for the same work as whites, but there has been no real mass movement inside the colonies.

The white working class suffers with wages, unemployment, job-related injuries that could be avoided, drafts, wage freezes, inflation, environmental pollution in water, air, and ground, utility hikes, and etc. that the Third World colonies suffer; as well as being organized by the state and ruling class to combat the liberation of Third World colonies. An antinuke movement to prevent the immediate destruction of the world appears from time to time, along with anti-draft movements.

However, there is no revolutionary mass movement within the white working class.

This is not to say that there are not any public revolutionary organizations or that there are not revolutionaries who clearly understand that the genocide of Third World people and the manipulation and exploitation of the working classes will not cease until there is revolution. Nor does this absence of a mass movement imply that there are no revolutionaries among any of the captured nations or of the white working class who have not historically or presently showed themselves to be truly heroic and deliberately revolutionary in their dealings. But it does mean that the need to organize a mass movement has not been appreciated to a large extent and that the formulas for doing this have not been developed.

Make no mistake about it, without a mass movement there is no revolution. An army without a mass movement can never achieve a balance of power necessary to defeat a government or build a mass movement to organize the people. A mass movement, on the other hand, can organize the people and set the conditions for the building of real people's armies, which will not only have the power to carry on protracted war but [will] build the forces strong enough to sweep the government and ruling class out of power...

Why the Collective First?
SMALL IS POSSIBLE ...

No one individual can carry out a revolution. If there were thousands of people gathered to carry out the revolution in any one place, these people would have to be organized to carry on in a coherent fashion within a strategic framework to fulfill the tasks of the revolution; they would have to be organized into companies, clubs, communities, or some type of political military or economic formation in tune with other formations, and it would take an organization to do this. It would take an organization as well to organize smaller groups of people and individuals. That is, to share a basis of understanding with them as to your objectives and means to carry them out and the reasons why these efforts are worthwhile. Moreover, it would take an organization to actually coordinate efforts by individuals into a means of doing practical and actual work, as well as coordinating efforts by this work into a coherent and consistent program that brings people collectively to the goals desired, while maximizing the effect of small actions and efforts and securing the progress made.

A collective that is from three to fifteen people is a starting point and functional unit, where these terms can be developed, where understandings can be confirmed, and where the potential of individuals can be maximized. A mass of people can be organized into a network of collectives, and a few people can build and expand a collective.

Once there are too many people to easily coordinate their actions, collectives can split in two, and tasks and programs can be coordinated between collectives. More importantly a collective has the greatest potential of maintaining a democratic one person, one meaningful vote process and can demonstrate clearly the power of organized people. A suggestion might be to keep the numbers in collectives odd, that way there are no tied votes.

The Collective
GUIDELINES, MEETINGS, RULES, AGENDAS, DISCIPLINE ...

Once you have formed a group, it's time to change that group into a political entity, a collective, if there are three or more people. You can set a list of things you collectively agree are priorities and make note of the things that you can deal with, to whatever extent, immediately, keeping in mind that you will have to work on matters for a long period of time and that, as you expect the collective to grow, you collectively establish guidelines.

For instance, even though you consist of a relatively small group of people, you would want the group to be self-reliant and yet responsive to the issues before you. You will want to establish ways for members to contact each other. A method of sticking with and following up on tasks once started. Criteria for recruiting new members, and standards for dealing with each other, potential friends and allies, and with enemies.

You will have to set meetings at regular times to deal with matters on your agenda. Decide what type of propaganda you may employ, share information with the group that may result in a collective advantage and advance for the struggle, and check in on projects, as well as setting aside time for group study and exercise.

Meetings should start on time and end on time and should cover the matters on the agenda and updates on work done before moving on to general discussion. They can be at homes on a rotating basis, in public parks, or at sites where tasks are being performed. Each collective should get two loose-leaf notebooks for the gathering of political and economics intelligence, with dividers between each topic, and notebook paper with ads, news clippings, and other printed items as a storehouse of information to be used in future research. That way when individual members run across information of value, the collective gets the opportunity to review it and gain by its storage. It is always a good idea rather than everyone buying the same newspapers to collectively buy them and collectively choose books and magazines. Particular members pick up particular publications at different meetings to share.

Rules should be within reason but definite. For instance, no member should be allowed to assault another member and yet continue to be a member. No member should have drugs or alcohol in his or her possession while at a project site or be under the influence of drugs or alcohol when doing collective tasks or representing the collective. No member should live off the proceeds of prostitution or sell hard drugs.

Agendas are necessary both in meetings and away from meetings, since they aid the collective in focusing input. At each meeting an agenda should be set and followed. At the close of each meeting the agenda for the period between that meeting and the next should be set, and every agenda should have an automatic re-check of tasks assigned or volunteered for from the next.

Discipline should be clear in regards to infractions. In relation to rules, for instance, if it comes to a collective's attention that a member sold heroin or was an informer that member would have to go. Obviously, a member who was late at meetings or who had failed to attempt a task or join in collective work wouldn't be subject to the same fate. However, if a member actually missed enough functions the collective would have to proceed as if that member wasn't there and under the circumstances decide the correct way to deal with minor problems. For instance, when a member misses a regular meeting he/she misses the opportunity to vote on whatever issues are before the collective, and if there is no advance notice of any particularly important matter, this cannot equal to being absent at a collective function where a task has been decided upon. Since all members are required to keep in touch and informed of meetings and collective tasks, the excuse of missing a task through ignorance by missing a meeting is not valid. There will more than likely be meetings missed and tasks for different reasons from time to time which the collective will have to pass judgement on. More than likely some members will drop out and return from time to time if that is permitted. As some drop out at only stages you should be as happy as you are when you recruit a new member and unless a member has committed a serious offense against the collective, or [against] the people while in the collective, they should be considered. When a member drops out due to commitment or differences they may reexamine their practice once away from the collective and renew their efforts once back in.

A collective must not be a group of vindictive individuals ready to take sides against anyone for petty reasons. At the same time for offences that fall between being late or absent from a meeting or task, and assault, theft, drug possession or sale, there should be not only a collective disciplinary proceeding and a punishment deemed fair by the majority but an extra task. An individual under discipline should have to write an essay on where his or her action or actions were wrong. The reasoning or their motive in the particular matter. Refusal to do this should result in expulsion, and all serious offenses should include permanent expulsion. If a collective finds out later that it was wrong, the members who voted for the expulsion, which should be a matter of record, should write an apology and self-criticism to the individual in question, just as the individual would be expected to write. In many cases it might be a good idea for members of the collective to write an essay before joining as to their aims and feelings.

Resources
PEOPLE, TIME, UNUSED SPACE ...

Starting out small and broke, the first objective of a collective is not to get in debt, either in terms of money or in terms of any patrons who may wish for any reasons to bankroll the organization. The desire to rent an office when in fact meetings can be held in homes, schools, parks, vacant lots, and in favorable conditions storefronts that can be taken over and occupied.

The task is to organize people through services that the government or corporations cannot perform, if they had the intentions, as well as the people themselves. The task before the collective is to initiate services and maintain self-reliance. Propaganda of the deed and mouth to mouth, as well as posters, graffiti, letters to the editors, and leaflets can accompany but cannot take the place of actual work and actual organizing. The desire to put out a paper which must be funded by a broke collective usually without an established system of distribution is crazy, and at the beginning is only an expressed view of small organizations.

A collective treasury should be designed before the details of money become a question, and by collective what is meant is that all funds brought into it are collective funds, and all funds leaving it do so after being accounted for collectively. If a bank account is set up then at least two members should have the power to withdraw funds only when at least both members are present. When funds are not held in banks and are held in safes, the safes should be in the homes of members who do not know the combination and should only be attended to by others when a vote has been taken. When commercial banks and safes are not used, the money raised collectively should be distributed after meetings have decided what should be the aim or needs to be taken care of.

Just as unused space in terms of a meeting place is a resource, time is a resource. Members are therefore required to invest time other than meeting-time into the organization, whether employed or unemployed. Investigation into resources should be made, as well as possible services to the community. For instance, it may be profitable and a good means of conducting propaganda to be in a babysitting service or to liberate an in-court lot and charge for parking or to develop a craft into a light industry and save the proceeds until a used car or a van can be bought to begin a gypsy car service.

At the same time, some investigation can be made into the whereabouts of recycling plants. At least one day a week a collective can converge on a vacant lot, bag aluminum and steel cans, bottles, and clear the particular lot of trash. At the same time, spraypainting or postering the area with the message you intend to get to people.

People seeing you at work get to wonder who you are and why you are doing what you are doing. At the same time a steady source of income enters the treasury to be saved until a bigger source of capital can be obtained. If, for instance, you buy a used car and start a car service where members of the collective alternate shifts, the money goes back into the treasury and the collective continues the process of accumulating collective capital.

Once the weather is favorable you plant Victory Gardens in the vacant lots close to members where they can water them straight from the building they live in, if possible. You invite the community to help you clear more vacant lots and turn them into gardens. After investigating what would be wisest and easy to grow and as vegetation ripens, you set up stands in areas people pass through and sell produce at a reasonable price; after dividing the produce between people in the collective and/or organizing gardens for people in the community to do with as they see fit.

Once you are known and recognized throughout the community and more than enough money is coming in, it is time, if you cannot simply liberate a place, to rent one and buy a press, even if just a hand crank model.

Arrangements should be made to have a public phone installed, which will not only be cheaper but discourage hours of sap rap. Then you can start turning out leaflets with a phone number to be contacted by and an address which should be occupied from noon to at least 8 p.m. so people can stop in after work as well as during the day. This place should be used for more than a contact and for meetings. A book exchange can now be initiated, where anyone can bring a book in and trade it for another book. A clothing exchange, likewise, could be initiated so as to not only serve people but bring them in contact with the organization on the basis of needs.

When profitable and no other use can be made of the rented space, political movies, decided upon by the collective, and plays should be staged. Dances, likewise, with no alcoholic beverages sold, on a weekly basis can be held. At the same time, periodicals from organizations friendly to us, as well as any periodicals thought appropriate to put out collectively, can be distributed.

However, at this stage the collective organizational goals include buying and taking an entire building big enough to cover all organizational functions. But not right away, unless someone donates a building, knowing that this organization wants things but never favors, then the regular publishing of a newspaper can be included.

At the same time this point, or early points, should mark the beginnings of rent strike organizing when it is clear that there are enough people to see the entire process through. Everyone who comes in contact with any of the collectives should be informed as to the goals and principles of the collective and rules of membership, if they are potential friends...

PART TWO

Although this is written in parts and is a suggested agenda, this is not to suggest every suggestion in Part One must be taken up before moving to the suggestions in Part Two, or that equal or better ways to reach people and be self-reliant are not to be found. Success must be measured in terms of how many people have been organized and participate fully in terms of developing and internationalizing the ideology of the group. Success must also be measured by the relationship with the community and area residents and the degree of self-reliance and freedom from counterrevolutionary influences.

In order for a revolutionary collective or organization to grow into a revolutionary mass organization certain requirements must be met, which include:

1. The acceptance of the organization by the people the organization intends to organize into an organization which is on their side and which places their interest before the interest of any individual or group of individuals. People must accept that the organization is theirs and intends to address and does address their needs.

2. People must know that the organization is firmly rooted and is not a "fly by night" group. That the principles and programs are sound and that the organization is guided in an intelligent manner that doesn't allow or tolerate corruption in any form.

People must feel that the goals of the organization can be reached and that the goals are worthwhile and deserve their participation and support...

Building and Aiding the Building of Other Collectives
SUGGESTING LINES ALONG FOOD, CLOTHING, AND SHELTER ...

A collective, besides carrying out its program and proving its program can work, must encourage the formation of other collectives. As new members are recruited, they must be given the opportunity to join a collective process, whether it's one new member or one thousand. Having a list of names in a book doesn't organize people or transform a group of people into an organization. Having people enter collectives, participate in study and discussion groups, attend meetings, vote on issues, do organizational work and participate in collective tasks, air their ideas, and organize other people, transforms people into revolutionaries and transforms groups of people into revolutionary collectives.

New members should join old collectives and form new collectives and be aided both in terms of encouragement and in terms of material support. For instance, if a collective already formed has tools and isn't using them on a particular day, they could lend them to a newly formed collective. [In] the case of sticks with nails for picking trash, any collective would look for suitable sticks when cleaning a lot, and it's cheaper to buy nails by the pound. Also, different collectives should help each other plow plots and harvest and look for other suitable vacant lots and areas. Food, herbs, or even green grass, cloves, and dandelions look better than trash-filled spaces between buildings. Spraypainting on the walls of abandoned buildings, flags, trash barrels for debris, for those who would otherwise litter, painted with the symbol of the organization is constant propaganda. A knowledge of the planting seasons for different vegetables carries this on from May until November.

Special attention should be made to aid squatters who live in abandoned buildings. They should be encouraged and aided to turn the lots adjacent to their dwellings into Victory Gardens, because they have begun to literally take back the land already. Collectives of squatters may be formed in the beginning of warm weather, equipped with camping gear and building skills. As squatters are many times unemployed, the investments of time and employment by their own collectives may be the actual material basis of the superseding society.

One of the objectives is to plant so many gardens that it becomes impossible to go through what were before ghost towns [without seeing them transformed] into areas where the best aspects of city and country living merge. Church groups, clubs, gangs should be encouraged as well to take over plots, as well as coordination for the purposes of trade between groups and forming of a "People's Market," where each group and collective can trade and sell their produce and carry on their own business independently.

At the point where there are a number of collectives in a given area attempts should be made of forming communes. First where buildings are taken over in a given area and where buildings are bought. Solid structures should be investigated for the purposes of establishing food co-ops.

None of this should be dealt with as ends unto themselves but as means to propagandize and organize the mass movement. Propaganda in front of structures, as well as bulletin boards outside and in, should alert all who enter to programs, activities, and meetings of the organization.

Possible employment outside of organizations for certain members may be investigated, in the ways of Veterans seeking loans and moneys from the government to buy houses and open businesses and government programs where houses can be bought for a dollar and repaired.

These ongoing programs are to continue year in year out with the goals of revolutionizing squatters' unions and organizing regional land banks, where groups of collectives pool resources to buy large tracts and connecting tracts of lands in given areas around and away from where the organization began, and most importantly until neighborhoods are transformed into commun-commun-e-ties. This is not only to initiate people's control over their lives and show the power of organization but to demonstrate the logic of socialism and justice and the desirability of revolution.

PART THREE

During this time, alternative energy sources that give independence from monopoly capital should be carried out and developed to as great an extent as possible. Wood-burning stoves should be built and installed in buildings taken over by squatters as quickly as possible, and there should be no inhibitions from collecting wood from structures less habitable.

Offices should set a fund aside for the buying and installing of windmills and solar heating equipment, this not only frees the organization of monthly bills, but demonstrates to a public that no donations are accepted without a good or service rendered, that the organization takes steps to be independent and cuts overhead so as to be able to serve more and better.

A building owned and propagated as being owned by a collective or an organization, with visible and independent sources of power and independence, is a permanent piece of propaganda.

A clothing exchange is a service that merely calls for the allocation of space and cadre to deal with the public. A food co-op is clearly an operation existing on the principle of buying bulk at the cheapest price and distributing at the cheapest price a wide range of wholesome foods, beverages, and herbs. To make a donation to see a movie, attend a dance, play, or recital of revolutionary content in such a place is to know that money is going into a revolutionary process.

Every member should have access to wholesale food and clothing and have tasks that include organizing and propagandizing and community service. Members not employed elsewhere may opt to join a manufacturing collective or a service collective. For example, money generated from a gypsy cab service, movies, dances, and open-air markets could be reinvested in collective capital, such as more gypsy cabs, etc.

Other capital investments may include machines and material for clothing production, videotaping of plays, canning of commune-grown foods, etc.

The task being to become free of capitalism and to better serve lumpen proletarian and proletarian people by the cultivation of revolutionary ideology through theory and practice on a mass scale. The building of alternative economic structures along socialist lines and building the grounds for the two classes to interact in a progressive manner by initiating the means for the two classes to interact along principled lines and adopting to a degree the role of the revolutionary proletariat.

PART FOUR

By the time an organization advances this far in one area certain processes should have been initiated in other areas, through members moving to other areas and initiating collectives but also through example which a revolutionary organization should be clear in both setting and explaining, especially with mass level participation. Once a federation of collectives is established in one area and progress is noted, the most progressive elements of other areas should be invited to witness and formulas should be shared, as this is not a competition. When an organization takes on the practices and guiding theories of another it becomes the organization. When a neighborhood becomes a commune, members should aid in building a federation of communes, just as collectives aid in building a federation of collectives.

A Word on Collective Business

Savings from individual collectives through enterprises that the members are engaged in, funds from a rotating basis from programs jointly carried out by collectives, and pooling resources are the means used to generate collective capital. No collective will receive government funding, except in the case of veterans from the U.S. armed services demanding their benefits. The organization should work with Third World and anti-imperialist veterans' groups, not only in aiding them to fight for their rights to benefits but to form collectives and be a part of the federation. However, funds from different government departments will always have strings attached and tend to direct interference from the U.S. government under the justification of protecting the American taxpayer. Likewise, money from corporations also leads to intervention, aiding to investigate the resources of a given collective and later the federation, tax investigations, fishing expeditions into what is being done with the money. Worst of all, these grants make the entire organization suspect to those who it serves.

The primary purpose of collective business besides building the infrastructure for a superseding society is of course to serve the needs of people we intend to aid, and in those regards not be a burden or a source of competition, except in cases where capitalist businesses from people who live outside or inside the community take advantage of conditions to exploit the community.

For instance, if there is only one laundromat in the area, which is exploiting the people, a group of collectives may pool resources and establish another laundromat that may merely come out even. We will encourage people to eat in family-owned and operated restaurants, rather than chain fast-food enterprises or expensive restaurants, as well as small stores, to pool resources and buy in greater bulk to make their prices cheaper.

At the same time, we will open food co-ops to give people the opportunity to be a part of an operation that helps them and to be able to get foods that are cheaper and of more variety than at established locations. We will not open a liquor store and at the same time will promote buying from community stores if you drink and making your own wines, whiskeys, and beers. We will not open a video or pinball parlor or otherwise engage in an enterprise whose motives are not clearly seen as practical fulfillment of needs.

At the same time, some vacant lots may be converted into picnic areas, flower gardens, playgrounds, small parks for the playing of checkers, chess, darts, horseshoes, etc.

When a certain strength is reached some collectives should open daycare centers, revolutionary cultural centers, and when possible schools.

Every advancement on our part must be seen as an advancement on the people's part. Rather than taking over communities we must initiate the reorganization of communities; reorganization, because communities are already organized, but not for the purpose of bettering the condition of the inhabitants or for their liberation. Our task is to revolutionize and neutralize all we come in contact with ...

Organizing Block Associations and People's Militias ...

Block associations are very important, and when members of collectives live in blocks that already have block associations, they should join, and collectives should take care to consider block association meetings when scheduling collective and commune meetings, so that members can attend both.

At the same time collectives should help to organize block associations whenever they conduct rent strikes or initiate Victory Gardens or any type of mass work in a given area. If there is already a block association where a rent strike is being organized, tenants should be encouraged to join in rather than set up a rival association, as well as when a Victory Garden is being initiated.

Candidates for recruitment into collectives should be asked to join and be familiarized with the programs and rules. This keeps the organization on ground level in touch with people who are familiar with what the organization is doing and makes a lot of work easier.

For instance, landlords often count on people not showing up for court and filing forms to contest evictions or conditions, and a particular tenant may indeed have to work or be at the hospital or otherwise be indisposed on a particular day. In that case an organizer who may represent people in court may have to get another tenant instead of the particular tenant to file a form. At the same time, as many tenants may have the same date in court from the same building, and many of these people may have to work, they may be replaced by people from other buildings who may need the same type of standing at a court date for a rent strike they are involved in. This is easier to arrange when an organizer can simply walk to the next building and talk to another tenant. This way no court days are forfeited, and landlords are contested every inch of the way. The more delay tactics are used the more money is withheld by the tenants.

Each time the landlord concedes the power, the tenants' union grows; each time a landlord is forced to give up a building and the organized tenants take it over directly, this should be noted and "celebrated." As the "city" is the landlord in many cases, actions should be sustained in an effort to force the city to give in. When through a crooked court a landlord receives a ruling in his favor, an organization fully prepared to make court dates should propagandize the struggle and appeal to civil court leaving the landlord to pay two sets of lawyers, the lower and higher court, while organizers train other tenants to be organizers and target other buildings of the same landlord with enough violations to initiate rent strikes and court actions.

With collective members involved in tenant unions and block associations consolidating mass power within the community, knowing that these organizers do in fact have organizational backup, former tasks that still have to be carried out become easier and advance becomes possible.

Collectives have a responsibility to protect patrons who come to dances, movies, and other organizational functions. From time to time members will volunteer to serve as security. To prevent assaults, stop alcohol and drugs from entering premises, search out electronic eavesdropping devices, etc. Those found to be satisfactory should be encouraged to be militia and perhaps represent the People's Militia while dealing with security.

In the same view, members of collectives who have formed people's car services and have shown themselves to be of the traits of militiamen/women should be harmonized with each other, as well as those living in the neighborhood. Their cars and radios give them the means to report enemy and criminal movements and transport militia to given areas quickly.

An intelligence network can be established and a People's Militia with members being known for their political practice over a period of time. Neighborhood people, fellow tenants, family members, schoolmates, club and gang members who have worked in vacant lots through turning them into Victory Gardens have had to concern themselves with the maintenance, administration, and protection of these plots from sabotage and theft. It is therefore possible to know these individuals' practice over a period of time, as well as their relation to the communities they have served. Those who check out as being responsible, principled, intelligent, and protective should be approached in regards to forming collectives/militias in the areas where they reside and continuing to do the services they've rendered.

This is in order to be complete people's warriors—rather than just fighters—as well as to have them protected by the fact that there are numerous people organized throughout the community who are not of the militia but support the militia.

For the police to stop the militia they would have to arrest the community.

Training and field military manuals should be bought and studied before these militias are officially formed, covering all aspect of military training. Physical fitness training should be universal throughout the organization. However, the militia should study military techniques, and etc. at militia meetings as well as having political cultivation universal throughout the organization, as they are not separate armed units and have other tasks as well; they are militia as well as cadre.

Some of these collectives will naturally be in contact with others. For instance, some radio connections between the cabs, regular automobiles, and apartments will be maintained. The formations will be based on standard military lines, a collective therefore equal to a squad will be the base.

Four collectives a platform, four to five platforms a company, four companies a battalion, two battalions a brigade, four or more brigades a division, this is so when a balance of power is reached with the enemy and regular formations literally occupy large land areas, an army is already established.

The object at the beginning being of course to work to the point of building a mass movement, and then a militia.

With an organization strong enough to run the heroin dealers out of town, this must be proceeded upon. As tenant organizations and the people in the community must be protected from robbers, muggers, arson, and rapists. This is where the militias sharpen their swords.

While this goes on, a health care program must be started to detoxify drug addicts. Space will have to be put aside to care for addicts while dealers are being attacked. Once addicts are detoxified they should be encouraged to form collectives to maintain themselves and to help others detoxify and to be organized for their own well-being, while an outright war is being waged against dealers. Which will include assassination with guns and bombs and expropriation of whatever money or arms can be found in the rubble. Addicts caught victimizing community people will receive vicious asskickings and be made to lick the habit through being kidnapped and cuffed for four days.

The next offensive by the mass organizations will be the building of alternatives for prostitutes. Which will include food, clothing, and shelter for them and their children and protection from pimps and graft-taking police. Members will simply approach them on the street and offer these accommodations as the means to develop collective enterprises increasing the organization.

Committees will also visit, send commissary money, letters, and food packages to prisoners, in state and federal penal and mental institutions, who are politically compatible with the organization. Encouraging them to form collectives before their release and aiding them in gaining parole by finding jobs, housing, and shelter. These visits, commissary money, food packages, and letters will appear to be from individuals, rather than members of an organization.

Next, and one of the most difficult, will be the organizing of shelters for homeless men and women, to offer immediate aid to those most in need. It is doubtful that, the economic conditions being what they are, much of a dent could be made. At the same time, in the winter some attempt should be made, and people should go into city shelters to organize what have to be malcontents.

Also, adoption of children should be encouraged by members.

Mass Public Moves
PARTY BUILDING

When a sizable number of the local community are in the organization, and in block associations, collectives, clubs, etc. favorable to [the] organizational principles and goals, the organizing of voter registration drives and voting blocks should begin, to determine local elections in schools and hospital boards, councilmen and women at large and State and U.S. Congressional Representatives. To influence community control of schools and hospitals to ensure that collaborators and outright enemies cannot misrepresent the aspirations of the communities by enacting laws and ordinances against our agendas and platforms and, likewise, to ensure that our members and allies enact local ordinances and influence laws that aid our efforts. This should only be undertaken when we feel that electoral victories are certain. All salaried staff members should be picked before elections so that each candidate runs as a leader of a team versus other staff members with mystery teams, likewise all candidates and staff members must vow before nominations to channel portions of their salaries and "operating expenses" into collective and federation enterprises and projects, to ensure that these are not individual victories and that these candidates already have the organization's backup to effect clear, practical, and well explained mandates. No conditions will be made with established party clubs and machines under any circumstances. No elections will be participated in without clear indications of victory beforehand, which can be measured by the registrations of voters through the block associations.

When half to three-fourths of the voters are registered under our designation in a given school district we run a candidate in that school district, and likewise at the hospital boards, Councilmen and women at large, and etc. Emphasis should be placed on community control and local elections, including that of judges, to the point where the election boards are of the federations and block associations. The only possible reason for defeat must be the rigging by authorities.

In running candidates for State Assembly and U.S. Congress the objectives must be just as clearly explained in practical terms. No enemy of the movement should be allowed to represent any districts where we and allies have substantial force. In certain instances, we may be able to form coalitions for the mere purpose of getting enemies out of office, such as mayoral races, State Assembly people, and etc. when they are the enemy...

Preparation for Armed Struggle

Some collectives not registered with the federation or visibly associated should remain covert as part of the militia. Members of these collectives should be eligible under the existing laws to obtain federal firearm licenses and work toward the collective planning of an amassing of funds for the buying of arms wholesale. With a federal firearms license, and structure and capital, a member should be able to open up a gun shop, order pistols, rifles, and shotguns and distribute them among the anarchist regular army, militias, and liberation armies, and anti-imperialist forces; who are in league with the federation politically and involved in armed struggle.

At the same time other collectives and in some cases the same collectives as above, will be organized to infiltrate members into the U.S. Armed Forces, correctional departments, security firms, and police departments, to obtain hard intelligence from the enemy, and training as well as access to arms. Obviously, members engaged in this area must be ideologically "tight," steadfast, and able to stick to a game plan; and to give up one way of life to literally go underground and play a role in the regular army...

The Socialization and Consolidation of the Left

The socialization and consolidation of the "left" must take place along principled lines. The term "left" must be redefined to be land, the means of production, and the power to really make decisions being in the hands of the masses, as opposed to the land, means of production, and power to make decisions being in the hands of a ruling class.

A. At the same time the principles of land and self-determination for the captive nations within the U.S. empire; that is New Afrikan, Native American, Puerto Rican, and Mexicano.

B. The socialization of all monopoly capital; such as electric and gas companies, phone companies, railroads, defense contractors, public works contractors, and etc.

C. This stage should be engaged in when the organization is established throughout the present confines of the U.S., and there are collectives and communes operating and advancing in different areas. As these collectives begin to interact publicly with other organizations along principled lines, efforts should be made to align, present our positions and support for:

- national liberations movements

- anti-repression movements

- anti-imperialist women's movements

- anti-nuclear reactor and anti-nuclear arms movements

- anti-urban renewal movements

- strikes by migrant workers, hospital workers, nursing home workers, prisoners, factory, plant, and mine workers, and all other workers, unionized or nonunionized, whose politics are compatible with the federation

Mass Media

At the point of consolidation of the "left," a nationally run independent weekly newspaper should appear. With a distribution system established throughout the hemisphere, made by the federation and organizations whose literature has been distributed throughout the federation.

This newspaper should carry news, editorial comments, ideological comments, support for national liberation movements, advertising of literature, and etc., from the federation and allies, human interest stories, children's stories, tips on living less expensively and more fully, exercises, preventive medicine, and the federation's political platform.

In heavily populated areas, legal and outlaw AM radio stations should be established with news, editorial comments, ideological comments, support for national liberation movements, community billboards set up free to allies to cover political and cultural events, and hours of non-interrupted music, except for news flashes and calls to the people.

At this point, this document ends.

2. ON TRAITORS

Introduction

Throughout the history of the Black Liberation Movement, there's been a literal plague of traitors. Perhaps every revolutionary movement can note the appearance of traitors; individuals who "roll over" once in the clutches of the enemy state, who sell out to the oppressors to make personal gains at the expense of former comrades, who use the power of the oppressors to attack those they may have had personal problems with, by volunteering themselves to be used by the state, who for whatever reasons make deals that involve the giving up of information which the state then uses to attack the revolutionary forces.

However, to say that this happens in every movement gives us no clue as to why these individuals could not be pointed out to the revolutionary forces prior to their ultimate transgressions or of how to spot those who very well may do harm intentionally to not only the armed political participants but to those who support the people's army, those who are sympathetic, and the colony as a whole. People are discouraged when they note that every offensive is defeated from within. Inhibited for good reason to pick up arms alongside those who may later finger them out, inhibited from opening their doors, or even speaking on the behalf of revolutionary forces. This is so to an extent today. The movement lays in frozen waste, not because New African People are generally loyal to the empire or think that there is no just cause, but because they think that war with the U.S. government is futile. Partly because of the tremendous firepower and technology of the U.S. government, but also that they have seen countless revolutionaries murdered and imprisoned due to betrayal. This compounds itself, in that we have not been able to contest the strength of the enemy along the lines of protracted war due to our failure to divert or weed out traitors. Once we get the information that someone has informed, it is after the fact, with a large portion of damage done.

Meanwhile, the toll of casualties and the weight of discouragement continues. In 1981 after an unsuccessful expropriation of one unit, the state picked up clues that allowed them to take the offensive. The U.S. government (federal) prosecuted one case under its RICO statue, the state of New York prosecuted another case. In the federal case eight people fought a legal battle against the prosecution armed with five informers who actually took the stand. Under the state indictment of four, one traitor had given literally pages of information without taking the stand—never disclosing what it was he said. In other words, out of a total of fifteen people allegedly involved in a war of liberation, six turned out to be informers—in two related cases. If you count those not on trial due to flight, six out of nineteen. All six informers came from the ranks and associations of the Black Liberation Movement. Counting as many people from this as were brought to trial, there were as many informers as there were those of us who took political prisoner, prisoner of war, and innocent citizen positions. Half of the people brought to trial under indictment were opposed by the same amount of traitors.

There are two major reasons for this; first, the means of acceptance by the clandestine forces, that is, the ways or methods that people were recruited and the type of behavior that was valued. The second is the overall lack of a counterintelligence program, which would have included observation and judgement on the character and political cultivation of all participants, by all participants. Every army in the world demands the loyalty of its troops, not only to the army but to the cause for the army's existence. Recruits should be questioned and tested as to their principles and motives, and more importantly when the actions of personnel are not consistent with revolutionary morality, aboveboard conduct with comrades, honesty in dealings with proletarians and lumpen proletarians, and the goals of the revolution, they should be expelled or terminated.

It is of note that the empire was not able to infiltrate actual trained agents of the state into the ranks of the BLA, which means that the only channel they had, the only sources of information, came from betrayal. That is, creatures who betrayed confidences, betrayed commitments, took advantage of situations to "help" themselves personally at the expense of former comrades. Had these traits been uncovered during times and circumstances of less gravity, these creatures could have been purged without disruption to the organization that is the cutting edge of New Afrikan resistance, with the effect of providing safety to the rest of the membership. This treatise is a personal inventory of traitors who were known personally by me, a listing of character traits that hopefully will enable others to see these types coming beforehand and purge them from their ranks, by having the guidelines to check and a historical account to be certain of the seriousness of the matter.

Character

There is a lot that goes into the makeup of a person's character, which should stand out in greater relief than the personality, for those who are in political association. Whether a person is outgoing or an introvert is a question of personality, whether a person is subject to twist the truth in order to have his or her way is a question of character. In other words, it's the quality of the relations, interrelations, and behavior that determines character; while, on the other hand, personality is a question of style. It is very important not to confuse these things, for, on the one hand, everyone who seems a bit odd shouldn't be purged right off the bat without any investigation into character, while anyone who doesn't take responsibility for mistakes or transgressions, who has a history of selfish actions, of victimizing people other than the enemy, of committing crimes against our side, should be purged immediately; there can never be a question as to where loyalties lay. Of course, a defector will insist that he or she is loyal up to the point where he or she turns their back on the revolution and embraces reaction, but both words and actions must be noted and judged.

A revolutionary, and a revolutionary combatant in particular, must have impeccable character. Those who support his or her actions should know that they will not be harmed through any intentional words or actions, and that the participant is deliberate in his or her behavior in that regard. Participants should be seen as competent and trustworthy.

It will be noted that Sam Brown at one point before he became a member of a cell of guerrillas habitually beat a woman with whom he shared an apartment. It was known that it wasn't and could not have been a case of self-defense, as the woman was beaten past the point of submission. It was obvious also that it wasn't a case stopping her from calling the police, as he had overpowered her to the point of being able to tie her up, and besides, even after his assault she turned to the revolutionary forces for justice.

Knowing that his acts were inexcusable he fled and hid for two years from the cell sent out looking for him. After that time, he plugged into a new group which had members who had been members of the group which had been dispatched to bring him to justice, who did not inform other members. Thus, without a trial or any collective discussion, or even a self-criticism, he was allowed to participate, when he should have at the very least been given the same kind of beating he had given out and been purged.

It will be noted that Tyrone Rison took collective money, which he used for his own purposes, and that when this was discovered he blamed the theft on another member of the collective. He was purged but allowed to be a participant after a sham disciplinary procedure where he was given the task of paying back the money, finding a military objective, and submitting a self-criticism. He never forthrightly admitted his crime, and therefore should have been purged and never allowed to reenter.

Peter Middleton, who was not an urban guerrilla, and who, if he had ever faced charges, faced charges of possessing small amounts of cocaine, was taken to be a revolutionary and allowed to be around revolutionaries. His associations gave his fabrications substance in the minds of reactionary and apolitical jurors. It was discovered that not only did he roll over — the FBI took over the clinic he worked in, but he had also met agents in Central Park to pass information to them prior to that. He was offered fifty thousand dollars to collaborate, just as were others who refused. He was a heavy user of cocaine who should have been purged because of that alone, but he was valued by other cocaine users who were in the collective.

Yvonne Thomas was obviously insane. Before burning down a safehouse and cutting her child with a razor and becoming an informant, she had disappeared and was found after being arrested for molesting another child. An instance of personal effects was missing from a person friendly to the guerrilla after she had visited, she had a habit of secreting away a few extra joints for herself, prompting suspicion when later a few rings and watches were missing. She was an associate through marriage to an actual political participant, and there is much to be said as to why she actually lived in a safehouse where she could witness the planning of military operations and financial transactions. However, the basic fact is she should not ever have been around any information of consequence.

It is supposed to be an honor to be a part of a liberation army, and membership and association is supposed to, in and of itself, denote a high degree of honesty, it's the basic requirement for the job, and once we see that requirement lacking in a member of a cell or a member of the support, that member has to go, either through expulsion or blood purge they must be put out of the way, not only because dishonesty will be the weakness by which the state will attempt to destroy the entire cell and everyone associated with it, but because each member is a representative of the cause and a member of the superseding society — if it is our desire to build a just society we must begin by being just and insisting on just participants.

Thomas should not have been shot for being petty, but that and clearly irrational behavior should have been the basis for her being outside the circle of any gravity.

Acts of contempt, especially violence against members who have not been collectively prescribed to be dealt with violently, is grounds for expulsion if not outright blood purge. There is enough opportunity for someone with a "bad" temper to find release, there is enough enemy to fight. Any charges against a member that one feels calls for a consequence should be brought before the collective, otherwise we could wipe ourselves out.

So bad character traits when exposed should be dealt with as soon as possible, not only because they are possible indications of someone being a political traitor, but because, in and of itself, dishonesty and contempt in the instances and in similar instances as described earlier makes for a band of rogues and not an army of liberation.

There will be other traits listed in the following inventory of the personality makeup of a few traitors; although many may not be as dangerous in and of themselves as some things mentioned, i do believe that they are indications that a member could very well be a traitor.

Certainly, a number of similar traits should indicate such, even when outside the boundaries of a collective, as there are certain things an honest and principled person will not do under any circumstances.

These cases, which call to our attention the need for full examinations, are also the subject of self-criticisms which have been written but do not fall within the scope of this work. It is our duty to compile personality inventories on all traitors, so as to be armed against them, and to complete and update criticisms, so as to be clear as to what we are doing.

Rison — Ego

1. Rison had more than a few ego problems that resulted in countless run-ins with comrades, which included him cutting people off in the middle of sentences during conversations and collective meetings. Coarsely, "shut up," and etc. If not to interject then usually so someone he agreed with could — he would never apologize for this

and said in so many words that he had rank just below the person who comrades collectively considered a leader. He asserted this based on seniority, even though this was challenged and no credence was paid to it.

2. Declared himself a weapons expert based on his experience in Vietnam, when he just had knowledge of the usual small arms most guerrillas are familiar with.

3. Although stating that he spent a lot of time in Vietnam and had been sent on countless patrols, etc., he never stated that the U.S. government had used him and others of African descent, the point was always how he survived.

4. Attempted to justify obvious security violations (see Security Violations, 1).

5. Rather than develop a front, to serve to satisfy inquiries as to his means of support he insisted that by simply telling police that he gambled and hustled to provide for himself and family. He went on to attempt this explanation when questioned by police in regards to a bank robbery.

6. Always had a lot of "ra ra shit" in the form of advice from an old vet. For instance, when children were being killed in Atlanta in what we agreed was the work of a conspiracy, he put forth that we should go there to kill white children as black children were killed. During an expropriation when a guard was disarmed without a shot fired, he insisted that the guard should have been killed for resisting, as well as all guards who resist.

Rison — Projections

1. Spoke on several occasions of how he would dread going to prison and the possibility of being raped by prisoners, and therefore never getting out because of having to kill his attacker.

Rison — Signs of Contempt

1. Pilfered money from collective war chest — never making an outright clear admission. When told that he would have to submit a self-criticism brought in a tape that never faced up to the charges.

2. Did in fact say that another collective member took money, he himself pilfered.

3. Rewarded himself with collective property after completing a task of transporting property, after it being collectively agreed that all property would be secured intact.

4. Borrowed money without any effort to repay borrowed money, only giving bullshit explanations when pressed.

5. Spoke at great length on how he and some of his army buddies tied up and skinned a woman to death in Vietnam, always being rather deliberate in his retellings, never expressing remorse and always sounding quite satisfied with himself.

Rison — Security Violations

1. Upon being bailed out on a bank robbery charge and brought home by relatives, he immediately got on his personal phone at his known residence to make a long-distance call to another city to inform comrades that he'd just been busted and released from jail. He further attempted to justify this by saying he had to make the call as soon as possible, when obviously he could have made the call from a booth.

2. Made long distance calls from residence prior to arrest, although told several times not to and although it was established collective policy to use phone booths. He continued this even after comrades had been busted and the state was in hot pursuit of several members of collective.

3. He indicated in conversations with people he hardly knew that he often had large sums of money and lived outside of legality.

4. At one point when two comrades were actively sought by police in a nationwide police hunt and at least one other comrade was in hiding, the collective was leaving a building with friends with the knowledge that the building was being watched by plainclothes police at a late hour (after 2:00 a.m.). Upon leaving the building, while knowing that police were looking at something unrelated, he went up to undercover police on his own to make clear that he knew who they were and beat on their windshield. He did this after it was collectively agreed that we would leave the scene as inconspicuously as possible, since it was a place subject to our return and we were too far away to scramble to our destination, and pigs would consider it no big deal to stop a crowded car of blacks, and that furthermore there were unarmed women with us.

5. Stated that certain people were slandering him and preventing him from seeing particular comrades, so that his personal value would not be acknowledged.

Brown—Ego

1. Stated that he had been a Yoruba priest, leader of the five percenters, a Lt. in the U.S. Army, 101 Airborne division, an engineer, among other things.

2. Talked a lot of "ra ra shit" about how down he was. At one point when it was suggested that he shouldn't be involved in a military action because he did not have a bulletproof vest, he stated that the speaker should exclude himself, rather than him, when the point was preparation.

Brown — Signs of Contempt

1. Stated to comrade during arrangement, "Fuck these ass-holes, let's go for ourselves."

2. Took up extra space in vehicles by sitting wide-legged, even though it was clear that other comrades would be packed in.

3. Beat a sister up past the point of subduing her — went on the run from the collective when this was discovered and it was clear that he would be dealt with because of what he did.

Brown — Projections

1. Spoke of the possibility of going to jail and being faced with having to decide whether or not to "bump the fags."

Thomas — Contempt

1. Made agreement to meet sisters in subway station on route to meeting, knowing that the sisters would get off of a subway to wait in the subway station for her. When this was discovered and she was confronted with her action of finding a ride and not telling the people who she knew would be waiting for her, she made no apologies.

2. She admitted that she hoped that military action by collective would not be successful. Her reasoning was that if the collective was successful in an expropriation, her husband would have money, would buy cocaine, would beat her, and since she wasn't gonna leave him, eventually he would kill her.

3. She asked questions that were tantamount to interrogation. Questions about acts, details, etc.

4. During social affairs would secrete joints given out for hospitality purposes in her pocketbook.

5. Displayed a sloppiness that was damaging to other people's property.

Thomas — Security Violations

1. Excessive talking in public to strangers about past that it was clear authorities knew about.

2. Would get high and disappear for days at a time. At one point was arrested for child molesting.

3. Display

At this point, this document ends. It is not known whether Kuwasi ever finished writing it, or if a more complete version exists.

3. THE VOCATIONS OF WARRIOR AND SOLDIER

The vocations of warrior and soldier have usually been risky. Cutting someone's head off has always implied the risk of having one's own head cut off. And so from time immemorial, there have been measures taken to ensure advantages in military exchanges and, likewise, measures taken to neutralize advantages or possible advantages by adversaries. Following the invention of the sword came the invention of the shield. Following the tactic of ambush came the tactic of advance point man, in order to warn the main body of troops. So integral to every type of combat are systems of intelligence—finding out what the enemy intends—and counterintelligence, preventing the enemy from succeeding in finding out what you intend and, in fact, giving the enemy wrong information that should result in a military blunder should the enemy follow up on it.

As well intelligence aims in finding the strength of the enemy, the whereabouts, the manner he conducts operations, the manner he lives, his covert and overt allies, and any piece of information that can be used to seek an advantage. Conversely, counterintelligence aims at denying this type of useful information to the enemy.

Intelligence and counterintelligence exist in the same realm of activity. The degree of intelligence in regards to the enemy indicates the amount of possible targets, weak points, response time, the consequences of the when and where, and dictates the lines of reasoning as to how to proceed. The less intelligence the more one is reduced to deciding matters simply by chance.

In those regards and in the framework and context of our struggle, a protracted war of national liberation by a numerically and technologically inferior force against a gigantic, resourceful, and sophisticated enemy, it behooves us to build a complete and comprehensive counterintelligence program and a complete and comprehensive intelligence program, in that order, not only because of the necessity of preserving our forces, or at least only engaging in exchanges only when we do maximum damage to the enemy, with the lowest cost in lives to ourselves, but also to develop cadre to their best; taking the maximum of enemy casualties in their heroic deed, so as to inspire the masses of our people to supporting the army.

As it is obvious that the opposing side inflicts casualty and captures, while inflicting even minor damage consistently against the enemy will eventually win, our first concern will be counterintelligence. Especially since we've taken heavy casualties and captures, because of the U.S. imperialist ability to find out who and where we are. It has also either been able to divine our intentions or fabricate them, as well. For our purposes here, the point is to keep out of reach of our opponents by forcing them to be ignorant of who and where we are, since in war, a soldier's fate does not rest upon acts committed when captured, but rather his or her connections with the liberation army and the ability to make good his or her escape.

Counterintelligence is the shield against the sword of intelligence. The counter to infiltration by outright enemy agents, defections of members misjudged, surveillance by counterinsurgency units by following known members, electronic listening devices, cameras, reactionary neighbors, pieces of evidence they may use to track down a suspected guerrilla, and police dragnets/roadblocks and random checks of the colonized population.

In building and maintaining a counterintelligence program there are two things that apply to all areas of operation. Firstly, that all measures adopted and employed must be adopted and enforced universally. Since if a countermeasure is not effected in one theater of operations or one cell, the consequences could very well harm and expose those members not only in that cell, but all other cells and support apparatus in contact with that cell. This again spills into other areas as the enemy may be informed of our countermeasures and be in a better position to counteract them than if they did not. Secondly, all information is to be transmitted to others on a need to know basis only; regardless of the rank or personal relationships particular individuals may have. Anyone who doesn't need information in order to carry out an assigned or agreed upon task simply should not receive such information; and anyone found to be transmitting information to a party not part of a formation with the particular task that calls for such knowledge should be dealt with for committing a security violation. This is so regardless of how long he or she or other members may have known the party in question. It should be kept in mind that people who are in fact cool don't want to know things that don't pertain to them. The less people who do in fact know our business, the less people we must suspect when it becomes obvious that there's a leak, the less trouble we have tracking down the source of a leak, and the less likely that a leak will develop. As historical and personal experiences abound where people who were supposedly cool "rolled over." There should be no question as to the gravity of this type of transgression, and anyone who has problems with this is a problem.

In this regard no critiques or other business will be carried out among nonmembers or with nonmembers having information as to what type of business is being conducted or where. No member will be introduced to a nonmember as a member. This may be implied where our organization is about to enter into a clandestine activity with another friendly organization. However, in the event we are purchasing equipment or information from an underground or underworld source, there's every reason to cover ourselves. Nicknames should be adopted as much as possible, and care should be taken when traveling with others underground. The police have a trick of asking those traveling with others the names of others on identification checks. So for instance if my ID says Joe Smith, and you are asked if you know me and say you don't, the next series of questions involve why are we traveling together. If you give a name other than Joe Smith, then: "How is it that you know him and don't know his name?" This is a ploy used when the ID actually checks out and police suspect they may be questioning some sharp operatives. If someone doesn't know your line of work, it is permissible to give them your adopted name, if someone does know your line of work and does not work with you, you should avoid travelling with them. The likelihood of someone outside and totally unconnected with the movement being stopped and questioned about the movement is less likely than someone who is, as well as the likelihood of them being followed. You should be ready to abandon a set of ID and adopt another persona in the event someone who knows the old persona is questioned, as once Joe Smith is in fact connected with who you are, police will be happy to check rent and telephone listings for that alias. Finding Joe is another story.

In the event you take residence with someone outside the formation, that someone should not be part of an aboveground political movement, should only know you by an alias, and should under no circumstances know what or who you are involved with outside of your cover involvements. As well, no underground or movement people should be introduced to them. A separate existence is just that — "Only a fool expects someone to keep a secret, he himself cannot keep."

If there's no one outside the organization knowledgeable of activities or personnel, and therefore no one outside the ranks capable of informing, the only way that information can be given to the enemy is by the members themselves. This is the most destructive to you and your cause, as it gives the enemy the opportunity to inflict maximum damage, and this forces those who you fight for to lose confidence in the struggle, which results in the lack of support for the existing apparatus and personnel and shortages of recruits. Without new recruits to take the places of those who die in battle or are captured — and who actually make expansion of the army possible, so as to enable us to achieve its historic tasks — the army has no future.

As recruiting is vital to building and maintaining an army, it deserves special attention and deliberation. Basically there are three types of people to be avoided: government agents assigned to infiltrate the army, those with characters that will fold and result in them going over to the side of the enemy, and those who through other character traits are subject to bringing attention to you by way of committing security violations that the enemy directs his attention to, in order to collect a chain of data to connect with other people, or places and events, past, present, or future, that are of our doing.

Agents

Agents are police who infiltrate organizations for the purpose of relaying information directly to their superiors. At times they may be staff members of politicians, GIs, or professional spies from a government agency. However, for all practical purposes, they are police. Although they are trained in how to relay information, endear themselves to leadership, and cover their tracks, they are the easiest form of the intelligence gathering apparatus to detect. At the same time, they are the most dangerous, because they are armed with the knowledge of who they are and who you are and are ready to get the jump on you if they suspect you are on to them. They know precisely what to look for, and have roundabout ways to make contact with their superiors.

At present the state has been unable to infiltrate the underground, as the tendency during the last few years of a mostly defensive strategy has been toward formations of people very familiar with each other. This has put an end to the period when an enemy agent could walk into an office, join an organization, and at some point be in touch with clandestine activities. However, as recruitment drives grow, the possibilities of infiltration will increase, as the enemy wants firsthand information before an operation takes place, after of course obtaining information on safehouses, medical units, arms, associations, strategy and tactics, resources and all else that will enable the state to thoroughly wipe as many units out as possible without any blows of consequence being delivered by said units. For these reasons, underground units should not be in contact with aboveground organizations, and people doing aboveground work shouldn't do underground work as well, as after your sentiments are clear, the enemy is left to only have to watch.

However, as a clear separation is still no guarantee in the future, if there is in fact no infiltration of government agents in the army at present, as aboveground organizations should protect themselves from agents, agent provocateurs, and the like, a step by step program of detection of enemy agents should be effected and maintained.

All recruits and new members should be questioned in regard to their employment, past employment, where they were born, raised, went to school, and if they had been in the armed forces. Additionally, they should be questioned as to their family, if they are married, have children, any physical or mental disorders, what they like to do, and etc. Since these questions are on rent and job applications everywhere and have been answered over and over an aboveground person shouldn't mind. In the case of an underground member who is not known by members of the unit in charge, refusal to answer these questions after volunteering to become a member should result in people's arrest; unless new members are to be arrested and held until they've answered the questions and the questions have checked out. On the aboveground level, prospective members should be turned away for refusing to answer or lying.

All new members should write an essay in regards to why they wish to become members, their ideology, why they believe the struggle is worth their living and dying. These essays should in turn be judged by people who have already gone through this, and once the essay is judged it should be destroyed.

Particularities or Give Aways

Agents are usually people who you don't know, and when you do come in contact with them to be successful they have to convince you that they are the genuine article. This will entail usually a bogus personal history, which may be remembered [illegible], but which will usually contain [illegible] places that are far away, along with places of residence during childhood, early adolescence, and likely up to the very recent past. This is because agents count on our inability to check their stories. In this regard comrades should pose as credit agents for banks, real estate agents, or whatever to check out the schools, past employment, and other particulars of the story while the recruit is still in front of a recruitment committee made up of individuals with proven records, universal acceptance by the organization, and no warrants.

This is how this procedure should unfold.

The recruit is told that if he intends to join the underground he must do so at this time, as we want people who are certain as to their intentions and want no other career except that of professional revolutionary, and asked if he or she finds the career of revolutionary the only acceptable occupation and if the applicant can read and write English, Spanish, Swahili, Arabic.

If all answers are assessed positive, the following questionnaire is put before applicant.

1. Name — First/Last/Middle

2. Date of birth

3. Religion

At this point, this document ends.

Distributed by :

RESISTANCE

Kuwasi Balagoon is a New Afrikan Freedom
Fighter and a Prisoner of War, charged with
the attempted expropriation of a Brink's
truck in Nyack, N.Y. on October 20, 1981.
He is being held captive at the Rockland
County Jail.

*Regarding the booklet reproduced in these and the pages that follow, as
Amilcar Shabazz recalls, Kuwasi "gave us some of his ideas on 'PT,'
or physical training, in his handwriting with sketches of different
exercises, especially what could be performed in the tight confines of
the small cells he spent many hours, days, and years of his life locked
up inside prisons and devoid of human contact. His body was as solid
as iron from his PT practice, which was a key to his life and power to
escape."*

Kuwasi Balagoon's Exercise Book

"...Without freedom (the ability to live in total), there isn't any big deal in living, since to accept fascism is to forfeit life."

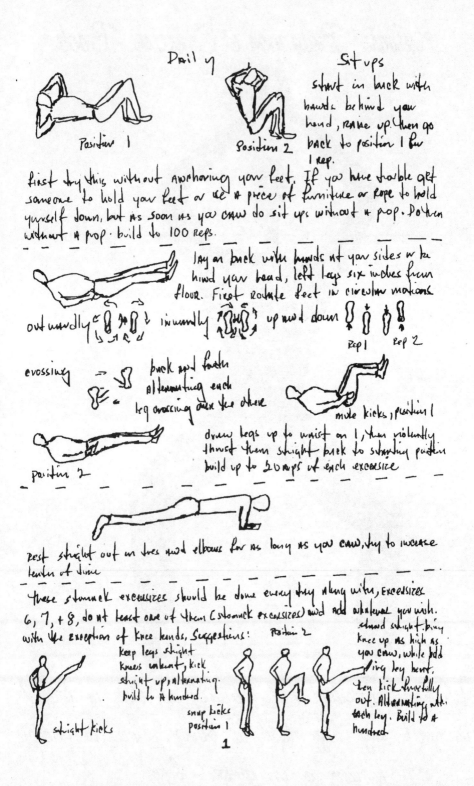

Daily

Position 1

Position 2

Sit ups
start on back with
hands behind your
head, raise up, then go
back to position 1 for
1 rep.

first try this without anchoring your feet. If you have trouble get someone to hold your feet or use a piece of furniture or rope to hold yourself down, but as soon as you can do sit ups without a prop. Do them without a prop. build to 100 reps.

lay on back with hands at your sides or behind your head, left legs six inches from floor. First rotate feet in circular motions

outwardly   inwardly   up and down
                                        Rep 1   Rep 2

crossing   back and forth
             alternating each
             leg crossing over the other

mule kicks, position 1

position 2

draw legs up to waist on 1, then violently thrust them straight back to starting position
build up to 20 reps of each excersize

rest straight out on toes and elbows for as long as you can, try to increase tenth of time

these stomach excersizes should be done every day along with, Excersizes 6, 7, + 8, do not leave one of them (stomach excersizes) and add whatever you wish. with the exception of knee bends. Suggestions:

keep legs straight
knees unbent, kick
straight up, alternating.
build to a hundred.

straight kicks

Position 2

snap kicks
position 1

stand straight, bring knee up as high as you can, while adding string toy bent. then kick forcefully out. Alternating with each leg. Build to a hundred.

1

The purpose of this manual is to give step by step instructions and suggestions into a good physical cultivation session, that can be started on immediately, improved upon gradually, and build strength and endurance within a minimum amount of space, time or props. Some of these EXERCISES are more difficult than others, and have variations that allow the practitioner to advance to the more difficult EXCERCISE in short order if workouts of at least twice A WEEK are consistently performed.

Given consistent application, correctly doing the excercises, and directly following each excercize with the next without delay, this system will leave anyone, in reasonably good health in not only good condition, but combat condition.

The session that follows should take less than and hour, indeed the less time taken provided that the excercises are done correctly, done to the maximum, the better, because that means that you are taking less time to recover, are excercizing while recovering and that not only are you working your muscles, but more importantly working your heart and lungs and getting you used to continuing when fatigued.

Along with this session done two times a week, all commanders should run at least four miles, three times a week and do at least one hundred sit ups a day. With that the proper diet and amount of sleep you will be in condition to carry on.

A mile and a half of which should be done under nine minutes.

2

1.st EXCERSIZE, side straddle hops.

count
1 Hundred

try not to slap hands together or to the sides

A good general warm up excersize.

position 1   position 2

2nd EXCERSIZE, KNEE bends, Part 1

Do not go down further than parallel.

position 1   Position 2   come up on toes

twenty five repretitions

| Part 2 | spread feet shoulder lentu for both excersizes

position 1   Position 2   keep feet flat

twenty five cunt repretition

take a deep breath at position 1, move to position 2, let air out when re turning to position 1 Part 1, After twenty five repretitions, begin part two take hands from hips and place behind head for position 1, take a breath, move to position two, keeping feet flat, continue for twenty five repretitions. Move directly from one EXCERSIZE to the next, 25 repres in part 1, in part 2 cunt 26 to 50, on back to part 1 - 50 to 75, to part 2, 75 to 100, to part 1, 100 - 125, part 125 - 150, Part 1, 150 - 175, Part 2, 175 to 200. If you can't go to 200 repretitions, try 100. If you can't do 100, try 50 - 25 of part 1s, 25 of part 2s, until you build up to 200. This is good for your legs, and good for your lungs. Now move right on to NEXT EXCERSIZE

3

3rd, EXCERCIZE, Knee lifts

position 1

position 2

stand with arms down to sides left knee to chest and bring back to floor - repeat to other side - alternate.

Count. one hundred reps.

this is good for your wind, hips + legs.

4th EXCERCIZE, side winders

position 1

position 2

stand with hands behind head feet shoulder length apart, at position. On a count of one move bending to the side, trying to touch the hip with elbow, then come back to starting position then of course, the same move to the other side and back.

Count. one hundred reps
this is good for your sides and back

5th EXCERCIZE Elevated push ups

If too difficult try 5 or ten regular push ups same as regular pushups Except you put your feet, and palms on chairs or boxes if the same height Go down as far as you can and back to where you started.
Try twenty five reps

This is good for the arms, shoulders, back + stomach

Airplane dives, 6th

position 2

starting Position

stand with hands on hips, feet shoulder length apart, move to second position touching opposite palm to foot. for instance left hand to right foot, Repeat to opposite.

twenty five reps.
try to overlook illustration please

This is good for the legs

4

Repete 5 and 6, then do 5 again.

7th, bend and reach

count 25

This is good for the stomach back and legs

Position 1   Position 2   Position 3   Position 4

On the count of one, hit your stomach with both fists, on the count of two reach down to touch toes, on the count of three hit your stomach again and on the count of four reach to the sky, tip toe at the same time.

Repete 5 and Repete 7 move right on to 8

start out with your hands behind you, bending forward at the waist, knees bend, and on your toes

on the count of one throw your arms up and jump as high as you can, do this twenty five times

If you need to "bounde" a couple of times for the sake of timing thats OK, but only count when you jump + reach.

Ah, thats wonderful comrade →

Position 1

Position 2

This is good for the wind and legs.

5

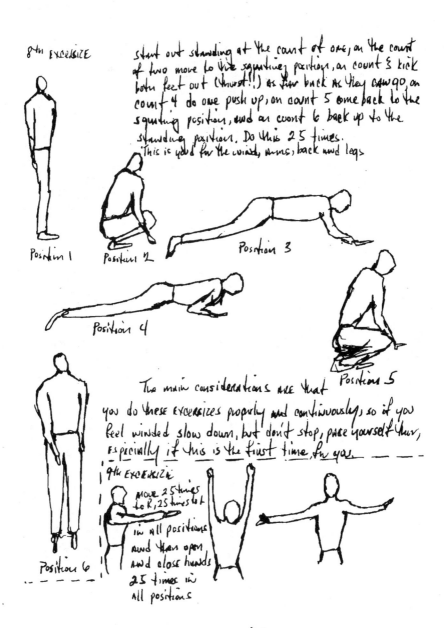

8th EXCERSIZE

Start out standing at the count of one, on the count of two move to the squatting position, on count 3 kick both feet out (thrust!) as far back as they can go, on count 4 do one push up, on count 5 come back to the squatting position, and on count 6 back up to the standing position. Do this 25 times.
This is good for the wrists, arms, back and legs

Position 1

Position 2

Position 3

Position 4

Position 5

The main considerations are that you do these excersizes properly and continuously, so if you feel winded slow down, but don't stop, pace yourself than, especially if this is the first time for you.

9th EXCERSIZE

move 25 times to R, 25 times to L

in all positions and than open and close hands 25 times in all positions

Position 6

This is good for the shoulders, arms, + fingers

6

EXERCIZE 10 chin up

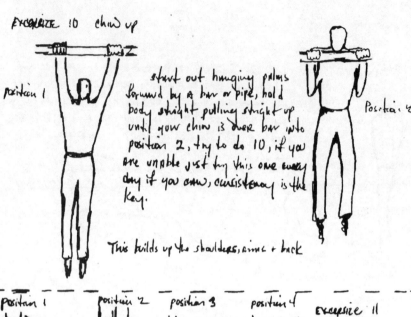

position 1

Position 2

start out hanging palms forward by a bar or pipe, hold body straight pulling straight up until your chin is over bar into position 2, try to do 10, if you are unable just try this one every day if you can, consistency is the key.

This builds up the shoulders, arms + back

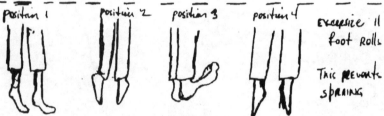

position 1   position 2   position 3   position 4

EXERCIZE 11
foot Rolls

This prevents
SPRAINS

start on your tip toes, roll to the edges of the inside soles of your feet, roll to your heels, then to the outside edges of the soles. Try this to 12 rotations, building up to 20 rotations. If inside try to USE a rug, if outside try to get a space of ground.

position 1   position 2

rotate the head twenty times to the right, twenty times to the left and then step out punching in whatever style you prefer, advancing ten feet or so

This exercize is good for the neck muscles and aids EXERCIZE 12
you in recovering from knock outs. 7

This system has been worked on & used by FREEDOM FIGHTERS and has been found to result in improved physical condition by all of us who has applied this system, just twice a week. Even though previous to this we had worked out and consistently used weights, yoga, isometries and other calisthenics, there done in sequence has proved to bring faster measurable results.

Again, these particular exercises done twice a week will not in view of themselves be all the physical conditioning that an urban guerilla will need. However we feel that with this system, the running of few miles three times a week with one and one half of those miles done in nine minutes, a hundred sit ups every day, and a few stretching exercises every day, consistently we will be better off.

We will build from practice and report a daily suggested routine in the near future, meanwhile please check this out and give us your criticisms and other thoughts on the matter.

Kuwasi Balagoon

Contributors

Sundiata Acoli was a codefendant of Balagoon's during the New York Panther 21 case. Subsequently a member of the Black Liberation Army, he was captured by the state in 1973 and is currently serving a sentence of life plus thirty years. His writings have most recently appeared in *Look for Me in the Whirlwind: From the Panther 21 to 21st Century Revolutions*, coauthored with Sekou Odinga and Dhoruba Bin Wahad, coedited by dequi kioni-sadiki and Matt Meyer (PM Press, 2017).

Ashanti Omowali Alston is a revolutionary, speaker, writer, organizer, and motivator. He is one of the few former members of the Black Panther Party (BPP) who identifies as an anarchist in the tradition of New Afrikan ancestor Kuwasi Balagoon. As a result of his membership in both the BPP and Black Liberation Army (BLA), he served a total of fourteen years as a political prisoner and prisoner of war. He is former national chair and currently on the Steering Committee of the National Jericho Movement to Free U.S. Political Prisoners. On top of all that, he is an Elder co-parenting two youngins, and a grandfather of a small "Maroon nation." Ashanti resides in Providence, Rhode Island.

Kai Lumumba Barrow has been an inspirational figure in grassroots organizing in the United States since the late 1970s. She is one of the founders of Critical Resistance, a prison industrial complex abolitionist organization, and she has played a leadership role in groups such as the Provisional Government of the Republic of New Afrika, the Malcolm X Grassroots Movement, the Black Panther Newspaper Committee, FIERCE!, INCITE!, UBUNTU, Southerners on New Ground, the Student Liberation Action Movement, and Queers for Economic Justice (to name but a few). In 2010, Kai formed the Gallery of the Streets. Kai's work fuses public art and organizing for social change to reconfigure the familiar and generate new ideas against the oppression of existing conditions.

Dhoruba Bin Wahad, a codefendant of Balagoon's during the New York Panther 21 case, was Field Secretary of the Black Panther Party and subsequently a member of the Black Liberation Army. Bin Wahad spent a total of nineteen years in prison on charges related to the illegal FBI Counter Intelligence Program (Cointelpro), after which he won release on his own recognizance and settled lawsuits against the FBI, the New York State Department of Corrections, and the New York City Police Department. A Pan-Africanist who has lived in Ghana, Guinea, and the USA, he is coauthor with Mumia Abu-Jamal and Assata Shakur of *Still Black, Still Strong: Survivors of the War Against Black Revolutionaries* (Semiotext(e), 1993), and of the recently released *Look for Me in the Whirlwind: From the Panther 21 to 21st Century Revolutions*, coauthored with Sekou Odinga, coedited by dequi kioni-sadiki and Matt Meyer (PM Press, 2017).

Joan P. Gibbs is a longtime activist, writer, and a lawyer. Joan has devoted her entire legal career to the practice of constitutional, civil rights, and immigration law and has worked at the American Civil Liberties Union, the American Civil Liberties Union Women's Rights Project, the Center for Constitutional Rights, and the Center for Law and Social Justice at Medgar Evers College, from which she retired in 2015. Over the years, Joan has represented a number of political activists and political prisoners, including members of ACT UP, the Malcolm X Grassroots Movement, the December 12th Movement, People United for Children, and political prisoners Herman Ferguson and Sundiata Acoli. Her writings, poems, stories, essays, and letters have appeared in a number of publications, including *Pambazuka News*, *Journal of Community Advocacy and Activism*, *Daily Challenge*, *Our Times Press*, *Sinister Wisdom*, *Iowa Review*, and *Azalea* (the first magazine published by and for lesbians of color in the United States, of which she was founding editor). Joan lives in Brooklyn.

David Gilbert was a founding member of the Columbia University chapter of Students for a Democratic Society (SDS) and the Weather Underground Organization. He went underground in the 1970s and participated in the same failed Brink's expropriation as Balagoon in 1981. He and Balagoon were code-fendants in that case and, as a result, he is currently serving a sentence of seventy-five years to life on the charge of felony murder. Gilbert is the author of *No Surrender: Writings of an Anti-Imperialist Political Prisoner* (Abraham Guillen Press, 2004) and *Love and Struggle: My Life in SDS, the Weather Underground, and Beyond* (PM Press, 2011).

Kim Kit Holder is an assistant professor of educational foundations and Africana studies at Rowan University in New Jersey. Dr. Holder earned his doctorate from the University of Massachusetts Amherst in Multicultural Education and African American Studies, his Master's in Early Childhood Education from Bank Street College of Education, and his BA in History from Hampshire College. Dr. Holder's primary interest is the education of underserved populations, and to this end he has worked in a wide range of settings including prison education and migrant education. His scholarly interests center on community and family involvement in the educational process, as well as fostering critical thinking.

Danielle Jasmine is a poet, author, performer, and real estate agent based in Atlanta, GA. As a young child, she visited Balagoon in prison and was part of his extended adopted family.

Karl Kersplebedeb is a Montreal-based publisher and distributor of anti-imperialist, anti-capitalist, and anti-patriarchal literature, as well as a longtime anti-prison activist. Working with comrades to publish the first edition of *A Soldier's Story* in 2001 remains one of the accomplishments he is happiest about.

dequi kioni-sadiki is the chair of the Malcolm X Commemoration Committee and was a leader of the Sekou Odinga Defense Committee, which waged a successful campaign for the release of her husband. A tireless coalition builder and organizer, dequi is a radio producer of the weekly show *Where We Live* on WBAI Radio, Pacifica, an educator with the NYC Department of Education, and a member of the National Jericho Movement to Free U.S. Political Prisoners. She is coeditor, with Matt Meyer, of the recently released *Look for Me in the Whirlwind: From the Panther 21 to 21st Century Revolutions*, coauthored with Sekou Odinga and Dhoruba Bin Wahad (PM Press, 2017).

Matt Meyer is the Secretary-General of the International Peace Research Association, Chair of the International Fellowship of Reconciliation Financial Advisory Committee, and the War Resisters' International Africa Support Network Coordinator. A noted educator, author, and organizer, Meyer focuses on an extensive range of human rights issues, including support for political prisoners, solidarity with Puerto Rico, the Black Liberation Movement, and all decolonization movements, and bringing an end to patriarchy, militarism, and imperialism. Meyer serves as Senior Research Scholar for the University of Massachusetts Amherst Resistance Studies Initiative. He is coeditor, with dequi kioni-sadiki, of the recently released *Look for Me in the Whirlwind: From the Panther 21 to 21st Century Revolutions*, coauthored with Sekou Odinga and Dhoruba Bin Wahad (PM Press, 2017) and author of *White Lives Matter Most and Other "Little" White Lies* (PM Press, 2018).

Sekou Odinga was a member of Malcolm X's Organization of Afro-American Unity and a founding member of the New York chapter of the Black Panther Party, as well as of the Black Panther International Section. He was, with Balagoon, a codefendant in the New York Panther 21 case. A citizen of the Republic of New Afrika and combatant of the Black Liberation Army, Sekou was captured in October 1981, mercilessly tortured, and spent the following thirty-three years behind bars—a prisoner of war and political prisoner of the U.S. empire. Since his release in November 2014, he has remained a stalwart fighter for justice and for the release of all political prisoners. He is a contributor to the recently released *Look for Me in the Whirlwind: From the Panther 21 to 21st Century Revolutions*, coauthored with Dhoruba Bin Wahad, coedited by dequi kioni-sadiki and Matt Meyer (PM Press, 2017).

Ajamu Sankofa is a trained educator and retired trial lawyer who specialized in prisoner rights. Since the 1970s, he has been a revolutionary minded activist who was a member of several ideologically diverse organizations, including the African Liberation Support Committee, the National Independent Black Political Party, the Socialist Workers Party, and the National Conference of Black Lawyers (NCBL). Sankofa remains very active in NCBL and lives in Brooklyn, NY, with his two beautiful black cats, Aries and Sunra.

Amilcar Shabazz is a professor of history and Africana Studies in the W.E.B. Du Bois Department of Afro-American Studies at the University of Massachusetts Amherst. Shabazz served as the department's seventh chair from 2007 to 2012 and currently serves as president of the National Council for Black Studies. From 2013 to 2016, he was the Faculty Adviser to the Chancellor for Diversity and Excellence at University of Massachusetts Amherst, where he still teaches, with an emphasis on the political economy of social and cultural movements, education, and public policy. His book *Advancing Democracy: African Americans and the Struggle for Access and Equity in Higher Education in Texas* (University of North Carolina Press, 2004) was the winner of the T.R. Fehrenbach Book Award and other scholarly recognition. *The Forty Acres Documents*, a volume he coedited with Imari Obadele and Johnita Scott Obadele, and for which he wrote the introduction, was one of the earliest scholarly works on the modern movement for reparations for slavery and the racial oppression of people of African descent in North America. Shabazz has been a Fulbright Senior Specialist and has done work in Brazil, Ghana, Japan, Cuba, and other countries. Once upon a time, before all this, he served as a young paralegal for Kuwasi Balagoon.

Meg Starr is founding member of Resistance in Brooklyn, a New York City–based anti-imperialist collective. When she began visiting Kuwasi in prison, she was the head of the Clifford Glover Brigade and a member of the Women's Committee Against Genocide. Since then, she has been a leader of the Free Puerto Rico Committee and subsequent solidarity organizations and efforts relating to Puerto Rican decolonization. Starr continues to serve as an early childhood educator and is the author of the award-winning *Alicia's Happy Day* (Star Bright Books, 2000).

Bilal Sunni-Ali is a world-renowned saxophonist and composer, famed for his work with the Gil Scott-Heron Band and comedy legend Richard Pryor. A founder of the New York chapter of the Black Panther Party, Sunni-Ali was a codefendant in the case of the U.S. vs. Mutulu Shakur, acquitted of all charges relating to the Brink's case. A lifelong revolutionary and citizen of the Republic of New Afrika, Sunni-Ali has been heralded as an ambassador of the movement. He is a contributor to the recently released *Look for Me in the Whirlwind: From the Panther 21 to 21st Century Revolutions* (PM Press, 2017).

Akinyele Umoja is associate professor and chair of the Department of African-American Studies at Georgia State University, where he teaches courses on the history of the Civil Rights and Black Power Movements and other Black political and social movements. He is the author of *We Will Shoot Back: Armed Resistance and the Mississippi Freedom Movement* (New York University Press, 2013). Umoja is a founding member of the New Afrikan People's Organization and the Malcolm X Grassroots Movement; he is particularly committed to work to support and gain amnesty for political prisoners and prisoners of war, to win reparations for African people, and in solidarity with the grassroots movement for democracy and self-determination in Haiti.

Albert Nuh Washington was a member of the Black Panther Party and Black Liberation Army, widely believed to have been framed as a member of the New York Three for his far-reaching political work. A stalwart fighter for Black liberation, Washington died of liver cancer as a political prisoner at the Coxsackie Correctional Facility prison in New York State, in 2000.

PM Press was founded at the end of 2007 by a small collection of folks with decades of publishing, media, and organizing experience. PM Press co-conspirators have published and distributed hundreds of books, pamphlets, CDs, and DVDs. Members of PM have founded enduring book fairs, spearheaded victorious tenant organizing campaigns, and worked closely with bookstores, academic conferences, and even rock bands to deliver political and challenging ideas to all walks of life. We're old enough to know what we're doing and young enough to know what's at stake.

We create radical and stimulating fiction and non-fiction books, pamphlets, T-shirts, visual and audio materials to educate, entertain, and inspire you. We aim to distribute these through every available channel with every available technology—whether that means you are seeing anarchist classics at our bookfair stalls; reading our latest vegan cookbook at the café; downloading geeky fiction e-books; or digging new music and timely videos from our website.

PM Press is always on the lookout for talented and skilled volunteers, artists, activists, and writers to work with. If you have a great idea for a project or can contribute in some way, please get in touch.

PM Press
PO Box 23912
Oakland CA 94623
510-658-3906
www.pmpress.org

PM Press in Europe
europe@pmpress.org
www.pmpress.org.uk

FRIENDS OF PM

These are indisputably momentous times—the financial system is melting down globally and the Empire is stumbling. Now more than ever there is a vital need for radical ideas.

In the many years since its founding—and on a mere shoestring—PM Press has risen to the formidable challenge of publishing and distributing knowledge and entertainment for the struggles ahead. With hundreds of releases to date, we have published an impressive and stimulating array of literature, art, music, politics, and culture. Using every available medium, we've succeeded in connecting those hungry for ideas and information to those putting them into practice.

Friends of PM allows you to directly help impact, amplify, and revitalize the discourse and actions of radical writers, filmmakers, and artists. It provides us with a stable foundation from which we can build upon our early successes and provides a much-needed subsidy for the materials that can't necessarily pay their own way. You can help make that happen—and receive every new title automatically delivered to your door once a month—by joining as a Friend of PM Press. And, we'll throw in a free T-shirt when you sign up.

Here are your options:

- $30 a month: Get all books and pamphlets plus 50% discount on all webstore purchases
- $40 a month: Get all PM Press releases (including CDs and DVDs) plus 50% discount on all webstore purchases
- $100 a month: Superstar—Everything plus PM merchandise, free downloads, and 50% discount on all webstore purchases

For those who can't afford $30 or more a month, we have **SUSTAINER RATES** at $15, $10, and $5. Sustainers get a free PM Press T-shirt and a 50% discount on all purchases from our website.

Your Visa or Mastercard will be billed once a month, until you tell us to stop. Or until our efforts succeed in bringing the revolution around. Or the financial meltdown of Capital makes plastic redundant. Whichever comes first.

KER SPLE EBE DEB

Since 1998 Kersplebedeb has been an important source of radical left-wing literature and agit prop materials.

The project has a non-exclusive focus on anti-patriarchal and anti-imperialist politics, framed within an anticapitalist perspective. A special priority is given to writings regarding armed struggle in the metropole, and the continuing struggles of political prisoners and prisoners of war.

The Kersplebedeb website presents historical and contemporary writings by revolutionary thinkers from the anarchist and communist traditions.

Kersplebedeb can be contacted at:

Kersplebedeb
CP 63560
CCCP Van Horne
Montreal, Quebec
Canada
H3W 3H8

email: info@kersplebedeb.com
web: www.kersplebedeb.com
           www.leftwingbooks.net

Kersplebedeb

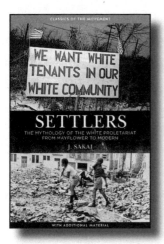

Settlers: The Mythology of the White Proletariat from Mayflower to Modern

J. Sakai • 978-1-62963-037-3
456 pages • $20.00

J. Sakai shows how the United States is a country built on the theft of Indigenous lands and Afrikan labor, on the robbery of the northern third of Mexico, the colonization of Puerto Rico, and the expropriation of the Asian working class, with each of these crimes being accompanied by violence. In fact, America's white citizenry have never supported themselves but have always resorted to exploitation and theft, culminating in acts of genocide to maintain their culture and way of life. This movement classic lays it all out, taking us through this painful but important history.

WHAT PEOPLE ARE SAYING

"*Settlers* is a critical analysis of the colonization of the Americas that overturns the 'official' narrative of poor and dispossessed European settlers to reveal the true nature of genocidal invasion and land theft that has occurred for over five hundred years. If you want to understand the present, you must know the past, and this book is a vital contribution to that effort."

Gord Hill, author of *500 Years of Indigenous Resistance*

"When *Settlers* hit the tiers of San Quentin, back in 1986, it totally exploded our ideas about what we as a new class of revolutionaries thought we knew about a so-called 'united working class' in amerika. And what's more, it brought the actual contradictions of national oppression and imperialism into sharp focus. It was my first, and as such my truest, study of the actual mechanics behind the expertly fabricated illusion of an amerikan proletariat."

Sanyika Shakur, author of
Monster: The Autobiography of an L.A. Gang Member

Look for Me in the Whirlwind From the Panther 21 to 21st-Century Revolutions

Sekou Odinga, Dhoruba Bin Wahad, and Jamal Joseph

Edited by Matt Meyer & déqui kioni-sadiki

Foreword by Imam Jamil Al-Amin

Afterword by Mumia Abu-Jamal

978-1-62963-389-3 • 648 pages • $26.95

Amid music festivals and moon landings, the tumultuous year of 1969 included an infamous case in the annals of criminal justice and Black liberation: the New York City Black Panther 21. Though some among the group had hardly even met one another, the 21 were rounded up by the FBI and New York Police Department in an attempt to disrupt and destroy the organization that was attracting young people around the world. Involving charges of conspiracy to commit violent acts, the Panther 21 trial—the longest and most expensive in New York history—revealed the illegal government activities which led to exile, imprisonment on false charges, and assassination of Black liberation leaders. Solidarity for the 21 also extended well beyond "movement" circles and included mainstream publication of their collective autobiography, *Look for Me in the Whirlwind.*

Look for Me in the Whirlwind: From the Panther 21 to 21st-Century Revolutions contains the original and includes new commentary from surviving members of the 21. Still-imprisoned Sundiata Acoli, Imam Jamil Al-Amin, and Mumia Abu-Jamal contribute new essays. Never or rarely seen poetry and prose from Afeni Shakur, Kuwasi Balagoon, Ali Bey Hassan, and Michael "Cetewayo" Tabor is included. Early Panther leader and jazz master Bilal Sunni-Ali adds a historical essay and lyrics from his composition "Look for Me in the Whirlwind," and coeditors kioni-sadiki, Meyer, and Panther rank-and-file member Cyril "Bullwhip" Innis Jr. help bring the story up to date.

At a moment when the Movement for Black Lives recites the affirmation that "it is our duty to win," penned by Black Liberation Army (BLA) militant Assata Shakur, those who made up the BLA and worked alongside of Assata are largely unknown. This book provides essential parts of a hidden and missing-in-action history. Going well beyond the familiar and mythologized nostalgic Panther narrative, *From the Panther 21 to 21st-Century Revolutions* explains how and why the Panther legacy is still relevant and vital today.